ABOUT THIS BOOK

Is there a crisis of world capitalism in our time, or has a truly global economy finally begun to pay off on the original promise of the greatest good for the greatest number? Has the leader of that global realm, the Unites States, reached the end of its hegemonic predominance, or is it in the robust middle age of its tenure, now bereft of serious antagonists?

The outlook of its authors is at once compelling and gloomy, a prophecy of a coming age of turmoil and disorder. Like Fukuyama's *The End of History*, this book will provoke a lively debate; unlike Fukuyama, Hopkins and Wallerstein know that *we* may forget about history, but history will not forget about us.

BRUCE CUMINGS
*John Evans Professor of International History and
Politics, Northwestern University*

ABOUT THE AUTHORS

IMMANUEL WALLERSTEIN is Director of the Fernand Braudel Center for the Study of Economies, Historical Systems, and Civilizations, and Distinguished Professor of Sociology, at Binghamton University. President (1994–98) of the International Sociological Association, he chaired the Gulbenkian Commission for the Restructuring of the Social Sciences in 1993–95, which led to the publication of its Report, *Open the Social Sciences* (Stanford University Press 1996). He is perhaps most well known for his pioneering theoretical work on the world-system, notably his *The Modern World-System*, 3 volumes (Academic Press 1974, 1980, 1989). His recent books include *Geopolitics and Geoculture* (Cambridge University Press 1991) and *Unthinking Social Science: The Limits of Nineteenth-Century Paradigms* (Polity 1991).

TERENCE K. HOPKINS is the founder and long-time Director of the Graduate Programme in Sociology (world-historical change) at Binghamton University. He is also a member of the Executive Board of the Fernand Braudel Center for the Study of Economies, Historical Systems, and Civilizations. Before going to Binghamton, he taught at Columbia University and the University of the West Indies. He is co-author of *World-Systems Analysis*.

JOHN CASPARIS is Associate Professor of Sociology at Binghamton University. GEORGI M. DERLUGIAN is Assistant Professor of Sociology at Northwestern University. RICHARD LEE is Scientific Secretary of the Gulbenkian Commission for the Restructuring of the Social Sciences. The remaining authors – SATOSHI IKEDA, SHEILA PELIZZON, THOMAS REIFER, JAMIE SUDLER and FARUK TABAK – are all Research Associates of the Fernand Braudel Center.

THE AGE OF TRANSITION
Trajectory of the World-System, 1945–2025

Coordinated by
Terence K. Hopkins *and*
Immanuel Wallerstein

with
John Casparis
Georgi M. Derlugian
Satoshi Ikeda
Richard Lee
Sheila Pelizzon
Thomas Reifer
Jamie Sudler
Faruk Tabak

ZED BOOKS
London & New Jersey

PLUTO PRESS AUSTRALIA

The Age of Transition was first published in 1996 by
Zed Books Ltd, 7 Cynthia Street, London N1 9JF, UK, and
165 First Avenue, Atlantic Highlands, New Jersey 07716, USA,
and in Australia and New Zealand by Pluto Press Australia,
PO Box 199, Leichhardt, NSW 2040, Australia

Second impression 1998

Cover designed by Andrew Corbett
Typeset in Monotype Garamond
by Lucy Morton, London SE12
Printed and bound in the United Kingdom
by Biddles Ltd, Guildford and King's Lynn

A catalogue record for this book is available from the British Library

Library of Congress Cataloging-in-Publication Data
Hopkins, Terence K.
    The age of transition : trajectory of the world-system, 1945–2025
Terence K. Hopkins and Immanuel Wallerstein with John Casparis
... [et al.].
        p.   cm.
    Includes bibliographical references and index.
    ISBN 1–85649–439–X. — ISBN 1–85649–440–3 (pbk.)
    1. Economic history—1945– 2. Capitalism—History—20th
century. 3. Economic forecasting. 4. Competition, International—
History—20th century. I. Wallerstein, Immanuel Maurice, 1930–
. II. Title.
HC59.H634   1997
330.9'045—dc20   96–16546
                                                           CIP

ISBN 1 85649 439 X Hb
ISBN 1 85649 440 3 Pb

In Australia
ISBN 1 86403 032 1

Contents

List of Tables and Figures

Preface

This volume is a product of the Trajectory Research Working Group of the Fernand Braudel Center for the Study of Economies, Historical Systems, and Civilizations of Binghamton University.

Participants in the Trajectory Research Working Group, other than those who are listed as co-authors of this book, who wrote working papers in the course of the project were: Farshad Araghi, Shuji Hisaeda, Hakiem and Margo Nankoe, and José A. Mota Lopes. In December 1992, the Group submitted its interim findings to a group of scholars who came to Binghamton for a three-day seminar: Bruce Cumings (History and Political Science, Northwestern University), David Gordon (Economics, New School for Social Research), Otto Kreye (Starnberger Institut, Germany), Saul Mendlowitz (World Order Models Project, New York), Alejandro Portes (Sociology, Johns Hopkins University), Robert Wade (Development Studies, University of Sussex, UK), and Boaventura de Sousa Santos (Centro de Estudos Sociais, University of Coimbra, Portugal). Their wise and lively comments forced us to reflect upon our arguments and reorganize the structure of our narrative. We greatly appreciate their willingness to assist us in this way, and are not authorized to absolve them of their inability to convince us about all the errors in direction we may have been taking. Finally, throughout the project, Satoshi Ikeda has served as Scientific Secretary with diligence and good humour.

The project was funded by the John D. and Catherine T. MacArthur Foundation as one-half of a project entitled 'Hegemony and Rivalry in the World-System: Trends and Prospective Consequences of Geopolitical Realignments, 1500–2025'. The three principal investigators were Giovanni Arrighi, Terence K. Hopkins and Immanuel Wallerstein. The other half of this project concerns a comparison of the historical patterns of different past hegemonies and transitions from one hegemonic regime to another. We are very grateful to the MacArthur Foundation, and in particular to Kennette Benedict, that they were willing to accept our thesis that, to understand the present dilemmas of the world-system, we had to start the story circa 1500.

1

The World-System: Is There a Crisis?

Terence K. Hopkins
and Immanuel Wallerstein

The 1990s is a period of great political uncertainty, intellectual unclarity, and diffuse social fear throughout the world-system. For some analysts, this is merely the result of a *fin-de-siècle* psychology, compounded by our coming not merely into another century but especially into another millennium. Many other analysts, however, take the evolving situation as reflecting much more serious matters. And the latter view finds more resonance in world public opinion.

The first great uncertainty is how we should collectively assess the period we have just lived through, 1945–90. It was in many ways a remarkable historical period. It was the moment of the most massive expansion the world-economy has experienced in the whole of the 500-year existence of the modern world-system. It was also the period of the most massive decolonization that has occurred since that of the Americas in the fifty years between 1775 and 1825, and this time it was not a decolonization by White settlers but by the non-White populations of the world. It was finally the period of an extraordinarily intensive so-called Cold War that embraced all the zones of the world-system and seemed to end spectacularly with the literal dissolution of one of its two formidable protagonists.

'Who won what?' is a question on the minds of many. And will we now enter into a new world order, as George Bush once promised us? To judge by current reports, it would scarcely seem so. Daily we read a litany in the newspapers of social disintegration in ever more parts of the world – the Balkans, the Caucasus, Africa, the Caribbean and Los Angeles, to start with. The long-standing Western faith in the inevitability of progress, the certainty that both greater prosperity and greater freedom would accrue to everyone's children and children's children has been called into serious question in recent years. Yet this faith underlay the rhetoric of the USA – its statesmen, policy-makers, and academics – throughout the Cold War. It is in the name of this faith that George Bush assured us a 'new world order'.

In this volume, we seek to assess what happened in the world-system between 1945 and 1990, in order to make plausible projections about the trajectory of the world-system in the next twenty-five to fifty years. The years 1945–90, however, cannot be appropriately appreciated without understanding that they are merely the latest period in the long history of the modern world-system, a historical social system which originated in the sixteenth century. For, since then a whole series of institutional domains have been constructed and reconstructed. These institutions continued to organize peoples' activities in the fifty years since the end of the Second World War and, in our view, will continue to organize them, perhaps with increasing difficulty, over the next twenty-five to fifty years.

We call these evolving institutional domains 'vectors' of the world-system, meaning complexes of processes that provide the continually evolving structured frameworks within which social action has occurred. Over its historical existence the modern world-system, in our view, has developed six such distinguishable but not separable vectors: the interstate system, the structure of world production, the structure of the world labour force, the patterns of world human welfare, the social cohesion of the states, and the structures of knowledge.

None of the six has (or, in our view, could have) developed in isolation from the others. The vectors are not at all to be thought of as loci of autonomous forces. They form, rather, the minimum array of interrelated facets of a single, imperfect, organic whole, each vector quite dependent on the others. Any shock, or blockage, or transformation within any one of them or among them affects all the others, and usually soon, visibly and consequently.

The interstate system is not something that has always been there. It was a creation of, and in turn a formative element of, the modern world-system. Its geographic scope and political depth have expanded in tandem with the spatial expansion of the axial division and integration of the labour processes forming its increasingly complex production system. It has been constructed of many pieces, including diplomacy and the rules governing extraterritoriality, the protocols governing interstate treaties, and the various trans-state institutions. But above all, the interstate system is a matrix of reciprocal recognitions of the (limited) sovereignty of each of the states, a framework that has been (more or less) enforced by the stronger on the weaker and by the strong on each other. Occasionally, but repeatedly, one power has been able to gain such a strong position that we can speak of its exercising hegemony over the system. When the interstate system is, rather briefly, in a phase of hegemony (as opposed to the more usual situation of a balance of power, or great power rivalry), one state credibly and continuously demonstrates its 'leadership' by shaping systemic structures, and having its systemic policies almost always accepted not merely by weaker states but by other strong ones as well. The hegemonic power has more say than that merely ensured by naked power, yet less than that which would be guaranteed to a fully legitimate authority. It is in short a hegemonic power in a world-economy, and not a world-empire. After 1945, the USA was in just such a situation of power.

The interstate system established the framework within which wars have so far been fought. But even more importantly, it created the framework that has constrained and shaped the workings of the ostensibly free (world-)market through which the world production system presumably has been operating. In the modern world-system, world production has been carried on by the rules of the capitalist world-economy in which the institutionalized primary consideration of those who own or control the means of production is the endless accumulation of capital. Not all producers have necessarily been individually so motivated, of course (nor have they always acted in accordance with transforming wealth into capital as their objective); but those which were in fact so motivated have recurrently survived and flourished better than those which were not. We call it a 'world' production structure because, across the 'world' in which it occurred (today the entire globe, but in the beginning only part of the globe), there has existed a network of commodity chains which linked production activities across multiple political jurisdictions, such that almost never could any single state place under its jurisdiction all the processes of production needed that are integral to any of the major economic activities located within its borders. Necessarily, then, the interstate relations governing the linkages affected in important ways the profitability of any production activity in that state's domain. Profitability has therefore been a function only in part of world market competitivity (the buzz-word of the 1990s). It has always been at least as much a function of the degree to which producers, with the aid of states, have been able to create conditions of relative monopolization of factors of production. And while old monopolies have always been disintegrating under the pressure of new entrants (from anywhere in the world-economy) into a (profitable) market, those with a combination of much accumulated capital, entrepreneurial skill, and extensive political access have always (or almost always) been able to create new monopolies, which again lasted for a while. Such global partial monopolies are often referred to by the less contentious name of 'leading industries' and it is the repeated creation of such industries that has accounted for the repeated great expansions of the world-economy, just as their exhaustion has accounted for the stagnations.

The process of accumulating capital on a world scale required the continual development of the world's forces and means of production. This process was a very uneven one, and thereby continually reproduced and deepened what we call the core–periphery zonal organization of world production, the basis of the axial division and integration of labour processes. The construction historically of the capitalist world-economy as world-system has entailed the establishment of commodity chains of production extending backwards from the organizing centres, at first all in Western Europe, into what were areas (and peoples) initially external to the relational processes and structures forming the growing world-system. This systemic and ongoing peripheralization, within the capitalist world-economy, of most of the world's peoples and production processes and the location of core processes in a few centres accounts in our view for the massive and ongoing inequalities of well-being among and within the state jurisdictions of the system.

Accordingly, just as there have been stronger and weaker states (gauged by military strength and political efficacy), so there have been core zones that have tended, by definition, to monopolize the high-profit monopolies while the peripheral zones housed production processes operating within truly competitive markets and hence characterized by truly low-profit activities. This relational inequality underlay the continuing political tensions among and within the states of the system. It is not one that can ever be overcome as long as the endless accumulation of capital remains the primary goal, since the endless accumulation of capital requires the existence of high profit (necessarily largely monopolized) economic activities. To the extent that everyone would seek to engage simultaneously in these high-profit activities, the boat would become 'overloaded' and accumulation would dry up. Hence the uneven distribution of rewards has been the necessary pendant of capital accumulation, and is fundamental to the system.

This requirement of unevenness has been integral to the continuing formation of the world labour force. If the ways in which labour was remunerated would everywhere have been the same, profit levels would have been everywhere the same and therefore low. While monopolistic loci in the extended commodity chains may themselves have had relatively small and highly paid workforces, their high levels of profit have been dependent on the much lower wage levels of those who produced the multiple inputs, and the inputs to the inputs, that they utilized in these loci. The world labour force has thus constituted a vested hierarchy within the multiple commodity chains.

Hence, as we look across the world at those segments of the commodity chains we call peripheral, we find modes of remuneration of labour where the bargaining power of labour has been politically constrained more strongly than in the core zone. One major mechanism of such constraint has been coerced employment (ranging from slavery to debt controls to various kinds of 'customary' arrangements). Another major mechanism, less obvious and less visible, has been the construction of forms of householding that require significant inputs of unremunerated labour to supplement wage income, thereby permitting reductions of labour costs to the employers of wage workers (which in effect involves a transfer of household members' surplus-value to the employers).

The world labour force, however, has been structured not only by the multiple employers and the states. The workers have themselves been involved in structuring the labour force – by syndical action, by migration, by the creation of solidarities and mutualities. Over time, the interacting pressures have frequently led to situations in which options for employers have been limited, reduced or transformed. One major form this has taken has been the putting forward by the workforce of new kinds of demands on state structures, which in turn have affected the ability of the states to operate geopolitically and, in particular, to house highly profitable economic activities. There has grown up a system of 'social wages' that has to be taken into account in calculating the real remuneration of workers. The three major fields in which such social wages have been located are education, health, and a generic field we may call redistributive allocations (such as pensions, unemployment payments, equity payments). The question that is always pertinent, of course, is whether there has been real redistribution from capital to labour, or simply a reshuffling of income already obtained by workers from one form to another.

It is only when we calculate all the forms of income that we can assess the vector of human welfare, but this vector is crucial in terms of the political stability and economic efficacy of the world-system. Not only is the true spectrum of human welfare a major evolving condition but so is the perceived spectrum. The unevenness of world productive activity has been reflected, even exaggerated, in the unevenness of world welfare outcomes – which have varied geographically, cyclically and historically. The belief in long-term welfare convergence has been a major ideological underpinning of the world-system. But the perception of convergence and of its converse, polarization, has been a function in large part of what has been measured, when, and by whom. One of the secular shifts in the world-system has been the increased collective ability to measure convergence/polarization of world welfare effectively. And the results of such a more careful look have not always been close to what official views have argued.

The realities of interstate conflicts plus worldwide competition for profits, plus the constant attempts to mould a world labour force that would be available, efficient but not too costly, plus the increasing attentiveness to the diverging quality of world welfare have added up to a tumultuous world-system, riven by constant violence and rebelliousness. What has held the system together more than anything else amidst this tumult have been the historic efforts to create ever more cohesive state structures and the elaboration of structures of knowledge that have served to legitimate the system.

The state structures have been getting steadily stronger for 500 years, their governments having sought to ensure internal order by an effort to monopolize the means of violence. They have sought to strengthen control of their borders, defining who and what may pass in either direction. To be sure, no state has ever achieved total internal or external control. And quite obviously some states have historically done much better in this regard than others – this is one aspect of what we mean by distinguishing between stronger and weaker states. But almost all states have been part of the long-term secular trend of strengthening the state, albeit with many short-term reverses of course.

The abilities of states to enforce order has been a function of their ability to command resources (taxation) and therefore personnel (bureaucracy), and of the acceptance of their rule because of services provided (security, infrastructure, expansion of human welfare levels). In all of this, states have not of course been 'neutral' arbiters (far from it), but all governments have regularly claimed to be both effective managers of 'national interests' and guarantors (along with the governments of other states) of the long-term stability of the world-system and its overall capacity to ensure the endless accumulation of capital.

Governments have increasingly utilized the glue of social cohesion in their efforts to achieve these objectives, and the major vehicle of this cohesion has been what we call nationalism (or patriotism). The basic theme of nationalism is that no matter how diverse the social situations and interests of those located within the state, they are (or should be) unified affectively by a common (and somewhat mythical) consanguinity and/or ascriptive allegiance, thereby legitimating the state's rule.

Nationalism has always involved one complication, the decision of who was to be included in the affective entity. The group was never defined as everyone merely resident in a state's jurisdiction. Nationalists often wished to include some who were not resident in the state (which in turn could become a call to irredentism), as well as to exclude some who were. Of course, a nation is a nation in the eyes of the beholder, and those eyes vary. In addition, to the degree that the requirements of the structuring of the world labour force have led to widely differing modes of labour remuneration *within* state boundaries, there has always been pressure to define the 'nation' as including only one part of the workforce, commonly defined by racial or ethnic criteria. And to the degree that these requirements have led to widely differing modes of labour remuneration *among* states, this pattern has commonly needed the justification of racism.

Thus 'nationalism' has quite frequently directly implied racism. But, of course, in historic reaction, the ideology of nationalism was appropriated by antisystemic movements in the struggle against racism – which is what we mean by 'national liberation movements'. Nonetheless, on the whole and over time, nationalism – as the principal legitimation of the state-system – has been more of a stabilizing than a destabilizing force of the modern world-system.

The story becomes clearer, if more complicated, when we look at the structures of knowledge. The single most important innovation in the structures of knowledge of the modern world-system was the displacement of philosophy/theology by science as the central organizing metaphor of knowledge, and indeed the dominance of one particular mode of scientific method (which we may label simplistically 'Newtonian'), which has claimed to be the only legitimate mode of scientific endeavour.

A crucial element in Newtonian science has been its claims to universalism, a theme that was directly reflected in liberalism, the dominant world ideology of the last two hundred years, and the one that came to define the geoculture of the world-system. The most reassuring element in liberal ideology was its argument concerning the trajectory of the multiple vectors of the world-system. Liberalism preached the inevitable triumph of an incrementalist convergence in human welfare as well as the eventual virtual elimination of violence that would result, it claimed, precisely from the increasing cohesion of the states resulting from the lessening of inequality. In a sense liberalism offered the practice of patient reformism to remedy tumult and civilization's discontents.

Liberal universalism seemed to be in direct opposition to racism and sexism. In fact it was in symbiotic tension with them, a relationship to which we have just alluded in the discussion of the role of nationalism in strengthening the social cohesion of the states. Liberalism's success as a mode of containing discontent and tumult was a direct function of the evidence its protagonists could present of incremental social 'progress', a thesis they were able to support quite well in the nineteenth century, but which has been much more difficult to argue consistently in the twentieth century.

Nonetheless, the combination of nationalism plus scientism/universalism/liberalism as the main elements in the geoculture of the world-system served for a very long time to obscure the tensions of the world-system and thereby in effect to hold them in check. The question today is: Are these tensions still in check? Or is there a crisis in the world-system?

To address this issue, we must first note one other feature of this world-system, a feature it has in common with all other historical systems. A historical system is both systemic and historical. That is to say, it has enduring structures that define it as a system – enduring, but not of course eternal. At the same time, the system is evolving second by second such that it is never the same at two successive points in time. That is to say, the system has a history, and it is what it is at any given moment not only because of its enduring structure but because of its particular (indeed unique) historical trajectory.

Another way to describe this is to say that a system has cyclical rhythms (resulting from its enduring structures as they pass through their normal fluctuations) and secular trends (vectors which have direction, resulting from the constant evolution of the structures). Because the modern world-system (like any other historical system) has both cycles and trends – cycles that restore 'equilibrium' and trends that move 'far from equilibrium' – there must come a point when the trends create a situation in which the cyclical rhythms are no longer capable of restoring long-term (relative) equilibrium. When this happens, we may talk of a crisis, a real 'crisis', meaning a turning point so decisive that the system comes to an end and is replaced by one or more alternative successor systems. Such a 'crisis' is not a repeated (cyclical) event. It happens only once in the life of any system, and signals its historical coming to an end. And it is not a quick event but a 'transition', a long period lasting a few generations.

In the terminology of the new science, this is the moment when the system bifurcates; that is, when the fluctuations away from equilibrium are so great that the curve flies off to form one or more new orbits. There is always more than one possibility at this point, and there is no way of determining in advance what the outcome(s) will be. All one can do is assess the likelihood that we are approaching a bifurcation (or are already in the midst of one).

This is the object of the research design for this book. When we look at the period 1945–90, we immediately notice a few things about it. It starts out as a period of incredible global economic expansion which then slows down. It starts out as the period of unquestioned US hegemony in the world-system and then this hegemony begins its decline. We have identified the moment of shift for each of these two phenomena as 1967/73.

Periods of global economic expansion and contraction are sometimes referred to as Kondratieff cycles. They typically have lasted 45–60 years, and are sometimes alluded to by historians when they speak of an era of prosperity or one of great depression. We believe that a Kondratieff expansion or A-phase began circa 1945 and reached its peak in 1967/73, whereupon it was followed by a stagnation or B-phase which is continuing into the 1990s. If we have stopped the story at 1990, it is partly because of the geopolitical chronology and partly because we did this research as of 1990.

Hegemonic cycles are far longer than Kondratieff cycles. It takes a long time for one major power to win a competition with another major power such that it can become fully hegemonic. As soon as it does so, it seeks to use its hegemonic position to prolong its power. Nonetheless, it is in the nature of the capitalist world-economy as a historical system that the very efforts made to prolong the power themselves tend to undermine the base of the power, and thus start the long process of relative decline (and, of course, of relative rise of other powers aspiring to establish a new hegemony).

The erstwhile hegemonic power, Great Britain, began its decline in the 1870s, and from that moment the USA and Germany began their long competition to become the successor world hegemonic power. After two world wars (really one long one with some interruptions), the USA won unconditionally in 1945. The real era of full hegemony began then, but already by 1967/73 US power had begun to erode.

Hence we see 1967/73 as the peak of two cyclical curves: the shorter Kondratieff cycle running from 1945 to 199?, and the longer hegemonic cycle running from 1873–(2025/2050?). This by itself is interesting, but in terms of the modern world-system is not unusual. Rather, it seems to reflect the normal cyclical workings of the system. The question we wish to pose, however, is this: Was 1967/73 *also* the peak of a still longer curve, the life curve of this historical system, running from circa 1500 to some point in the relatively near future? The life curve of a historical system is not bell-shaped, like Kondratieff cycles or hegemonic cycles. Rather, the curve of a historical system tends to go upward monotonically until it reaches its peak, and then to fall with relative precipitousness. It is not the graph of a cyclical rhythm but that of the combination of secular trends.

How can we know the answer to such a question? Our methodology, we think, is quite straightforward, and speaks directly to the question posed. We have studied the six vectors previously outlined. We have sought to describe each of these vectors of the world-system as a whole twice – once for the period 1945–1967/73 and once for the period 1967/73–1990. We have found considerable differences between the two periods for each of the six vectors. This exercise constitutes Chapters 2–7 of this book.

We have then tried (in Chapter 8) to put the pieces together into one encompassing whole. In comparing the second or B-period findings with those of the first or A-period, we have asked how much of the changes can be accounted for by what we know of the recurrent workings of Kondratieff cycles and hegemonic cycles. Once we have thereby 'eliminated' the changes attributable to these two cyclical rhythms, how large a residual is there? What kinds of changes in the second period cannot be accounted for via either Kondratieff or hegemonic cyclical rhythms? We have found some significant ones. And we then ask how likely it is that such changes might be the sign of 'crisis', of the beginning of a bifurcation?

Finally, in Chapter 9, we try to project a middle-term future (1990– 2025). The logic of our exercise is as follows. If indeed 1967/73 is *also* the beginning of a systemic crisis, of the precipitate downturn, what might we expect *during* the bifurcation – that is, in the middle run? The short answer is disorder, considerable disorder. But we try to give this projected disorder more specific characteristics, to elaborate the picture, and to suggest what we see as some of the real historical alternatives before us.

If the outcome is not determined in advance, and hence cannot be predicted, that does not mean we must sit by helplessly waiting for the hurricane to envelop us. As in any kind of real historical crisis, there exist real choices that can be made. Those who discern them lucidly and act on them with concerted effort are less likely to lose the outcome they prefer than those who put their faith in the unseen historical hand. It is to help in this effort that this book is written.

Part I

The Institutional Vectors, 1945–90

2

The Interstate System

Thomas Reifer and Jamie Sudler

From 1945 to 1967/73: The Creation of the Cold War Structure

After 1945, the United States, the world's number one military power and the only power to have nuclear weapons, took the lead in establishing a new structure for the interstate system. After dropping atomic bombs on Japan on 6 and 9 August 1945, the USA felt itself somewhat released from the limitations on its freedom of action inscribed in the agreements negotiated by the three Great Powers at Yalta (Alperovitz, 1985; Davis, 1986: 182–3). The USSR, though some distance behind the USA in terms of military power, was nonetheless the second great power, and it is not surprising in retrospect that two blocs developed around this military dichotomy (Gaddis, 1987: 221). Still, although the US and Soviet blocs or spheres of influence were actually in place before the war was over, it would be some time before Roosevelt's one-world universalism would be replaced by Truman's two-bloc Cold War order and the attendant remilitarization of interstate relations (Schurmann, 1974: 3–8, 13–16, 39–107).

The Yalta Conference in February of 1945 set the seal on the creation of these two blocs (Barnet, 1983: 96). The USA agreed to limit itself primarily to its own bloc, as did the Soviets (Keal, 1983: 84, 93–4; Barnet, 1983: 107; Davis, 1974: 167–8, 184). For example, the USA, long dominant in Latin America, reaffirmed this domain, obtaining Latin American adhesion to the Act of Chapultapec in 1945, which sealed a military alliance for the Western hemisphere (Keal, 1983: 108).

It was, however, the monopoly of strategic nuclear weapons by the United States that more than anything else allowed it 'to claim rights to intervention in what amounted to a "sphere of predominant influence" that ran right up to the borders of Soviet or Chinese occupation every-where in the world', creating a 'historical legacy' that would live on throughout the postwar era (Ellsberg, 1981: xi). Thus, with the end of the Japanese Empire and as British and French imperial power waned in the Middle East and Asia, the USA picked up the baton, first with the Truman Doctrine for Greece and Turkey (thus securing US influence over Middle East oil) and later in Northeast and Southeast Asia. The USA thereby locked its allies into a dependent relationship through its provisioning of global security combined with its control over the flow of both oil and agricultural goods.

A second key element was the fact that all the major industrial economies other than the USA had been destroyed or massively damaged by the war. Economic conditions throughout Europe were very difficult in the years immediately after the war, a situation exacerbated by un-usually bad weather (Barnet, 1983: 110). There was hunger, disease and extreme cold, all of which took their toll on people and animals (Solomon, 1982: 14). Additionally, there was much economic disruption resulting from the postwar nationalizations and the absence of eco-nomic coordination among the European states (Barnet, 1983: 113). Conditions in Japan were equally difficult, because of both economic disruption and political turbulence, including a large left-led labour movement (Moore, 1983), as was the case, of course, in France and Italy as well.

The third crucial ingredient at war's end was the wave of revolt sweeping through the colonial world. The largest colonial areas were in Asia and in Africa. In Asia, all the colonial zones in Southeast Asia had been occupied by the Japanese during the war, a fact which had further stimulated local nationalism. In general, all the major colonizing powers – Great Britain, France, Belgium, Portugal and the Netherlands – had lost both power and prestige in their colonies as a result. This put the colonial powers in the awkward situation of having to *re*-establish their authority, often in situations where local nationalist movements had established *de facto* control.

The demands for self-rule and independence by the colonized peoples posed both an opportunity and a dilemma for the USA. The USA was finally in a position to break open the closed trading blocs of Europe's and Japan's territorial empires in pursuit of its worldwide Open Door policy. Still, the USA had to be careful. Its European allies were strongly opposed to the dismantling of their colonial empires, and in addition the USA wished to avoid a revolutionary process of decolonization that could pose a threat to US plans to maintain the Third World within the core–periphery structure of the capitalist world-economy.

As the dominant world power, the USA faced the challenge of reconstructing the unity of the capitalist world market based on multi-lateralism – 'the absence of barriers to the transfer of goods and capital across national borders' (Borden, 1984: 6; see Gardner, 1980: 13, 42–47, 56–62) – while simultaneously creating a favourable balance of power. The main threat to multilateralism after 1945 was the dollar gap, the $10 billion trade surplus of US exports over imports which caused a great shortfall in foreign dollar accounts (Borden, 1984: 6; Leffler, 1992: 164).

Ironically, it was the very supremacy of the USA in world production and trade that posed the greatest threat to the reconstruction of the capitalist world-economy, as fiscal insolvency in Europe and Asia threatened to close the USA out of overseas markets and hence to destroy the possibilities of multilateral economic integration. The USA saw these countries as markets for its exports, yet Japan and Western Europe did not have enough dollars to buy US foodstuffs, raw materials and other goods that they depended on for reconstruction (Wallerstein, 1991a: 26). Furthermore, US–Soviet competition threatened Western Europe (and later Japan) with a cutoff of traditional markets and sources of supply in Eastern Europe, China and elsewhere (Borden, 1984; Cumings, 1990: 37). This only increased the dependence of Western Europe and Japan on supplies from the dollar area, thus exacerbating the dollar gap.

Before the war, the USA had regularly run a large trade surplus with Europe, a trade that was brought into balance by US purchases of primary products from Europe's colonies in the Middle East, Africa, Asia, and elsewhere. European countries then acquired these dollars by exchanging manufactured goods for raw materials and foodstuffs from their colonies and through repatriation of profits from large-scale colonial investments. This triangular trading pattern thus provided a basis for multilateral trading relations (Borden, 1984: 21–2). As Europe was forced to convert many of these investments into cash to pay for the war, it could no longer acquire billions of dollars through profits from colonial investments alone and was thus forced to increase its own exports in order to generate foreign exchange to meet its import needs. This was no small problem given the waning of colonialism and the cutoff of markets and non-dollar sources of supply in the Communist bloc.

US leaders feared that economic collapse or disorder would increase Communist gains in Western European elections and thus reorient continental trade towards the USSR and away from the West (Leffler, 1992: 163, 188–92). Likewise, in Japan, the USA feared a leftward drift and, after 1949, was concerned about the political-economic implications of a renewal of Japanese commercial relations with Communist China (Borden, 1984: 22). The USA saw a real danger that if the triangular trading patterns – through which Europe earned dollars through US purchases of raw materials from their colonies, as described above – were not re-created worldwide, Europe and Japan would form soft-trading currency blocs with other countries in their respective areas, including the USSR, Eastern Europe, and later Communist China. This would then upset both the multilateral trade relations and the balance of power that were so essential to the operations of the capitalist world-economy and interstate system.

The USA sought to establish the prerequisites for multilateral economic integration and intra-capitalist cooperation under US leadership by reconstructing Japan and the Federal Republic of Germany as the regional workshops of Asia and Europe and reintegrating them with their peripheral zones. Specifically, US planners aimed to re-create triangular trading patterns by restoring Europe and Japan as industrial producers so they could trade manufactured goods for primary products with their former colonies, thus earning dollars and reducing their dependence on US primary products and other goods, which was a major factor in their dollar shortage (see Leffler, 1992: 468–9). This planning also came to include development programmes for the Third World, as highlighted in Point Four of Truman's 1949 inaugural address, which were seen in part as a way to create alternative markets for Europe in the Middle East and other regions (Leffler, 1992: 291).

In essence, Japan and the Federal Republic of Germany were the central props in the maintenance of a favourable balance of power, while their revival as industrial workshops was a crucial part of the material underpinning for a renewed expansion of the capitalist world-economy (Borden, 1984: 15; see Leffler, 1992: 498). As always, power and plenty, or balance of power and balance of trade/payments considerations, were inextricably linked.

The Bretton Woods institutions – the International Monetary Fund (IMF) and the International Bank for Reconstruction and Development (later the World Bank) – were wholly inadequate for solving these balance-of-payments problems and thereby creating the conditions for currency convertibility. It was the Marshall Plan that served as the stop-gap measure to deal with the dollar gap and to begin the task of forcing multilateralism on the European economies (Wood, 1986: 38; Hogan, 1987: 130, 133; Leffler, 1992: 233; Block, 1977: 86–92). Still, the Marshall Plan provided only a temporary fix to the dollar shortage and a fiscally conservative US Congress was reticent to provide sufficient aid to Europe and Japan to overcome this gap (Borden, 1984: 11).

The USSR, for its part, feared the influence of the Marshall Plan and other US programmes which were predicated on the supposition that the Eastern European economy would be reintegrated into that of the Western European core in return for US aid. The USA also aimed to prevent the emergence of a united Germany that was either aligned with the USSR, or even neutral. To this end, US planners viewed aid programmes as means to ensure the integration of the western zones of Germany – most notably the coveted Rhine–Ruhr industrial complex – into the orbit of the West (see Leffler, 1992: 277–86; cf. Loriaux, 1993: 83–110). This conflicted with Stalin's desire to protect the Soviet periphery from Western or nationalist influence. As Leffler (1992: 185–6, 204) notes, 'US officials recognized that they were confronting the Kremlin with unpalatable choices. National self-interest, Kennan realized, would probably force the Russians to clamp down on Eastern Europe' (see also Alperovitz and Bird, 1994: 10). The Soviets did exactly this, rejecting Marshall Plan aid for itself, pressuring Poland and Czechoslovakia (who were tempted) not to participate, and completing the Communist seizure of power in Eastern European states by a takeover in Czechoslovakia, which was particularly worrisome to the West since it had had a functioning parliamentary system (see Leffler, 1983: 249).

Then in June 1948, the Berlin crisis erupted when the USA announced it would implement currency reform in the western zones of Germany. The USSR saw this as a move towards the creation of a separate government in the western zones of Germany and the subsequent integration of the Federal Republic of Germany within the Western orbit. They moved to blockade goods coming into Berlin. In turn, the West responded with an airlift (Leffler, 1992: 184–6, 203–20; Bird, 1992: 309–11; see Feis, 1970: 267–412). The USA argued that moves such as this by the USSR were evidence of aggressive intent, invoking memories of Munich and casting the USSR as the successor to fascist regimes in Germany and Japan that had previously sought to build world-empires (see Dehio, 1962).

By the late 1940s, the USSR had consolidated its domination of Eastern Europe, while the USA had found the beginnings of a solution to both the balance of power and balance-of-payments problems in Europe and Asia. First articulated with the Truman Doctrine (1947), and later with the establishment of NATO (1949), the USA made it clear that Communist/Soviet (no distinction was made between these two) threats against Western Europe, Greece or Turkey would be met by US dollars and force. The 1945 division of Germany into four occupation zones was replaced by a more enduring division, the establishment of two German states. With its atomic superiority, the USA had the confidence it needed to integrate (and eventually rearm) the Federal Republic of Germany as part of NATO despite Soviet fears of German power and the risks, noted by Senator Vandenberg, that these moves 'would institutionalize a permanent cold war', which indeed they helped to do (Leffler, 1992: 204, 208–10, 218–19, 277–86, 308, 351, 498; Alperovitz and Bird, 1994: 3–20; Bird, 1992: 311). Besides, the Cold War and NATO were useful, allowing as they did for the containment of both the USSR and thrusts towards independence by the allies of the United States (Costigliola, 1989: 25).

Nuclear superiority, while crucial for NATO, was also useful in backing up US interventionary forces in the Third World (Ellsberg, 1981: i–xxviii; Leffler, 1992: 443–4; Betts, 1987; Alperovitz and Bird, 1994: 13–16; Davis, 1982: 35–64). In a circular logic of causation, however, US intervention in the Third World further increased the need for European rearmament and US strategic superiority, lest the USSR escalate ongoing Third World conflicts in which the two great powers found themselves supporting opposite sides by moving the confrontation to Europe, where they had a conventional advantage (Leffler, 1992: 384). In any event, the establishment of NATO was immediately countered by that of the Warsaw Pact, as the Marshall Plan agencies were countered by the construction of COMECON. The Cold War was being fully institutionalized, at least in Europe.

The long-term solution to both the balance of power and the dollar gap problem in the balance of payments, however, came only in the 1950s. Dean Acheson, US Secretary of State, and his aide Paul Nitze, saw rearmament, or 'international military Keynesianism' (1969), as the solution to Congressional reticence to tackle the dollar gap problem and related security issues. Nitze outlined this strategy in a key policy document, NSC 68 (Borden, 1984). The difficulty arose in finding a compelling reason to implement the policy while overcoming the divisions between the two seemingly incompatible currents in foreign policy, the nationalist and internationalist, that prevented Congressional authorization of the package.

Congress (especially right-wing Republicans) typified the nationalist current, representing as they did mostly local/regional business interests and constituencies rooted in the home market, and were extremely reluctant to increase taxation to rebuild their former economic and military competitors. The internationalist foreign-policy current, symbolized in the cosmopolitan lawyers of the Eastern Establishment such as Dean Acheson and John J. McCloy, represented instead the interests of multinational corporations and bankers with their keen interest in international trade and overseas markets (Borden, 1984: 10; Schurmann,

1974: 60–65; Bird, 1992: 15–20, 663; Cumings, 1990: 23–31, 79–121; Issacson and Thomas, 1986). There was only one issue, fundamental to the American people, that could bring the nationalist and internationalist currents together: security (Schurmann, 1974: 65–8, 76–107).

North Korea's onslaught against the South, coming on the heels of both the Soviet atomic explosion and the Chinese Communist revolution, provided the political crisis that allowed for the Congressional authorization of the massive increase in military expenditures necessary to both overcome the dollar gap and reinforce the Cold War balance of power in Asia and Europe. With international military Keynesianism, the USA was able to distribute the liquidity necessary to rebuild what Acheson called the two great workshops of Europe and Asia (Gilpin, 1975: 110) while at the same time enmeshing US allies into a US-dominated security structure. US security obligations included guaranteeing an Open Door for free enterprise in the Third World, which US planners deemed essential for multilateralism (Leffler, 1992: 314, 355–60). The Korean War was the occasion for pursuing all these objectives at once, as intimated by Acheson's later remark: 'Korea saved us' (Hershberg, 1993: 498; cf. Cumings, 1990: 761, 918).

US military expenditures increased more than threefold during this period, setting off the Korean War boom. US troops in Europe, replete with nuclear weapons to back them up for purposes of extended deterrence, provided tangible evidence of the credibility of the US commitment to defend Western Europe against superior Warsaw Pact conventional strength. At the same time, these US troops acted as a 'migratory city' (McNeill, 1982: 74–5, 82), so that by 1954 $2.3 billion were flowing into Europe annually to purchase European-made military equipment for NATO and other allied troops through 'offshore procurement' and related programmes (Sanders, 1983: 113).

Furthermore, the boom increased prices of primary commodities by as much as 150 per cent, allowing Europe and Japan to earn dollars from trade with their peripheries, helped along by US programmes such as 'coordinated aid' which tied dollar grants to the development of non-dollar sources of trade (Borden, 1984: 25). Policy document NSC 48/5 outlined similar schemes for Asia, centring initially around production for the Korean (and later the Vietnam) War. By 1964, $7.2 billion in military procurement had thus flowed into Japan (Borden, 1984: 155, 220; Elliot, 1955: 312–17). By 1970, on an annual average basis the USA spent $500 million a year for twenty years in Japan, a $10 billion windfall (Borden, 1984: 220).

Although the Korean War was instrumental to the construction of US hegemony on a global scale, one can also trace its origins back to the

Asian region, specifically to what Cumings (1981: 117) has called the 'first postwar act of containment', the partition of Korea into US and Soviet zones of occupation in 1945. Document NSC 48 was outlined under Acheson's guidance in 1949 immediately after the explosion of the Soviet A-bomb, the Chinese Communist Revolution, and what 'Americans sensed [as] an expansion of pressure all along the Soviet perimeter, but especially in Asia'. It essentially extended *formally* Truman's containment doctrine to the whole of the Far East (Cumings, 1990: 45, 160, 166). This key US policy document for Asia reflected Acheson's vision of the 'Great Crescent', outlining as it did a programme for regional economic integration centred on Japan that included both Northeast and Southeast Asia, and stating: 'In view of the desirability of avoiding preponderant dependence on Chinese sources, and the limited availability of supplies from prewar sources in Korea and Formosa', Japan would have to turn instead to Southeast Asia to meet its needs (McGlothlen, 1993: 191–2, quoting NSC 48, 23 December 1949 draft; NSC 48 draft in Etzold and Gaddis, 1978: 252–69; see Cumings, 1990: 45–58, 168–77, 761–5; Schaller, 1985; Leffler, 1992: 253–60, 298–304, 333–41).

In 1950, the North Korean press was full of articles that voiced rather different concerns, articulating fears of a revival of Japanese imperialism (in alliance with the South Korean regime) and of Japan turning into a staging ground for US military operations in Northeast Asia (Cumings, 1987–88: 89). For the USA, North Korea was a mere client of the Soviets, with no autonomy (Cumings, 1990: 443). North Korea's attack can be seen, though, as an attempt to unify a divided country in which a civil war was raging while seeking to prevent the emergence of a regional political economy based on Japan as the workshop, reintegrating its former empire in northeast and southeast Asia under the auspices of US hegemony (Cumings, 1990: 763–5; Cumings, 1987–88: 89).

US aid to the French in 1950 and beyond was also driven by the NSC 48 logic of shoring up the Pacific Rimlands, containing and ultimately rolling back Communism by cutting the economic links between Japan and China, ensuring the former's economic access to Southeast Asia and by driving a wedge between the Soviets and Chinese until the latter could be reintegrated into the Asian political-economy under US patronage (Cumings, 1990: 165; Cumings, 1993: 34–63; Leffler, 1992: 298–304; *Pentagon Papers*, 1971: 375–81). In addition, losing Indochina would surely have been politically catastrophic at a time when the Democrats were still reeling from an offensive led by Asia-first right-wing Republicans blaming the Democrats for losing China, with the related McCarthyite accusations of treason and betrayal that led to the subsequent purge of suspected Communists from the State Department (Ellsberg, 1972: 41–141, esp. 82–141; see also Cumings, 1990: 79–122; and Davis, 1986: 162–7). Furthermore, Soviet and Chinese support for the Vietnamese and other revolutionary movements only increased US fears of the so-called domino effect, the 'superdomino' being Japan (*Pentagon Papers*, 1971: 450; Dower, 1972: 101–42).

The Cold War structure permitted in turn the use of Cold War anti-Communism against labour movements in the USA, Western Europe and Japan. In the USA, the wave of anti-Communism got a boost as the Soviet army's move into Eastern Europe increased anti-Communist sentiment among those of Hungarian and Slav descent, who had in fact been key groups in the formation of the Congress of Industrial Organizations (CIO) and totalled up to half its membership, quite apart from the fact that it ensured the ascendancy of right-wing Catholicism in general (Davis, 1986: 90, 94; see Wallerstein, 1954, cited in Cumings, 1990: 788; Fraser, 1989: 55–84). The combination of anti-Communist purges within the CIO and Truman's reliance on the Republicans and Southern Democrats to support the Cold War virtually assured the defeat of the CIO's Southern organizing drive, Operation Dixie, dashing the hopes that had been raised by labour's 1946 postwar strike wave (Davis, 1986: 96–7; Lichtenstein, 1982: 233–41).

In Europe and Japan too, the Cold War came into play, as US intelligence efforts working in conjunction with the AFL–CIO ensured Communist defeats in electoral contests and the weakening of left-led labour movements. Labour was instead integrated into the discipline of Fordism and the Cold War, while in the Eastern bloc, independent unions and non-state-sanctioned political activity were brutally repressed (Arrighi, 1990a: 29–63; Davis, 1986: 184–90; van der Pijl, 1984: 150–56; Chomsky, 1991: 331–50; Eisenberg, 1983: 283–306; Filippelli, 1989; Moore, 1983).

Along with curbing left-labour movements in Europe and Japan, the USA aimed to check Third World radicalism even as it sought to break up the old colonial system. US plans for a new multilateral world order were, to be sure, in conflict with the old world order of European territorial empires, with their overseas colonies and closed trading blocs. Furthermore, colonial rule was increasingly leading to revolutionary decolonization. These were the two reasons why the USA was generally favourable to decolonization. The USA pursued this reform of the inter-state system in part through its establishment of the United Nations, in part by direct pressure on the colonial powers.

On an ideological level, the UN was a promissory note to the peoples of the periphery that they too could enjoy political independence, progress and equality in the same manner as the powerful states (Schurmann, 1974: 69). The UN promise was a contradictory one for US hegemony, providing the framework for dismantling the old colonial empires while at the same time providing space for radical anticolonial movements and for non-alignment policies by Third World independent states.

Politically, the UN was no less than 'revolutionary' in that 'for the first time in world history, there was a concrete institutionalization of the idea of world government' (Schurmann, 1974: 71) with the General Assembly providing for one country, one vote. At the same time, much of the real power resided with the five powers that comprised the Security Council – the USA, the USSR, Great Britain, France and China. Nevertheless, the United Nations was another mechanism through which the USA helped restructure the interstate system to include the heretofore denied rights of the colonized people of the world, as citizens of sovereign states. Indeed, when all is said and done, this radical restructuring of the interstate system through worldwide decolonization is one of the most important legacies of the US cycle of hegemonic rule (Arrighi, 1990b: 401).

Still, the US fear of independent nationalist or Communist movements that might threaten its Open Door policy marked the limits of its support for decolonization. This is why the USA at times acceded to the desire of European governments to slow down decolonization, the support for the Portuguese in Africa and for the French in Vietnam providing two illustrations. Along with sometimes backtracking on its promise to push forward on decolonization, US covert operations limited the sovereignty of nominally independent states. From 1945 to the late 1960s, the USA aggressively pursued its policy of the Open Door, engaging in military actions around the world, such as in Iran in 1953, where the USA helped to overthrow Mossadegh and install the Shah (Bill, 1988: 51–97), and in 1954 in Guatemala, where the USA ousted the incumbent government when it challenged the prerogatives of US multinational corporations.

The Cold War itself developed in the context of the stirring of nationalist forces in the Third World, as the movement for decolonization accelerated due to the pressure of the anti-colonial movements. The process was pushed still further with the Bandung Conference in 1955 and the birth of the non-aligned movement (NAM), at which all of the twenty-nine states that were independent at the time in Africa and Asia (except for the two Koreas) were represented. The NAM states attempted to steer clear of Cold War superpower alignments which limited their sovereignty, supporting the rights of Third World states for self-determination in all aspects of social, economic and foreign policy (Singham and Hune, 1986: 66). These positions were merely the restatement, if not the logical extension of, 'rights' that had been codified in the UN Charter, and for that reason it might have been expected that non-aligned leaders would not encounter hostility from the USA. Non-alignment, however, threatened US plans for multilateral economic integration and was thus seen as a serious challenge.

The USA opposed nationalist threats to its Open Door policy not only from the Third World but also from the colonial powers. Nominal independence for the Third World was necessary as colonial blocs also threatened multilateral economic integration. An important example of the benefits the USA derived from its decolonization policy is the 1956 Suez crisis. Egypt under Nasser had emerged as one of the leaders of the NAM and the 'Bandung generation'. After Nasser nationalized the Suez Canal, Great Britain, France and Israel invaded Egypt. Though opposing Nasser's radical nationalism, the USA balked at this blatant attempt at recolonization, turning on its allies and forcing their withdrawal. In the process, the USA displaced the British and French from much of the Middle East, thereby strengthening its own control over the region's oil. Suez provides but one example of the US refusal to back the reimposition of colonial rule, in sharp contrast to its reaction to the crushing of the Hungarian uprising by the USSR in the same year, where the USA (despite much rhetoric) in fact deferred to Soviet domination of Eastern Europe as per the postwar balance of forces and related agreements.

By 1960, nearly twenty countries in Black Africa had won independence and the wave of decolonization was going ahead at full steam. The USSR and the USA sought to win the allegiance of these and other newly-independent states, while the European powers attempted to slow down the whole independence process. The efforts of the European powers to stem the tide of decolonization were legion. The Dutch had engaged in counterinsurgency operations in the East Indies in the immediate postwar period; the British had done the same in Malaya and the Gulf, and had put down the Mau-Mau anti-colonial revolt in Kenya in the 1950s as well. The French were drawn into long and bloody colonial wars in Vietnam and Algeria. And the Portuguese fought anti-colonial movements in Guinea-Bissau, Mozambique and Angola (which would only achieve independence in 1975).

During this whole period Cold War competition was on the rise. In 1961, Khrushchev exacerbated US fears of Third World nationalism by talking about the certain spread of Marxism through 'wars of national liberation' (Noer, 1989: 258). The essentially counterrevolutionary

response of the USA in the Kennedy years was built on the premiss
that the USA should promote nation-building and economic development as the alternative to the Communist road (Paterson, 1989: 13).
Kennedy's Alliance for Progress was one such programme designed to
support pro-systemic governments in Latin America, including via pre-
emptive counterinsurgency (Rabe, 1989: 105–22; McClintock, 1985;
1992). Unsuccessful in its attempt to overthrow the Cuban Revolution
and fearful of its spread, the USA allied itself with Latin America's
oligarchic elites, supporting the overthrow of the Brazilian government
in 1964 (Black, 1977) and invading the Dominican Republic in 1965.

Time and again, the USA would support decolonization only to turn
around and use covert operations to ensure that Third World regimes
were pro-American. In Indonesia, the USA had successfully pushed the
Dutch to grant independence, yet later contributed to the destruction
of the Communist Party of Indonesia and its suspected supporters in
1965 after the overthrow of nationalist leader Sukarno (with possible
US involvement), in what the CIA called 'one of the worst mass murders
of the 20th century' with somewhere between a quarter of a million to
over one million killed (Kadane, 1990a; 1990b; cf. Scott, 1985: 239–64;
Brands, 1989: 785–808; Crouch, 1978).

The long crisis in the Congo (rich in natural resources) provides
another example of US covert intervention after independence to ensure
a pro-American regime. In 1960 when Belgium sent troops ostensibly to
protect its citizens after Congolese troops mutinied shortly after independence day, the Congo's President Kasavubu and Premier Lumumba
called on the UN to force out the Belgians. In fact, they served as tacit
support for the secession of the province of Katanga. The UN sent in
troops whose political role was ambiguous. When Lumumba thereupon
sought Soviet aid to regain the province of Katanga, Kasavubu (with US
and Belgian encouragement) fired Lumumba who in turn dismissed
Kasavubu. Soon thereafter, Eisenhower and CIA director Allen Dulles
opened up the possibility of assassinating Lumumba and putting Joseph
Mobutu, a senior army officer, in his place, which the CIA then set out
to do (US Congress, 1975: 13–70). Lumumba was eventually assassi-
nated by the leaders of the Katangese secession, who had captured him
in suspicious circumstances (Gleijeses, 1994: 209). What stability there
was then in the Congo came from the UN troops. Katanga province
was finally reintegrated in 1964. When, however, the UN forces made
ready to leave in 1964, there was another wave of rebellion against the
Kasavubu government initiated by Lumumba supporters. As the
Congolese army crumbled, Kasavubu appointed the very leader of the
Katanga rebellion, Moise Tshombe, to be prime minister. Some African

states, along with the USSR, China and Cuba, provided some small support to the Lumumbist rebels while the USA moved in 1964–65 (assisted by Belgium) to organize, fund and transport a White mercenary force to ensure the country's pro-American stance, with hundreds arriving from South Africa and Rhodesia (Gleijeses, 1994: 217–20, 235–7). As a result of this US-orchestrated intervention, the military situation stabilized. The political situation, however, grew increasingly confused under the new prime minister, Tshombe, until Mobutu, the long-time US ally, took over in a military coup in 1965 (Gleijeses, 1994: 235).

Africa, Asia, Latin America and the Middle East were now the zones experiencing turbulence, while Europe and Japan were back on their feet. Consequently, the USA shifted gears. In the early 1950s, US military and economic aid had gone mostly to European countries and to select East Asian locales; in the late 1950s and 1960s, most US aid went to pro-American Third World governments.

Out of the postwar disorder, therefore, a world order was constructed that for a time guaranteed US predominance in the world-economy, although it was simultaneously sowing the seeds of its own undoing. The glue for the newly reconstructed interstate system was found in the decisive formalization in 1950 of the fault lines between East and West, announced first in Truman's containment doctrine of 1947. In this, the Korean War was instrumental to establishing the border zones between these two blocs while leaving much of the Third World as the zone where superpower competition could continue without igniting World War III (Cumings, 1990: 756), despite the ever-present risks of escalation, as evidenced in the Cuban Missile crisis and the new round of super-power competition it spawned (see Ellsberg, 1986a; see Hershberg, 1990: 163–98; see Lebow, 1987; cf. Bundy, 1988).

In addition, albeit that both the USA and the USSR officially pro-claimed anti-imperial ideologies (Barraclough, 1964: 121, 123), this bi-polarity of the Cold War was instrumental for both powers in justifying intervention and maintenance of dictatorial client states in their respec-tive spheres of influence. In the USSR this was largely confined to Eastern Europe (Afghanistan and select Third World states being notable and much later exceptions), while for the USA it ran the gamut from Latin America to the Middle East (Chomsky, 1982: 192, 422). Thus, through various policies, the USA and the USSR, at times in reaction to each other, created blocs and security relationships. These relation-ships created an order in the interstate system and assured for a time the mutual reinforcement of the two blocs.

The two main thrusts of US foreign policy during this formative period were the reconstruction of the Federal Republic of Germany and Japan as the regional workshops of Europe and Asia; and the general push toward decolonization balanced by a 'global logic of counterrevolutionary violence' (Davis, 1986: 183) to ensure an Open Door to foreign trade and investment in the Third World, thus maintaining the core–periphery structure of the world-economy required for multilateral trading relations and economic integration.

By the late 1960s, however, the security functions of international military Keynesianism began to overtake its economic functions, as the USA moved to crush revolutionary movements that threatened the Open Door policy. The USA, however, would confront the limits of its own power once again when it attempted to impose its will on the Vietnamese people. The Vietnamese challenge demonstrated to the world the potential power of the South against the North, as the Tet offensive in 1968 showed in dramatic fashion how a peasant army in a small underdeveloped country could defeat the world's hegemonic superpower (Arrighi, Hopkins and Wallerstein, 1989a: 36, 103).

The Vietnam War in turn played a critical role as well, in causing a major reversal in the position of the US balance of payments, starting in 1968. In a stunning reversal, whereas the early postwar years saw a US $10 billion trade surplus of exports over imports that caused an enormous dollar gap, in 1971 and 1972 the USA showed a balance-of-payments deficit that reached nearly the same amount (Schurmann, 1987: 356; see Borden, 1989: 57–85). The printing of dollars by the USA to pay for the war was causing inflation and this led other core countries to prefer gold holdings rather than dollars. The resulting gold drain led to the end of dollar–gold convertibility, as the USA closed the gold window in 1971.

As during the Korean War before it, high levels of US foreign aid and military spending for the Vietnam War provided a 'windfall' to US allies, especially the East Asian states of Japan, South Korea and Taiwan. In addition, as part of its geopolitical strategy in Asia, the USA continued to open its market to East Asia's exports, creating a pronounced single-market dependency, while tolerating the region's mercantilism, in a kind of 'Reverse Open Door' (Woo-Cumings, 1993: 146; Havens, 1987: 92–106; Woo, 1991: 92–7). Over time, this high level of military spending and the opportunities it created for US allies (especially in East Asia), made the US economy weaker relative to the other core states and their economic regions, the growth of which was fostered by the interstate order created by the USA.

In retrospect, rebuilding the regional workshops of Europe and Asia proved relatively easy when compared with ensuring multilateral trade patterns with the periphery through enforcement of the US Open Door policy. Ultimately, it was this contradiction between the global expansion of the US informal empire and the growing strength of Third World nationalism that was the most decisive factor in prompting US hegemonic decline. At the same time, the USSR was also losing power in its bloc, as exemplified by its invasion of Czechoslovakia in 1968 and the growing split with China. The bipolar world order was giving way to renewed competition and multipolarity.

From 1967/73 to 1990: Changes in the Interstate System

The period after the Tet offensive saw dramatic changes in both the world-economy and the interstate system, as US hegemony declined and the world-economy went into a downturn. Western European states and Japan became less dependent upon the USA by the late 1960s as a result of the real increase in their economic strength vis-à-vis the USA. Despite, however, their desire to play a more active role in world affairs, they were cautious about hurting their special relationship to the USA, whose military role remained crucial for them (McCormick, 1989: 173; Barnet, 1983: 338). The West Germans began in the late 1960s to open up relations with Eastern Europe, the so-called *Ostpolitik*. They signed both the nuclear non-proliferation treaty in 1969 and a non-aggression pact with the USSR in 1970 (McCormick, 1989: 174; Barnet, 1983: 294); later, they formally recognized the postwar boundaries in Eastern Europe.

In many ways the *Ostpolitik* became a driving force that propelled a change in the previous relationship between the East and the West (McCormick, 1989: 173). The USA now tended to follow the Federal Republic of Germany's lead at times, instead of the USA always leading its allies as it had during its phase of maximum hegemony of the previous twenty-five years (Lundestad, 1986: 109). At the same time, the 'relaxation of tensions' between East and West loosened the Soviet hold over its Eastern European satellites, as many of its client states in Eastern Europe increased their economic relations with the West (McCormick, 1989: 182).

By the late 1960s, then, the Tet offensive and the growing independence and competitiveness of the Federal Republic of Germany and Japan all began to underscore the limits to US power. The 1969 Nixon Doctrine, in recognition of these limits, brought an end to the policy of being always in the front line of global containment, first put into practice with the Korean War (see Litwak, 1984). In this important policy shift, Nixon and Kissinger moved to devolve power to select semiperipheral states, such as Brazil, South Africa, Israel, Iran and Saudi Arabia, which were instructed to act as regional subimperial powers for the USA. The USA backed off on sending its own ground troops into combat, relying on proxy states and the use of air and naval power instead (Klare, 1972: 322–3).

The geopolitical consequence of this policy shift was the pursuit of détente with the USSR, combined with profiting from the Sino-Soviet split by the dramatic US opening to China. The new triangular diplomacy of the USA in the late 1960s/early 1970s was designed to pressure China and the USSR into a full acceptance of the norms of the US-dominated interstate system. At the same time, triangular diplomacy allowed the USA to play China and the USSR against each other. Furthermore, as China moved toward being a US ally over the next decade (or at least a consistent opponent of the USSR), the result was a significant change in the global balance of power to the decisive benefit of the USA. Indeed, it had been the threat posed by the Chinese Revolution that led the USA into its wars with Asia in Korea and Indochina. With the *rapprochement* with China, the USA could now disengage somewhat from its Asian commitments.

The early 1970s also witnessed the growing economic power of Third World oil producers (Nwoke, 1987). OPEC's oil shock of 1973 raised US oil costs from $5 billion in 1972 to $48 billion in 1975 (McCormick, 1989: 164; Itoh, 1990: 54). The rise of OPEC was even more consequential, however, for the United States' main competitors. As oil was dollar-denominated, the rise in oil prices absorbed dollars the Europeans and the Japanese had been accumulating overseas, damaging their trade balances and pushing up their production costs (Schurmann, 1987: 271, 354, 371, 373; Bromley, 1991: 135, 141). The oil price rise also bolstered Nixon's and Kissinger's strategy of reliance on subimperial powers to help police the world-system, by allowing the exchange of US arms for petrodollars (Bromley, 1991: 141). By opening up a new circuit for surplus capitalization in the Third World, OPEC allowed for the recycling of petrodollars to the USA not only through arms sales but also through the granting of construction contracts, purchases of Treasury Securities, and other investments (see Bromley, 1991: 150). This recycling of petrodollars shored up the dollar's value and illuminated the centrality of oil and arms in maintaining US hegemony.

The increased dollars from the USA and other oil-consuming nations were lent via Western banks to industrializing countries in both the US and Soviet blocs. Over time, these loans made the recipient states much more subject to the power and dominance of lending governments, banks and the IMF/World Bank (Korner et al., 1986; see Payer, 1974;

R. Broad, 1988). Third World states used much of this borrowed money to buy large quantities of arms imports, primarily from Europe and North America, with up to $400 billion on arms spent mainly by semiperipheral states between 1960 and 1987 (George, 1992: 151). Arms sales to oil producers, especially Iran and Saudi Arabia, the 'twin pillars' of US policy in the Gulf region, served both economic and military security functions. Under the Shah, Iran purchased over $30 billion in arms mostly from the USA (Klare, 1984: 126; Bill, 1988: 200–12). In part, the USA saw these high-tech weapons sales as a tool of foreign policy, making recipients into clients dependent on US goodwill for the continued supply of weapons, spare parts and training (Ellsberg, 1986b).

The USSR also involved itself in this trade, sending military aid to Syria, Egypt and Iraq. US and Soviet arms sales around the world in this period were aimed at creating a favourable balance of power, using weapons sales not only for the substantial profits they brought but also as currencies of influence. For the USA, there was some irony in this, since beginning in the 1950s it had bought arms overseas in order to redistribute dollars to its allies, while now the USA sold arms to garner foreign exchange to prop up its own balance of payments.

The détente that came about in the early 1970s was over by the end of the decade. Tensions between the USA and USSR increased as the latter turned to renewed support of revolutionary movements and postcolonial regimes in the Third World. The USSR had done this earlier in Cuba, Egypt and India. It had been the hope of Nixon and Kissinger that détente would end this, leaving the USA to pursue alone its manoeuvres in these areas, if on a more subdued scale. Instead, changed Soviet perceptions of the relationship with the USA led to increased involvement by the USSR in particular peripheral areas (Garthoff, 1985: 502, 671; McCormick, 1989: 182). The main thrust of Soviet activity was in Southern Africa (Angola, Mozambique), the Horn of Africa (Somalia and Ethiopia), South Yemen, and Afghanistan (Lundestad, 1986: 125–32).

The 1970s and 1980s also saw other factors contributing to worldwide militarization, including the drive for military self-sufficiency, most noticeable in the semiperipheral zone. South Korea launched its heavy chemical and industry programme, in part to achieve self-sufficiency in military items following the decline in aid flow from the USA and the opening to China. In the 1980s, Iran embarked on an all-out effort to produce domestically the weapons it needed when an embargo virtually grounded the Iranian air force (Klare, 1991: 179; see Ellsberg, 1986b; Catrina, 1988: esp. 224–8). South Africa and Israel both developed a substantial capability to produce arms, including nuclear weapons (Klare,

1991: 179). Finally, we now know that Iraq and North Korea launched a major drive for weapons self-sufficiency, coming at least very close to producing nuclear weapons, despite being signatories (as non-nuclear states) to the Non-Proliferation Treaty (NPT) and thus subject to inspection and monitoring by the United Nations' International Atomic Energy Agency (IAEA) (Burrows and Windrem, 1994: 25–59, 424–38).

Along with the growing diffusion of weapons promoted by the arms industry and interstate conflict, there was a growth of second-tier arms suppliers specializing in low-to-medium-technology weapons. Third World producers cut into the market share of weapons producers in Europe/North America. Second-tier weapons-producing states included Brazil, China, Israel, North Korea, South Korea, Chile, Poland, Spain and Czechoslovakia. Brazil's military sales grew from $670 million in 1976–81 to $2.6 billion in 1982–87, and military sales in China grew from $1.25 billion to $7.8 billion in the same periods (Klare, 1991: 181).

Overall, Third World states vastly increased their military spending after 1970. From the 1960s to the early 1970s average annual military spending by Third World states was $4–5 billion; in the period 1973–79 the amount was $20 billion, followed by an increase to $40 billion during the period 1985–89 (Sivard, 1991: 6, 11).

Along with this progression of worldwide militarization was an increase in the growth of the UN network, with UN peacekeeping operations increasing from 1956 right up to the 1990s, though its troop deployments were still small (if growing) relative to that of the superpowers (see Karns and Mingst, 1994: 188–215). At the same time, institutions regulating the interstate system have grown by leaps and bounds. The UN alone grew to comprise more than a dozen specialized agencies (Arrighi, Hopkins and Wallerstein, 1989a: 44), from the IAEA, which acted as a supranational authority monitoring and regulating weapons development (primarily of Third World states), to the World Health Organization.

With the work of formal decolonization largely complete by the 1970s, the Third World stepped up its demands in the UN and other forums to press for political-economic reform in the world-system. The UN Conference on Trade and Development (UNCTAD), a structure established under Third World pressure, pushed for a New International Economic Order. UNESCO, in the period when Amadou Mokhtar M'bow of Senegal was secretary-general, sought to establish a so-called New World Information Order, the objective of which was to reduce Western *de facto* control over world media (Preston, Herman and Schiller, 1989). In addition, on the basis of the Universal Declaration of Human Rights, the UN Human Rights Commission and related agencies moved

towards formal investigations that aimed to limit the impunity of governments in dealing with citizens or residents of their states. By the end of
the 1970s, then, the growing strength of the Third World in mobilizing
against the political and economic inequities of the world-system seemed
to be reflected in the UN as well, as could be seen by looking at voting
patterns in the UN General Assembly (see Karns and Mingst, 1991:
281–3; Kay, 1993: 169–70).

This institutional upheaval had as its counterpart a growing social
upheaval in semiperipheral and peripheral states during the late 1970s
and into the 1980s, which the superpowers could do little to control
(McCormick, 1989: 225). There was social unrest in Iran, Nicaragua, El
Salvador, the Philippines, Brazil, South Africa, South Korea, Poland,
and later in all of Eastern Europe. In particular, the Iranian Revolution
and the seizure of the US embassy was a major challenge to the interstate order, a symbol of the decline of US power (Barnet, 1983: 400–
401), and of the increasing power of the South in relation to the North.

The Iranian Revolution led to the partial abandonment of the Nixon
Doctrine. The loss of the United States' regional gendarme sent shock-
waves through the US establishment, leading directly to a sense of need
to renew a Cold War ambiance (Chomsky, 1982), this occurring even
before either the seizure of the American embassy or the Soviet invasion
of Afghanistan. The trajectory of Soviet policy was somewhat different.
Since détente, the Soviets had mistaken the USA's low-visibility strategy
as a sign of its own growing strength. Eventually, the USSR repeated
the US Vietnam disaster in Afghanistan.

Like the Korean crisis that allowed for the implementation of NSC
68 and the first Cold War, the Soviet invasion of Afghanistan enabled
the USA to go forward with plans for a renewed Cold War that were
already in place. In fact, a stronger US military posture was being pressed
for by influential elite policy-making groups such as the revived Committee on the Present Danger, which originated in 1950 to lobby for a
strong military at the beginning of the first Cold War (Sanders, 1983:
238–40; see Hershberg, 1993: 491–553).

The USA attempted to move away from relying primarily on subimperial powers and instead increased its military expenditures and
preparedness in order more directly to confront the USSR and turn
back challenges in the Third World. US readiness to intervene *directly*
around the globe was illustrated with programmes such as the Rapid
Deployment Force (Ellsberg, 1981), while the 'revitalization of its proxy
networks' (as was revealed in Iran–Contra and related scandals) showed
the US residual dependence on subimperial allies and mercenary forces
(Klare, 1989: 97–118). Reagan's new aggressive unilateralist strategy also

involved a campaign against the UN to eliminate independent initiatives of the Third World there (see Preston, Herman and Schiller, 1989).

Many of the changes in the world during the 1980s were directly associated with the US deficit economy that financed its military build-up, starting under Carter and continuing under Reagan and Bush. In the 1980s the Reagan administration's spending on the military vastly increased the annual federal budget deficit, as under Reagan the USA went from being the world's largest creditor nation to the world's largest debtor in record time (see Deger, 1990: 191, Table 5A 2). By the mid-1980s, the US military budget hovered at around $300 billion, while the total cost of the Reagan–Bush round of military Keynesianism from 1981 to 1991 totalled over $3 trillion (Morrison, Tsipis and Wiesner, 1994: 38). Thus, the US attempt to revive its hegemony through military superiority exacerbated its economic decline (Itoh, 1990: 93; Halliday, 1990: 12; see Markusen and Yudken, 1992).

During the 1980s, the US economy grew more slowly than those of its major trading partners, with its share of world production and the net profit rates of US corporations going down while that of its corporate rivals in the Federal Republic of Germany and Japan went up (Zysman, 1991: 86, 90; Itoh, 1990: 73, Table 3.4). Growth in the Federal Republic of Germany and Japan relative to the USA was such that, during the 1980s, the world-economy began to be grouped around three major zones: Japan-led East Asia, by far the most dynamic region (see Ozawa, 1993: 129–50; Cumings, 1994; cf. Selden, 1994), the European Community, and the US-led Americas.

In addition, the USA began to compete with poor countries on world financial markets to fund its deficit-financed military Keynesianism, regressive tax cuts, corporate debt, and other related programmes, and this was probably 'the most important single factor in the sudden collapse of Third World incomes in the early 1980s' (Arrighi, 1991: 52). For instance, the rise in US interest rates led directly to the growing crisis in Third World debt arrears, with debt increasing to nearly $1 trillion by 1988 (see Sen, 1990: 203–6, Tables 6.2, 6.3).

Despite this enormous debt burden, the combination of semi-peripheral and peripheral military rivalries combined with Soviet and Western intervention to set off numerous regional wars and arms races. In Africa, the devastation was particularly great as South Africa (with support from select Western allies) continued its 'total strategy' of regional destabilization, supporting guerrilla forces in some cases and relying on direct invasion and incursions at other times in Mozambique and Angola, and to a lesser extent Zimbabwe (Hanlon, 1986). This strategy effectively destroyed the economies of at least Angola and

Mozambique; between 1980 and 1988 an estimated 1.3 million people in Angola and Mozambique died as a result of direct or indirect effects from South Africa's war, with the economic losses of all the southern African (SADCC) states coming to over $60 billion (UNICEF, 1989: 10, 24–5, 35–8, cited in Davies and Martin, 1992, 363).

Along with regional conflict, the Third World has also seen the proliferation of nuclear, chemical and biological weapons, along with a growing capability to produce nuclear and other weapons of mass destruction. Missiles and modern jet aircraft, including ballistic missiles with nuclear and chemical capability, have also been acquired by a growing number of Third World countries. Between 1981 and 1988, out of $341 billion worth of arms going to developing countries, 69 per cent, or $235 billion, went to the Middle East and South Asia. Top buyers were India, Iran, Iraq, Israel, Libya, Pakistan and Syria, all of which had been involved in wars and/or arms races in their regional settings (Klare, 1991: 172). The emergence of Third World military powers, helped along by superpower rivalry and increasingly equipped with weapons of mass destruction, including nuclear weapons, is one of the most important trends of the 1969 to 1989 period.

By the end of the 1980s, however, the most glaring change in the order of the interstate system was the total disintegration of the Soviet bloc and with it the collapse of Marxism-Leninism as a strategy of development for the Third World. The USSR, having been bankrupted by Cold War military spending and economic mismanagement, and facing revolt in Eastern Europe and ethnic unrest on its periphery, sought to open up to its common European neighbours so as to stem its economic decline. To accomplish this, Gorbachev took unilateral steps to end the Cold War. As revolt mounted in Eastern Europe, Gorbachev proceeded with his April 1988 UN agreement for a planned withdrawal from Afghanistan, with the last Soviet troops leaving by mid-February of 1989 (Chaliand and Rageau, 1990: 11).

In December of 1988, Gorbachev announced in a speech to the UN deep unilateral cuts in Soviet armed forces plus a withdrawal of the Soviet forward-based troops and offensive tanks from Eastern Europe that had given tangible credibility to US fears of a Warsaw Pact blitzkrieg invasion of Western Europe. In January 1989, the USSR declared that it was going to withdraw 200,000 Soviet troops from Asia (Ambrose, 1983: 362). 1989 was also the year in which Gorbachev announced that the USSR would no longer uphold the 1968 Brezhnev doctrine; this helped set off a tidal wave of revolts that shook Eastern Europe, toppling Soviet-supported Stalinist regimes along with the Berlin Wall, and finally freeing the region from Soviet domination. In the next two years, the USSR disintegrated while Germany achieved reunification. Gorbachev's reforms were too little, too late, apparently, to stop either the loss of Eastern Europe or rising ethnic/national revolt at the Soviet periphery that ultimately paved the way for the disintegration of the Soviet empire.

The US–Soviet order that had organized interstate relations in Europe after 1945 was over (Halliday, 1990: 8). No other order or scheme as cohesive as the Cold War division of Europe had been substituted in its place. Preceding the political changes in Eastern Europe, conflicts between East and West began to end in other parts of the world, including Cambodia, Afghanistan, Ethiopia, Somalia, Angola and Nicaragua (Halliday, 1990: 6). In other words, the conflicts that had begun after the ambiguous, mid-1970s détente between the USA and the USSR were being wound down, though leaving regions awash with weapons that could and often would be used in ethnic-cum-national conflicts.

With the former Soviet stranglehold on Eastern Europe lifted, people within the former Soviet satellites were now competitors for a share of the world accumulation of surplus. Rather than contributing to order and stability, Eastern Europe, like numerous other regions, saw a resurgence of ethnic and religious hatreds once held in check, leading to widespread uncertainty and instability when contrasted with the 1945–89 order. Disintegration and growing conflict in the former Yugoslavia and the former USSR are but two examples of this, with nuclear weapons in the latter making the situation all the more dangerous.

By 1989–90, the principles upon which the USA had organized an international order were no longer applicable to the world-system. In forty-five years the setting had changed drastically. No longer could world security be organized around two competing blocs. The reunification of Germany and the disintegration of the Soviet bloc put an end to two major aspects of the postwar interstate order, though the Cold War still lingered in the Asian zone, symbolized in the division of Korea. Still, now there was no threat from the Soviets, real or otherwise. With the dissolution of the Warsaw Pact the rationale for NATO was gone as well (Wallerstein, 1991a: ch. 1). The USA, however, still aimed to continue its hegemony by keeping its allies locked into a dependent relationship through US control over the flow of oil, agricultural goods, and the provisioning of security.

Unlike Reagan's unilateralism that sought to focus on the bipolar conflict between the USA and the USSR, however, Bush found it necessary to revive multilateralist alliance diplomacy based on the UN Security Council in order to gain support for what was in essence a unilateral US war to turn back Iraq's August 1990 invasion of Kuwait

(Schurmann, 1993: 192–4, 201–2). In a new twist, though, Bush's solicitation of allied contributions to fund the war indicated US plans to shore up its hegemony by institutionalizing protection payments from its allies.

With the bipolar Cold War order gone, new threats to world security have emerged, the most notable of which are the proliferation of weapons of mass destruction such as nuclear weapons, 'failed states', ethnic/national violence, and the rise of Third World regional powers. Still, with the collapse of the Warsaw Pact, and with the Soviet Union no longer politically and ideologically committed to supporting enemies of the USA, it would appear that US costs for maintaining an Open Door in the Third World and protecting the core countries could be dramatically reduced. Rather than curbing its arms sales or attempting to seek global curbs on the proliferation of conventional weapons, though, the USA has instead stepped up arms sales to the Middle East and Far East, where regional arms races continue (Klare, 1994: 134–54). In this, the USA seems determined to preserve its specialization in the protection industry by playing up the dangers posed by Third World regional powers such as Iraq, even as it contributes to the problem.

Les Aspin, chairman of the House Armed Services committee and later Secretary of Defense, stated that the Persian Gulf War should be 'a model for future wars. The Iraq experience would be transplanted around the global to measure the relative strength of other troublesome regional powers as a means to plan forces to defeat them' (*New York Times*, 3 February 1992). Aspin termed this method 'Iraq equivalents'. Though even Aspin's own assessments made it clear that no country, with the exception of China, has air or ground forces as strong as those of Iraq before the Gulf War, US military planning and related budget requests, as in the *Bottom Up Review* and the *1994 Annual Report of the Secretary of Defense*, still go 'beyond worst-case planning' (Forsberg, 1994: 3–6).

These documents call for a US force structure large enough to fight two Gulf-like wars 'simultaneously' in the Far East and Middle East, and further assume that the USA will face adversaries that are comparable or stronger than that of Iraq before the Gulf War (Forsberg, 1994: 4). Defence analyst Randall Forsberg (1994: 3–6, Table 1–3) has shown that it is wholly unfeasible for any of these regional challengers to develop forces equivalent to that of Iraq's 'before the year 2000, or even, for all but Syria and North Korea, before about 2010'. Still, to maintain the force level necessary to counter these inflated threats, the USA intends to spend $1.2 trillion between financial years 1995 and 2000 on the military, despite its current $4 trillion deficit, itself primarily caused by the last round of military spending (Forsberg, 1994: 3–6; Burrows and Windrem, 1994: 500).

At the same time, the world does face new security threats in the form of the horizontal proliferation of nuclear and other weapons of mass destruction, as well as the problem posed by the nuclear weapons in chaotic regions such as the former USSR (see Burrows and Windrem, 1994; Hersh, 1994: 61–86). Attempts by the nuclear states to maintain a monopoly on nuclear and other 'superweapons' will probably only serve to exacerbate the problem. Third World regional powers have long known that the monopoly of high-tech weaponry by the USA (and Western Europe) limits their real sovereignty and power, and have therefore pursued military self-sufficiency (see above, and Burrows and Windrem, 1994: 17).

Recent continuing efforts of the IAEA to control the production and acquisition of these weapons in the Third World (through monitoring adherence to the NPT, for example) have shown themselves to be woefully inadequate. The UN Security Council, composed of five nuclear states, all of whom are among the top arms makers in the world, has little moral authority in the eyes of Third World states in this area. In the absence of reductions in these weapons by the great powers (especially the USA) as well as a genuine effort to curb the spread of these weapons, it is hard to imagine their widespread proliferation being stopped. Thus, even as the superpower arms race has ended, a new arms race has already begun.

Rather than pursuing leadership in world security and arms control through diplomacy, the USA seems set on maintaining its role through military means. A recent Pentagon document gives a picture of the US hopes for a resurgent hegemony in a one superpower world, noting that the USA 'must maintain the mechanisms for deterring potential competitors from even aspiring to a larger regional or global role' (Tyler, 1992b). This document is but one illustration that, though the Cold War between the USSR and the USA is over, it lives on in US policy toward the Third World and in its attempts to contain the independence of its allies, as might be gleaned from the US invasion of Panama and the Gulf War (see Ghilan, 1991: 25–36; cf. Kaufmann, 1992). Despite US intentions, the relative strengths among the great powers has now changed so much that the USA can no longer dominate its core rivals as '*de facto* client states', as it had during the heyday of the Cold War (Wallerstein, 1984: 39). Attempts to maintain its status as both the world's hegemonic power and only superpower, while perhaps temporarily shoring up the US role, will in the long run only exacerbate US economic decline, as US comparative advantage in the protection industry saps its still great residual economic strengths in world production, commerce and finance (Markusen and Yudken, 1992).

Furthermore, the 1980s have also seen a generalized collapse of developmentalist efforts in the Third World, thus leaving the hopes outlined originally in Truman's Point Four unmet. The reformist proposal to bring all the former colonized areas into the 'family of nation-states' has been played out, yet during the 1980s most of these areas suffered increased immiseration rather than movement toward the economic equality that the UN Charter and the USA had promised (see Arrighi, 1991: 39–66). As the bipolar world of the Cold War ended, centrifugal tendencies in the interstate system have re-emerged and a world awash with weapons struggles to deal with the dangerous legacy of increased militarization, immiseration and disintegration left in the wake of the Cold War.

3

World Production

Satoshi Ikeda

The world production system in the period 1945–90 possessed five principal features. First, the overall productive capacity of the world-economy expanded, allowing an unprecedented increase in world production. The growth in productive capacity, however, was not linear over time, nor was its spatial distribution uniform.

Second, the world-economy was significantly further integrated, after the brief interruption of the interwar period, by a vast increase in the movement of goods, services, capital, people and information within and across national boundaries. The degree and mode of integration, however, were also not uniform for the different parts of the world-system, nor was the rate of integration constant throughout the period.

Third, the first half of this period, 1945–1967/73, seemed to be one of invincible US economic power represented by the technological advantage and institutional strength of US firms. However, in the period 1967/73–1990, the US share of world production declined noticeably as these firms faced formidable challenge by European and Asian firms. Nonetheless, while some industrial activities shifted away from the USA, it is far from true to say that the USA had lost its lead in all technological areas and that all US firms failed to adapt their organizational structure to meet competition.

Fourth, the postwar institutional framework regulating global trade and financial activities was continuously adjusted in the general direction of 'liberalization'. Successive rounds of negotiations within the structure of the General Agreement on Tariff and Trade (GATT) removed a large part of the trade barriers for the global flow of manufactured goods. State regulations over private financial flows among the core countries were lifted in the 1960s and 1970s, and those over foreign exchange transactions in the 1980s. The direction of such institutional changes, however, was not always linear, and sometimes the changes were in contradiction with the overall liberalization of the world-economy. For example, in spite of the success of multilateral GATT negotiations, the principle of non-discrimination of GATT was undermined by the formation of the European Economic Community (EEC) and the European Free Trade Area and by the practice of bilateral trade restrictions.

Fifth, there was a substantial expansion in the role played by the state. In addition to its role as the regulator of domestic economic activities and the negotiator of interstate economic regulations, the state expanded its role as the provider of basic social services and income redistribution and as the regulator of aggregate economic activities through monetary and fiscal policies, especially in the core zone, at least up to the 1970s. Although the welfare provisions helped to legitimate capitalism in the core regions, the resulting higher labour costs accelerated factory relocation from the core to the periphery in the economic downturn, particularly since 1974. While the policy of economic stimulation supported growth in the 1945–1967/73 period, such a policy backfired in the second half of the 1970s, resulting in stagflation, and growing US government spending in the 1980s resulted in a huge US government debt that has potentially limited private-sector investment and reduced fiscal flexibility.

These features of the world-economy in the postwar period are analysed here from a specific angle of vision, the transformative processes of the major business enterprises, which came to be known as transnational corporations (TNCs). The joint-stock or incorporated companies have been the principal units of accumulation in the world-system for at least two centuries. When we direct our focus on the enterprise system, the major features of the postwar world-economy described above turn out to describe a process wherein major business enterprises expanded the scale and scope of their activities and became increasingly worldwide in their spatial scope and trans-statal in their legal jurisdiction.

While both European and Japanese corporations historically had had symbiotic relations with the state, the postwar process was one in which they grew less dependent on it as they expanded their activities abroad. The growth and allocation of the productive capacity and activity in the world-economy was the result of the activities precisely of these enterprises – research and development (R&D), production, transportation, distribution and financing. The integration of the world-economy was brought about by the expansion of the spatial scope of the enterprise activities. The relative decline of US economic power was a process concomitant with the rise of European and Japanese enterprises. However, once again we should emphasize that the processes of expansion and transnationalization of business enterprises, the rise of non-US enterprises, and the increasing domination of large-scale business enterprises in the world market was not a continuous process; nor was it uniform across geographic space and the spectrum of industrial activities.

We shall discuss three major themes. First, we shall survey the structural transformation of the world-economy. Using national macroeconomic data, we shall see that 1967/73 marks a turning point of the Kondratieff cycle. Second, we shall describe the changes in the major business enterprises and their networks, on the understanding that the TNCs were the principal agent that brought about the world-economic transformation. We shall look at this separately for the manufacturing sector and the service sector. Finally, we shall analyse the impact of the transformation of the world-economy and its agencies of accumulation on the hegemonic position of the United States.

Expansion, Integration and Polarization

The productive activities in the world-economy expanded at a much faster rate in the second half of the twentieth century than in the first half. Total gross domestic product (GDP) of thirty-two major countries representing about four-fifths of world output and population doubled in the thirty-seven years between 1913 and 1950, but in the thirty-seven years from 1950 to 1987, total GDP increased by 4.6 times (Maddison, 1989: 113, Table A-2). However, the growth of production was not constant over time. The data Maddison assembled show a golden age of fast growth between 1950 and 1973 and a period of slower growth and accelerated inflation between 1973 and 1987 (1989: 31). The total GDP of the thirty-two countries grew at an annual average compound growth rate of 5.1 per cent in the 1950–73 period and only 3.4 per cent in the 1973–87 period. This confirms that 1973 (or more precisely 1967/73) marked the turning point of a Kondratieff cycle.

In addition to temporal discontinuity, there existed spatial disparity in growth performance. According to the figures from the same table, GDP shares were calculated for developed/developing country groupings and regional country groupings (see Table 3.1). The share of the Organization of Economic Co-operation and Development (OECD) countries dropped by 9.2 per cent between 1950 and 1987 while the share of the developing Asian countries increased by the same amount.

The increase in the share of developing Asian countries is mainly due to China, which increased its share between 1950 and 1987 by 7.4 per cent. Among the OECD countries, the US share declined from 1950 to 1987 by 10.3 per cent and the pace of decline was faster in the 1950–73 period than in the 1973–87 period. The share of European OECD countries also declined from 1950 to 1987, but this decline took place mainly in the 1973–87 period. Japan's share increased from 1950 to 1987, but the pace of increase slowed down in the 1973–87 period. Regionally grouped data show that the share of the three regions – North America, Europe and East Asia – was approximately equal as of the late 1980s, the result of the rapid increase in the East Asian share (a gain of 15.3 per cent between 1950 and 1987).

The standard of living, as measured by per-capita real GDP (which is not the best indicator, but serves as a fair approximation), improved between 1950 and 1987, with a break in the trend again in 1973. The annual average compounded growth rate for the thirty-two countries was 3.3 per cent in the 1950–73 period and 2.2 per cent in the 1973–87 period. When this global record is broken down into two subperiods and country/regions, the trend change and regional differences become apparent. The principal features are that developing Asian countries increased the growth rate of their living standard in the 1973–87 period, except for the Philippines (from 1.9 per cent growth rate in 1950–73 to 0.6 per cent in 1973–87) and Taiwan (from 6.2 per cent to 6.0 per cent, which represents a drop but is still impressive overall). A slowdown of the pace of improvement in the standard of living was observed for all the OECD countries (except Norway), the Latin American countries, and the USSR (Maddison, 1989: 35, Table 3.2; see also Kenwood and Lougheed, 1992: 245–60).

The comparison of per-capita GDP does not reveal to us, however, the trend of polarization in the absolute standard of living in the world-economy (see Table 3.2). The gap between OECD countries and Asian developing countries widened markedly between 1950 and 1987, even though the per-capita GDP of the latter improved as a percentage of the average per-capita GDP of the OECD countries. Latin American countries and the USSR also experienced a significant widening of the gap between them and the OECD countries. In terms of country performance, the absolute difference of per-capita real GDP has been widening between richer and poorer countries, the only exceptions being the cases of Taiwan and South Korea. Even in the case of China, whose world production share increased tremendously between 1973 and 1987, the gap widened. It should be noted that there exist exceptions to the above trend also among the oil-producing countries, which were excluded from Maddison's study, although in many of these cases the gap, having narrowed in the 1970s, once again widened in the 1980s.

The expansion of productive activities in the world-system was accompanied by further integration of these activities among the households, governments and business enterprises within and across national boundaries. The expanded flow of goods, services, capital, people and information resulted in a complicated interaction among the multiple agents. For example, a household in the USA may today participate in a pension fund which purchases Finnish government bonds that in turn makes it possible for Finnish households to purchase commodities manufactured by Indonesian women under the subcontracting arrangement of a US distributor. Such integration, however, was not homogeneous across different parts of the world-economy.

The deepened integration of the households into the world-economy took the form of an increasing share of their income being earned by participation in the production of goods and services sold in the market as well as an increasing share of consumption goods being purchased in the market. If we use GDP as an indicator of market activities, the volume of such activities definitely increased in the postwar period. However, there is a countertrend, which is that an increasing proportion of the population in certain parts of the world is being separated from the officially recognized market activities. Even within the core zone, there is an increasing number of less privileged in the urban centres whose degree of market participation is decreasing, as discussed by Tabak in Chapter 4 (see also Portes, Castells and Benton, 1989; Feige, 1990).

The government sector has expanded its economic role in the postwar period markedly. As Table 3.3 shows, the average total government expenditure as a percentage of GDP for six OECD countries expanded steadily in the twentieth century, to reach the level of nearly one-half of the GDP in the mid-1980s. The role of the government as the supplier of services as well as employer has become quite important today, as indicated in Table 3.4.

It should also be noted that the states in the core zone play not only the role of demand creator but also that of financial surplus absorber. About 60 per cent of world bond capitalization was issued by various governments in both 1966 and 1989 (Ibbotson and Brinson, 1993: 204–5, Figs 10–2, 10–3). The absorption of oil dollars in the 1970s by semiperipheral and peripheral states via US bank lending was a further instance of the degree to which the states have expanded their long-standing direct integration into the workings of the world-economy.

The ever-growing crossflow of goods, services and capital also implies further integration of the activities of various agents of the world-economy. Through the international trade of finished goods, the households of the importing countries are connected to the enterprise of the exporting countries. Through the international trade of raw materials and intermediate goods, the enterprises of different countries are connected into the commodity chains of the world-economy. Foreign direct investment (FDI), the activity of setting up an affiliate or subsidiary in a foreign country, extends the scope of enterprise activities beyond national boundaries. The new forms of investment (NFI) (OECD, 1987: 24; Oman, 1989: 15), together with equity investment, cross-border licensing, and sales agent agreements, expand the scope of enterprise networks. The cross-border financial investment handled by banks and security firms integrates investors (individual, corporate or institutional) and borrowers (governments, enterprises and supra-states) from multiple state jurisdictions.

This expansion of the cross-border flow of goods, services and capital has been greater than the growth of productive activities in the postwar period. However, the growth of these flows did not take place simultaneously; nor was the resulting integration uniform over different parts of the world-economy. The general trend observed was a cycle of different modes of integration leading the integration process successively. Trade led world integration in the 1950s. In the 1960s, while trade continued to expand, FDI became the primary mode of integration. International bank lending boomed in the 1970s, and international security flows became the fastest growing mode in the 1980s.

The expansion of international trade in the early postwar period was perceived to be the engine of growth (Soete, 1991: 51). While the value of world exports expanded 1.23 times in thirty-seven years between 1913 and 1950, it expanded 9.6 times in thirty-six years between 1950 and 1986 (Maddison, 1989: 142, Table D-5). The break in the growth of trade again occurred around 1973, as shown in Table 3.5.

In the general trend of world trade expansion, trade in manufactured goods expanded the most, and the growth of manufacturing trade was much larger than the growth of manufacturing production. From 1963 to 1979, manufactured exports rose by 281 per cent, while manufacturing rose by 149 per cent. In the same period, exports and production of minerals rose by 99 per cent, agricultural exports by 94 per cent, with agricultural production growing only by 45 per cent. From 1980 to 1988, the annual growth rate of manufacturing trade was 5 per cent, while that of manufacturing production was 3.5 per cent (Kenwood and Lougheed, 1992: 286–7).

The growth of trade activities occurred primarily among OECD countries, whereas the redistribution of manufacturing activities showed a more worldwide pattern. As the figures in Table 5.6 indicate, exports from the OECD countries led the integration of the world-economy throughout the postwar period. In terms of regional composition, the decline of North America and the rise of East Asia as the source of exports stand out.

As the integration of the world-economy through international trade slowed down after 1967/73, cross-border capital movements, such as FDI, international bank lending and international portfolio investment successively picked up the baton as the major mechanisms of world-economy integration, supplementing trade flows. For example, the current value of exports increased 3.5 times between 1975 and 1989 while the FDI outflow increased 7 times in the same period (UNCTC, 1991: 5, Fig. 1).

The growth of FDI activities is summarized in Tables 3.7 and 3.8. The annual FDI outflow and inflow almost doubled in every five years between 1970 and 1988. Generally speaking, FDI expansion in the 1950s and 1960s was led by US corporations which were attempting to circumvent the tariff wall of the EEC. FDI in the 1970s was, however, led by European and Japanese corporations in an attempt to secure markets in the core zone and to lower production costs by using cheap labour in the periphery. FDI expansion in the 1980s was led once again by the European and Japanese corporations, but now primarily in service sectors such as finance. As a result of FDI expansion, the share of FDI inflow in gross domestic capital formation increased (see Table 3.9). In terms of the country share of FDI outflow and inflow, the integration of the world-economy achieved through FDI was predominantly among the countries of the core zone. Also, there was a marked decline in the share of FDI outflow from the USA and an increase in that from Europe and Japan, while the share of the USA as a recipient of FDI increased, together with a continuation in the importance of Europe as the principal FDI destination.

International banking activities also expanded since the second half of the 1970s. The expansion of international bank lending increased after 1974, as US banks (re)circulated the oil dollars to governments in the periphery and semiperiphery. This took the form of syndicated loans, in which short-term loans were rolled over to create long-term loans at variable interest rates. The second oil price increase in 1979–80 combined with the anti-inflationary tight monetary policies instituted by the states of the core zone, however, resulted in an accumulated debt problem for a large number of developing countries and the consequent erosion of US bank dominance in the early 1980s (Okumura, 1988b: 17–18). Since then, international bank lending has been led by Japanese and European banks (Nishimura, 1988).

At the end of 1991, the total stock of international bank assets was $6,147 billion, and liabilities were $6,084 billion (BIS, 1992: 163). International assets became a large portion of total bank assets. For example, the total assets of the top thirty Japanese banks was $5,609 billion in 1989, ranging from the world's largest bank (DIK) with $413.2 billion to the world's one-hundredth largest bank (Shizuoka Bank) with assets of only $47.5 billion (*Fortune Directory*, July 30, 1990: 324–7). The international assets held by all Japanese banks, which showed the largest national concentration of that year, were $1,969 billion (BIS, 1992: 163). This implies that about one-third of Japanese bank assets were international assets. The ratio of international bank lending to GDP is a further measure of its great expansion. For the OECD countries, the ratio increased from 6 per cent in the mid-1970s to 10 per cent in 1980, and to 17 per cent in 1989 (Bosworth, 1993: 9).

Portfolio capital movements expanded greatly as well in the 1980s. This form of investment includes the sale and purchase of the foreign bonds issued both by governments and by private enterprises, as well as investment in foreign equities which do not result in takeover by foreign equity holders or a substantial increase in their control. According to the BIS (1992: 94), the average annual outflow was $2.48 billion in 1975–79, $8.36 billion in 1980–84, $35.36 billion in 1985–89, and $214.6 billion in 1990–91. The major sources of portfolio investment were European Community (EC) countries and Japan, and the major recipients were EC countries and the USA, although portfolio investment inflow into Japan increased substantially in 1991 ($115.3 billion).

We see the importance of international portfolio investment by comparing the size of world equity and bond markets and the share of cross-border transactions in equities and bonds. World equity market capitalization expanded from $500 billion in 1960 to $8,300 billion in 1990, and during these years the US share dropped from 73.3 per cent to 33.2 per cent, Europe raising its share from 21.5 per cent to 23.9 per cent, and Japan increasing its share markedly from a negligible level to 33.2 per cent (Ibbotson and Brinson, 1993: 106, Fig. 6-1). Cross-border equity flow increased especially in the 1980s, amounting to $1,441 billion in 1990 (Goldstein et al., 1992: 37, Table 7). This means that 17.4 per cent of total world equity was in the hands of foreign owners.

The total amount of outstanding bonds, both domestic and international, at the end of 1989 was $12,516 billion, out of which $1,348, or 10.8 per cent, was in international bonds. At the end of 1991, the

total figure increased to $15,040 billion while the international bond
figure increased to $1,651 billion, or 11.0 per cent of the total world
outstanding bonds (as calculated from the figures in BIS, 1992: 177).

The growth of international financial flow has resulted in the evolution of world capital markets from a set of loosely linked national
markets to a single global entity (Bosworth, 1993: 7). One of the
distinctive features of this development is the increasing role of the
Eurodollar and other offshore markets which are not regulated by any
state agency. By 1988, the size of the Eurodollar market had grown to
$1,500 billion, and other Euro-currency markets to $1,000 billion
(Kenwood and Lougheed, 1992: 267). Under the condition of stagnation
in the world-economy, global financial transactions have expanded
tremendously to the point that no state interventions, singlehandedly or
jointly, were able to manage or control the global financial markets
(Wriston, 1992; Miyazaki, 1992).

As a result of liberalization and the integration of financial markets,
the opportunities for an investor in one country to invest in financial
assets from all over the world have increased. For example, out of
$44,425 billion financial wealth of the world in 1990, over 50 per cent
of the total ($22,417 billion) was available to US investors (Ibbotson
and Brinson, 1993: 15–16, Figs 1-4, 1-5).

The integration of the world-economy in terms of the movement of
people and information also steadily increased throughout the postwar
period. In particular, migration from the periphery to the core, or even
to the semiperiphery, increased in the 1967/73–90 period as developmentalist experiments failed in many developing countries. At the same
time, expanding telecommunications networks and quickly expanding
data-processing capabilities were the key elements in the growth of the
world capital markets and the global business service industries.

The above trends taken together reveal the following features of the
expansion, integration and polarization of the world-economy in the
postwar period. First, the expansion in the intra-national and international flows of goods and services promoted further separation of
the loci of production and consumption (trade in final goods) and the
increasing integration of productive activities conducted at different
places (trade in raw materials and intermediate products) through the
formation and expansion of the enterprise networks.

Second, the expansion of international financial flow and self-
regulating capital markets resulted in the formation of a heterogeneous
structure of markets in the world-economy – the labour markets where
cross-border migration was relatively tightly managed by the states, the
goods and services markets where restriction over cross-border move-

ment had been removed gradually, and the financial markets which became increasingly global and self-regulating.

Third, the integration of the world-economy progressed primarily as an intra-core affair in the second half of the twentieth century in contrast to the period of colonial imperialism in the previous era. This, however, does not mean to deny the crucial and expanding role of the periphery and semiperiphery as the suppliers of low-cost, labour-intensive manufactured goods as well as underpaid workers for the core. Furthermore, core-centred expansion resulted in a widening absolute income gap between the populations in the core and those in the periphery and semiperiphery.

Fourth, there emerged a tripolar regional structure, the so-called Triad of North America, Europe and East Asia (Ohmae, 1985). The Triad countries accounted for 65 per cent of the world GDP in 1987, 50 per cent of world trade in 1989 (UNCTC, 1991: 36), and nearly 100 per cent of world financial flows (BIS, 1992). The intra-Triad integration proceeded at a faster rate in the 1980s. According to UNCTC (1991), between 1980 and 1988, intra-Triad FDI stock nearly tripled, from $142 billion to $410 billion. In 1980, the stock within the Triad accounted for 30 per cent of the worldwide stock of inward investment; by 1988, intra-Triad stock had increased to an estimated 39 per cent of worldwide inward stock. Thus, interactions within the Triad have outpaced both interactions in the rest of the world and interactions between the Triad and the rest of the world, indicating a faster rate of integration within the Triad than between the Triad and the rest of the world (UNCTC, 1991: 36). As of the early 1990s, the world's top industrial corporations and banks are primarily from the Triad as Tables 3.10, 3.11, and 3.12 indicate.

The Expanding Role of Transnational Corporations

The above structural changes in the world-economy in the second half of the twentieth century have been caused primarily by the expansion of the activities of capitalist enterprises which are increasingly transnational and trans-statal, renewing earlier traditions. Let us review the expansion of the role of transnational corporations by looking at the FDI and other data.

The emergence of large-scale business enterprises whose activity spanned several state jurisdictions has often been described as the 'late 20th century development sequence' (Taylor and Thrift, 1982b: 24, Fig. 2.1). In fact, it renewed an important capitalist tradition of the early modern period, which has declined in the nineteenth century. Many large US national business organizations grew into multinational business organizations, mainly since the 1950s. The FDI outflow balance of the USA which led the growth of world FDI activities in the early decades of the postwar period, more than doubled between 1950 and 1957, from $11.8 billion to $25.4 billion, and then doubled again between 1957 and 1966, to $51.8 billion (Okumura, 1988a: 284–5, Table B-1).

Beginning in the 1960s, the term 'multinational corporation' (MNC) came to be used to describe those corporations that 'operate production facilities in a number of different countries' (Ethier, 1983: 266). As the MNCs grew further and gained relative autonomy from state regulation and intervention through their operation in multiple countries, the term 'transnational corporation' (TNC) was frequently substituted for 'MNC' – for example, in the publications of the United Nations Centre for Transnational Corporations (UNCTC). In the late 1980s, a third term, 'global company', was suggested, reflecting better the degree to which the scope of corporate activities was worldwide (see, for example, Julius, 1990), but it did not catch on, possibly because there exists some scepticism about the degree of true globality of the TNCs (*The Economist*, 27 March 1993: 5). Although there are no official estimates of the number of TNCs, available information suggests their steady increase in the postwar period. In 1980, the number of TNCs was estimated to be over 10,000, controlling at least 90,000 foreign affiliates (Stopford and Dunning, 1983: 3). By the early 1990s, these figures had increased to 35,000 and 170,000, respectively (*The Economist*, 27 March 1993: 5). In 1984, the number of total non-bank US transnationals was calculated at 2,088, with 16,892 foreign affiliates (Dunning, 1993: 81, Table 6.1).

Expansion of the subsidiary networks, the outcome of increased FDI activities, may be seen in Table 3.13, which summarizes the subsidiary networks for 315 major TNCs between 1950 and 1970. It is clear from the table that the majority of large TNCs expanded their subsidiary networks beyond six countries in the two decades. Although comparable data for the 1980s are not available, the number of subsidiaries and affiliates expanded in the 1970s and 1980s, especially in the second half of the 1980s, as we can see from the spurt of FDI growth in that period.

These TNCs dominate world industrial production. The high degree of concentration may be seen in the data collected in *Market Share Reporter* (1992) for selected industrial sectors (see Table 3.14). The TNCs played an important and expanding role in the world-economy in terms of the share in world production and trade. Humes (1993: 26) states that 'by 1989, the total sales [more than $3,800 billion] generated by the

50 largest industrial corporations significantly contributed to the total GNP [less than $18,000 billion] of the countries of the world'. Furthermore, '[t]he combined assets of the top 300 firms now make up roughly a quarter of production assets in the world' (*The Economist*, 27 March 1993: 5).

Another measure of TNC production activities was direct foreign production, a measure suggested by Clegg (1987), who shows that the proportion of overseas production of the TNCs of a country to the total production in that country has increased in all countries (see Table 3.15). Furthermore, the pace somewhat quickened between 1970 and 1975 as compared to the period 1965–1970. Stopford and Dunning (1983) analysed the data of the world's largest 500 TNCs listed in Stopford (1982). According to Table 3.16, which reproduces a part of their analysis, the production share of foreign-owned firms out of total manufacturing increased in the 1970s. It is suspected that the rapid increase in intra-core FDI in the 1980s, together with the phenomenon Gordon (1988) called the 'recentralization of capital in high income countries', the contribution of foreign-owned firms (from the core) has expanded in the core countries.

At the same time, the production of overseas subsidiaries as a percentage of total worldwide production of major TNCs increased overall between 1977 and 1981 from 30.7 per cent to 33.2 per cent. As Table 3.17 indicates, the performance differed by industry and nationality. Furthermore, the degree of transnationalization in terms of the sales share of foreign affiliates in total sales of non-bank US TNCs is given in the same table. We can conclude that the activities of foreign subsidiaries and affiliates are a quite significant aspect of TNC activity today.

The share of subsidiary production for total production by TNCs varies according to the home country of the TNCs. The share was high for the TNCs from small European countries, low for newcomers in transnationalization, and intermediate for the old home countries, as shown in Table 3.18.

The share of TNC-related trade out of total trade also indicated the degree of TNC network expansion. Intra-firm trade, which is primarily cross-border transactions between the subsidiaries and the parent company, takes about one third of trade in the USA and Japan, as shown in Table 3.19. Julius (1990) introduced the concept of FDI-related trade to capture trade activities of TNCs that are not included in intra-firm trade. FDI-related trade refers to all trade involving at least one TNC or its affiliates on either side of the trade. As Table 3.20 indicates, about one-half or more of the trade of these countries was handled by the TNCs.

The large corporations were responsible for a good proportion of capital formation in their home countries, and, as the transnational network expanded, TNC investment abroad increased in importance as well. The FDI share in gross domestic capital formation is one measure that indicates the transnational expansion of enterprise networks (see Table 3.9). In the 1980s, the share of foreign enterprise investment in gross domestic capital formation increased in the developed market economies more than in the developing countries, although the level was substantially higher for the developing countries. The share increased for the UK, the USA and the Federal Republic of Germany, but that for Japan remained low, and the share actually declined in Latin America and the Caribbean countries. Overall, however, we can conclude that the TNC network expanded substantially in the core through FDI, and the dependency on FDI increased in the periphery.

The Industrial Sector

The above figures indicate that the role of TNCs has expanded in the second half of the twentieth century. This expansion was a direct result of the formation and transformation of corporate networks, which differ according to the country of origin of the TNC and in different industries. Let us trace the network formation of the TNCs' industrial activities by examining the country data of FDI outflow and inflow. FDI is a record of overseas investment activities that is one mode of cross-border expansion of the corporate network. Through FDI, a source country TNC opens either subsidiaries (defined as 100 per cent ownership) or affiliates (less than 100 per cent ownership). Although there are other means to expand the corporate network abroad, such as international subcontracting and licensing, comprehensive data for these other forms are not available in many cases.

If we refer back to Tables 3.7 and 3.8, we see that, while FDI grew by increasing amounts throughout the period, there was a fluctuation in the rate of growth. For example, the pace of growth slowed down in the 1980–84 period. The yearly FDI performance summarized for the G5 countries (USA, UK, France, Federal Republic of Germany, and Japan) by Julius (1990: 21, Fig. 2.2) shows a spurt of FDI activities in three periods: 1970–73, 1977–79 and 1983–87. While the decline in FDI outflow from G5 between 1973 and 1974 was small and temporary, the trend in decline between 1979 and 1983 was significant and longer lasting.

The country share in FDI flow tells us the temporal shift in active expansion of the TNC networks in different countries. In the 1960s and the first half of the 1970s, US TNCs were responsible for more than 50 per cent of world outbound investment. The transnationalization of US TNCs in this period needs to be placed in the context of the effort of US corporations to maintain the domination they had had in the world market since the immediate postwar period. In the 1950s, the major industrial corporations of the USA dominated the most important segments of the world market – the US and West European markets – through trade. Under conditions of currency non-convertibility, the purchasing power for US exports was provided to European countries through the Marshall Plan. By 1950, the network of US TNCs spread mainly to Canada and Latin America, which accounted respectively for 34.5 per cent and 29.3 per cent of US FDI outflow balance in 1957, and in the manufacturing and petroleum sectors, which accounted for 31.5 per cent and 35.7 per cent of the outflow balance, respectively.

As currency convertibility was restored in the late 1950s, some West European countries moved toward the formation of the EEC, which served among other things to provide partial protection for their enterprises from the competition of US companies. The US industrial corporations responded to this by investing directly in Europe and setting up subsidiaries to serve as the manufacturing base for the European market in the 1960s. By 1970, the share of Europe in total US FDI outflow balance increased to 33.5 per cent from 14.7 per cent in 1950 (Canada's share dropping to 27.8 per cent and Latin America's share to 14.7 per cent), and the share of manufacturing industry increased to 41.1 per cent (the petroleum sector dropping to 26.2 per cent) (Okumura, 1988a: 284–5, Tables B-1, B-2).

By the combination of the policy of industrial protection and promotion undertaken together with US government assistance justified by the objective of containing Communism, the West European and Japanese states managed to create industrial corporations which could compete with US TNCs in the 1960s. In the late 1960s, US domination in world production and trade in manufactured goods eroded, and in the early 1970s, West European corporations deployed their networks within each other's boundaries and into North and South America, coming to surpass the USA as the major source of FDI.

For example, the FDI outflow balance of the UK shows a marked increase of FDI in Europe from £455 million in 1962 to £2,867 million in 1974 (13.4 per cent and 27.5 per cent of the UK total) and in the USA and Canada from £785 million to £2,271 million (23.1 per cent and 21.8 per cent) in the same years. In the case of the Federal Republic of Germany, the share of Europe was 52.9 per cent and that of the USA was 17.2 per cent in 1976 (Okumura, 1988a: 296, 300, Tables C-1,

D-1). This trend marks a major shift in the direction of capital flow from one from core to periphery to one that was intra-core in the 1960s.

In contrast to the market-oriented intra-core FDI of the USA and European TNCs, the transnationalization of Japanese industrial enterprise took a more periphery-oriented direction (see Kojima, 1978; Yoshihara, 1976; Ozawa, 1979). Starting from small-scale FDI in Taiwan in the 1960s, Japanese firms shifted their labour-intensive manufacturing operations to East and Southeast Asia in the 1970s. Although the Japanese TNC network extended into the USA and the EC in the 1980s, periphery-oriented Japanese enterprise network expansion still continued even amidst the surge of service-sector FDI into the EC and North America in the 1980s. For example, developing countries accounted for 55 per cent of total Japanese FDI outflow balance (of which 28.2 per cent was in Asia) in 1976, 54 per cent (26.9 per cent in Asia) in 1980, and 46 per cent (20.6 per cent in Asia) in 1986 (Okumura, 1988a: 309, Table E-2).

As a result of the growth of European and Japanese TNCs, US domination of world industry eroded in the 1970s, and this process continued in the 1980s. Let us examine the national composition of the major industrial TNCs. Tables 3.10 and 3.11 summarize the top 50 and the top 500 industrial corporations listed in the *Fortune Directory*. The lists contain the major industrial corporations, which are the trend-setters of TNC activities. As may be seen, whereas in the 1950s and 1960s US corporations dominated the world industrial scene, by the 1970s European TNCs had made gains at the expense of US TNCs, and in the 1980s, Japanese TNCs made gains once again at the expense of US TNCs.

The 1980s saw three major trends in industry-sector TNC network expansion: (1) increased intra-core FDI, prompted by bilateral protectionism (primarily on the part of the USA and France), and the further anticipated integration of the EC scheduled for 1992; (2) integration of selected peripheral sites for low-cost manufacturing by the core TNCs; and (3) expanding collaboration and alliance among the TNCs from the Triad.

Intra-core TNC network expansion is indicated by FDI inflow in the 1980s. As compared to the 1970s when the major destination of FDI was Europe, in the 1980s the USA emerged as the principal destination of FDI, although still followed closely by Europe (Table 3.8). The share of industrial-sector FDI inflow balance in the USA remained stable in the 1980s (Okumura, 1988a: 284–5, Table B-1), indicating a significant expansion of the networks of non-US industrial TNCs in the USA.

The TNC network expanded further into East and Southeast Asian countries in the 1980s in order to integrate low-wage (and reputedly docile) women's labour there. The FDI was supplemented by so-called 'new forms of investment' (NFI) (Oman, 1989: 10), which included minority shareholding by the TNC as well as international subcontracting; this was already the principal strategy of Japanese TNCs in the 1960s, and it subsequently spread among the TNCs from other core countries. Through NFI, the host country's financial resource was mobilized without the TNCs exposing themselves to the potential risks of financial loss and prosecution for violating local labour and environmental laws. Furthermore, the TNCs were able to continue to have full control over the operation of their local affiliates, since the latter were completely dependent on the TNCs' technology, distribution, and marketing capability.

According to Halbach (1989: 10, Table 2), minority shareholding joint ventures played an important role in developing countries in industries such as motor vehicle manufacture, electronics, machinery and precision instruments. The share of minority shareholding joint ventures out of all ventures in the developing countries was 50 per cent, 56 per cent, and 57 per cent for these three industries (based on questionnaire results from 30, 41, and 24 TNCs in the respective industries). Eight TNCs in the food-processing industry that participated in the same study did not have any minority shareholding arrangements, indicating the variation among industrial sectors in terms of the need and preference concerning minority/majority shareholding. The expansion of minority shareholding overall indicates the expansion in mobilization of host country capital. The shift from 100 per cent owned subsidiaries to NFI, especially in developing countries, enabled the TNCs to expand their control over local capital and enterprises without committing their own capital, which was devoted to high-return generating activities in the core regions.

Intra-core TNC competition in the 1970s and 1980s involved transnational network formation in different regions, resulting in a different pattern of integration of the periphery and semiperiphery by each TNC group. The Japanese networks were deployed mainly in East and Southeast Asia, the EC networks in Central and Eastern Europe, and the US networks in Latin America (UNCTC, 1991: 56, Fig. VII; cf. Michalski, 1991: 8). This, however, was not a mutually exclusive cross-deployment of the networks. For example, out of $7,067 million FDI in South Korea between 1962 and 1989, 50.3 per cent came from Japan. However, the US share was a healthy 27.5 per cent; and Switzerland, the Federal Republic of Germany, the UK, the Netherlands and France combined accounted for another 13.3 per cent (Dehm, 1990: 142).

The role of East and Southeast Asian networks deployed by the Japanese TNCs was to export low-cost goods to the Triad. Some 68 per cent of total exports of Japanese manufacturing affiliates in Asia were to the Triad (35 per cent to Japan, 23 per cent to the USA, and 10 per cent to the EC). The regional network of Japanese TNCs in Asian countries serves the 'three-legged strategy' (UNCTC, 1991: 47) of Japanese TNCs through the supply of low-cost goods. The UNCTC (1991: 63) predicts that 'the role of EC transnational corporations in Central and Eastern Europe may come to resemble the relationships of Japanese transnational corporations with their Asian subsidiaries and United States transnational corporations with their Mexican subsidiaries, especially if Central and Eastern European countries are allowed to trade freely with the EC.' Thus three regional networks were formed (Humes, 1993: 26–30). It should be noted once again that the regional networks are not regionally closed. Instead, they are open to the entire world market, especially the Triad, based on the strength coming from the regional linkages (see Amin, 1993).

As a result of the expansion of the scope of transnational corporations, world industrial activity not only increased in the core region but also spread into periphery and semiperiphery. Table 3.21 summarizes the annual growth rate of manufacturing. The growth centres in the 1960s were Latin America, the so-called centrally planned economies (or CPEs – Eastern Europe and the former USSR), Japan and Israel (indicated by the difference between the total for Asia and Asia excluding Japan and Israel). In the 1970s, while growth in Western Europe lagged behind the world average, developing countries and CPEs led the list in growth rates. In the first half of the 1980s, however, Latin America collapsed, together with Western Europe and Oceania. Above average growth rates were achieved only in Asia, North America and the CPEs, but the performance of the CPEs was dismal compared to their previous performance. In the second half of the 1980s, world manufacturing growth recovered, but growth in Western Europe remained weak, together with a further deceleration in the growth rate in the CPEs. By contrast, the performance of Asian developing countries was particularly impressive in the 1980s, together with a remarkable recovery on the part of Latin America in the second half of the 1980s.

As a result, there was a shift of manufacturing activities from the Americas and Western Europe to Asia, while the USSR and Eastern Europe maintained their share. Furthermore, the rapid increase in manufacturing activities in developing Asian countries involved a substantial relocation of industrial activities from Japan, which was the core in this region, primarily to the Asian newly industrializing countries (or

NICs, which included South Korea, Taiwan, Hong Kong and Singapore) which constituted the semiperiphery of the region, and also to Thailand, Malaysia, Indonesia and China, which constituted the periphery of the region.

Those industries that were relocated to the peripheral and semi-peripheral zones in largest measure were the labour-intensive industries, the capital-intensive industries tending to stay in the core. The domination of the core in capital-intensive industries was exemplified by the location of automobile production, while marked intra-zonal shift in labour-intensive industries was exemplified by production of cotton woven fabrics and also television receivers (see Tables 3.22, 3.23 and 3.24).

The marked rise in the share of industrial production in Asia since the 1970s was due in part to the spread of an organization of production called the multi-layered subcontracting system (Arrighi, Ikeda and Irwan, 1993: 48–63). In contrast to the vertically integrated operation typical of the US TNCs, this system reduced labour and capital costs through the use of subcontractors. With the application of flexible production (Friedman, 1988: 20–26), Japan integrated East Asia (excluding North Korea, but increasingly China as well as Southeast Asia) into its sphere of accumulation, lifting up the entire region to be a major centre of production and accumulation.

The importance of East Asia as a location of manufacturing production has thus been increasing. The manufactured export share of the so-called dynamic Asian economies (DAEs, which include the Asian NICs, Thailand and Malaysia) in total manufactured exports of all developing countries has increased from less than 10 per cent in 1965 to more than 45 per cent in 1988 (OECD, 1993a: 22, Chart 2). In fact, DAEs are the most important trade partner of OECD countries among non-OECD country groups, and their trade share was increasing rapidly in the second half of the 1980s (OECD, 1993a: 25, Chart 4). The DAEs were the host of FDI from the core, and the share of Japanese FDI increased in the second half of the 1980s while the US share declined (OECD, 1993b: 35, Chart 1).

Furthermore, the industries which went from the core to the periphery and semiperiphery were not limited to labour-intensive manufacturing. For example, although crude steel production involves a capital–labour ratio higher than the average of all industrial categories (calculation based on employment and capital formation data in UN, 1967; 1981; 1991), production has spread from the core to the periphery and semiperiphery (see Table 3.25). However, this industry had a low R&D content, as indicated by Soete and Verspagen (1991: 256). Indeed, crude steel production technology has been standardized, and its technology 'rent' is already depleted. The steel manufacturing TNCs of the core survived by upgrading their product mix from low-technology, mass production items to high-technology, specialty items in the 1970s and 1980s, as such semiperipheral countries as Brazil and South Korea expanded their production capacity in low-technology items (see Yachir, 1988: 47–9).

Thus, there emerged a separation of the location of high R&D/high-technology production and the location of low-technology production. Although we cannot present exact data, the share of production costs in retail price was probably quite small, and the rest was composed of distribution, advertisement, retailing, product development, production technology development, insurance and finance costs, and profit. When the entire operation was under the control of a TNC, then the value-added component conducted in a peripheral or semiperipheral zone could become quite small, even if the production figure showed a larger contribution.

Location of R&D activities and high-technology production was determined principally by the core TNCs and core states in spite of the effort on the part of semiperipheral states to catch up with the core. If the core TNCs let the enterprises and states of the semiperiphery and periphery import advanced technology, it was not the most advanced and best technology. Only lower-level technology was transferred (Henderson, 1989: 44–8; Yachir, 1988: 47–9). Even if a core TNC located production assemblage of a high-technology item, like advanced electronics products, in a semiperipheral zone, the production of key components such as integrated circuits or microprocessors tended to remain in the core.

Japanese companies, for example, have been very reluctant to transfer higher technology to other Asian countries (*New York Times*, 13 October 1991: F1, F6; 5 December 1991: D1, D22). In addition, the rise of inter-TNC collaboration for high-technology development excluded access to such technology on the part of states and enterprises of the periphery and semiperiphery (Ohmae, 1985: 134–44; *New York Times*, 1 January 1992: 1, 48). The spread of the production of high-technology products in the semiperipheral and peripheral zones under TNC control implied a further integration of these zones and dependence on global TNC operations. Peripheral states and enterprises were left with increasingly fewer possibilities to achieve self-sufficiency because the high value-added segments of activities were monopolized by the core.

The intensified competition among TNCs under the condition of slow economic growth since 1974 has resulted in the expansion of corporate networks into the peripheral and semiperipheral zones of the world-system, seeking cheap labour for manufacturing without spending much capital under the NFI strategy. At the same time, there was an intra-core network expansion, in particular in the service sector. This was in part a response to financial liberalization in the 1980s which eliminated restrictions on foreign exchange transactions, and in part a result of the pressure of investing surplus capital under conditions of slower economic growth.

In addition to the TNC network expansion, intra-core TNC alliances became an important strategy from the mid-1970s. Soete (1991: 61) observes that, in contrast to the period from 1950 to 1970 when manufacturing joint ventures were gradually expanding, the period since the mid-1970s saw a dramatic expansion in joint ventures involving R&D activities. The international TNC alliances were the result in part of the increasing requirement of R&D investment involving high risk (UNCTC, 1991: 37; Yoshitomi, 1991, 20).

Hargert and Morris (1988) studied cooperative agreements and collaboration, as reported in major European business journals. First, they found that the number of cooperative agreements among TNCs from different home countries increased substantially in the 1980s. The number of cooperative agreements involving US and EC TNCs increased from fewer than ten in 1979 to nearly two hundred in 1985. Likewise, those involving EC and Japanese TNCs increased from almost zero in 1979 to about eighty in 1985, and those involving US and Japanese TNCs increased from almost none in 1979 to about sixty in 1985.

Second, international collaboration was observed in the R&D-intensive industries such as aerospace (19.0 per cent), telecommunications (17.2 per cent), computers (14.0 per cent), other electrical (13.0 per cent), and motor vehicles (23.7 per cent). Third, the principal purpose of collaboration was joint product development (37.7 per cent), production (23.3 per cent), and development and production (16.8 per cent). Fourth, the predominant collaboration partners were rivals (71.3 per cent). Finally, the composition of collaboration partners was intra-EC, 30.8 per cent; EC–USA, 25.8 per cent; EC–Japan, 10.1 per cent; USA–Japan, 8.4 per cent; intra-USA, 8.4 per cent; and others between Triad TNCs and non-Triad TNCs, 16.6 per cent. Since the source of information was European publications, collaborative arrangements among Japanese TNCs and those between Japanese and US TNCs may be underrepresented. Taking that into consideration, it is clear from their figures that collaborative ventures were sought equally by the TNCs from all members of the Triad (also, see Soete, 1991: 61). The continuation of the above trend is confirmed by Hagedoorn (1993), who extends the study of Hargert and Morris to 1989.

Given the emergence of a Triadic world-economic structure, the TNCs have been seeking to expand market shares in all three major markets – the EC, the USA and Japan – through FDI, collaboration, and merger and acquisition (Bleeke and Ernst, 1993). Increasingly, low-wage countries in Asia, Central and Eastern Europe, and Latin America have been integrated into the expanding and intensifying regional networks controlled by the Triad TNCs as low-cost manufacturing zones.

Humes (1993) describes the change in the strategy of the TNCs, which attempt to cope with a rapidly changing and increasingly complicated market situation. The desire to spread the costs and the risks and to speed up the development and distribution of new products has led not only to more mergers and acquisitions but also to a variety of forms of joint ventures and other types of alliances for R&D, manufacturing and marketing. Differences in the cost of staffing, raw materials, manufactured components and money (which change as currency exchange rates fluctuate) force transnationals to develop globally flexible sourcing strategies. The impact of these forces has been reinforced by differences in the extent to which countries engage in protectionism, the variety of tariff and non-tariff means countries use to apply protectionism, and disparities in the application of their protectionism. All of these factors have increased the extent to which multinationals not only market but also manufacture and source multicontinentally (Humes, 1993: 25–6). While labour-intensive manufacturing activities have been shifted to the periphery of the world-economy, the 'brains' of the TNC networks – product and process research and development, advertising, marketing, financing, distribution, and so on – have been kept in the core.

The Service Sector

In the environment of slowed economic growth, some service sectors became the most profitable sectors in the capitalist world-economy. While some industrial activities spread to the periphery and semi-periphery in the postwar period, the most profitable service activities are currently and will be in the future monopolized by the TNCs from the core. Who gains control over a few growing service sectors will probably decide the structure of world-level accumulation in the coming decades.

As the USA lost its supremacy in production and trade in the 1970s, the service sector, such as banking, financing, business services, transportation and telecommunications became the principal area of US TNC operation. Increased international lending on the part of US banks, together with increased portfolio investment abroad in the 1970s, marked the shift from industry to business-related services. European and Japanese service TNCs, however, caught up with the US service TNCs rather quickly (see, for example, Table 3.12). The world service market came to be dominated by a small number of major TNCs from the Triad.

The tertiary or service sector, which is usually defined as residual of the primary (agriculture and extracting) and secondary (manufacturing) sectors, has been increasing in importance. Table 3.26 shows that the importance of the service sector as measured by its GDP share increased significantly in the past two decades. Also, the growing importance of the service sector in the world-economy was reflected in the rapid rise of service-sector FDI as compared to the rise of industrial-sector FDI.

The sectorial distribution of FDI showed a cycle where raw material extraction, manufacturing and services took turns as the leading sector in transnationalization. UNCTC (1991: 15) observes that '[d]uring the 1950s, foreign direct investment was concentrated in raw materials, other primary products and resource-based manufacturing; today, it is mainly in services and in technology-intensive manufacturing'.

In the case of the USA, the share of service-sector FDI (trade, transportation, banking and financial sectors) increased from one-quarter of total FDI in 1950 to one-third in 1986. As Table 3.27 shows, the share of service sectors in total inward and outward FDI balance became significant in the USA, the Federal Republic of Germany and Japan. The increase in the stock of service-sector FDI was a result of the rapid change in the flow of service-sector FDI as summarized in Table 3.28.

The rising share of FDI in the service sector in recent decades – 40 per cent of world FDI stock and 50–60 per cent of annual flow by the end of the 1980s – was brought about by the decreasing cost of data processing and telecommunications (Aharoni, 1993: 1–2). At the same time, invisible trade as a percentage of total trade increased. The share of invisible trade receipts (which reflects trade in services) in total receipts increased from 23.4 per cent in 1960, to 25.2 per cent in 1970, to 26.2 per cent in 1982. The share in payments increased from 23.2 per cent in 1960, to 24.9 per cent in 1970, to 29.4 per cent in 1982 (Enderwick, 1989: 9, Table 1.2). The world export of services is dominated by the core. As Table 3.29 shows, the top ten countries controlled about two-thirds of the world total in 1980.

The most important service items whose trade and FDI activities were increasing were business-related services such as financial services, legal advising and consultation, insurance, transportation, and telecommunications and data processing. Although the market was expanding in these sectors, it was dominated by the TNCs, which were expanding their networks throughout the world.

The banking sector is one of the oldest business services in the capitalist world-system. Transnationalization took place at an early stage in this sector, but the expansion of cross-border networking has been quite remarkable in recent decades. And, as a result, 'all of the industrial countries have a large number of branches and representative offices in other industrial countries, as well as in developing countries and the two major Communist countries, the USSR and China', and the number of multinational banks increased from 2,744 in 1968 to 5,814 in 1983 (Grubel, 1989: 63).

Table 3.30 shows the growth of the assets of the world's top fifty banks. It is clear that the banking sector experienced tremendous growth of its top corporations. Japanese banks increased their share significantly, which is reflected in the change of the composition of the world's top fifty banks (see Table 3.12). Between 1970 and 1990, the number of US banks in this group dropped substantially while the number of Japanese banks increased. European banks maintained their presence in the list without much change. The ranking by the *Fortune Directory*, however, is based on the total amount of assets, which does not necessarily reflect the profitability of these banks to investors. According to *Euromoney* (February 1993: 102), J.P. Morgan, a US bank, is the world's best bank in terms of shareholder's equity, return on equity, and so on. Indeed, the best Japanese bank, Sumitomo Bank, was ranked only in forty-third place.

The growth of banks measured by the growth of total assets of the top fifty US banks was faster on average than that of the top fifty US industrial corporations (see Table 3.31). However, the growth of banks slowed down in the 1980s while the total assets of the top fifty US diversified service companies kept growing at a high rate. This reflected the trend of 'securitization' where corporations and other borrowers obtained money not through bank lending but through bond and equity sales in the financial markets. Financial market liberalization with unrestricted foreign-exchange transactions triggered a worldwide trend toward securitization.

The relative importance of banks in financial activities of corporations and households was decreasing in the 1980s. Bank deposits as a proportion of corporate financial assets declined in Germany from 57.5 per cent in 1980 to 43.8 per cent in 1990. In Japan, there was a quite sharp drop especially in the second half – that is, from 78.9 per cent in 1980, to 77.8 per cent in 1985, to 46.5 per cent in 1990. In the USA, the proportion had been low for some decades due to the earlier development of the financial markets; in 1990, the figure was only 18.8 per cent. Bank deposits as a proportion of household financial assets declined in the 1980s as well in the Federal Republic of Germany and Japan. The share of bank loans as a proportion of corporate liabilities also declined during the 1980s (Goldstein et al., 1992: 3, Table 1). These changes indicate that corporations and households were increasingly integrated directly through sales/purchase of equity and bonds, while indirect channelling of money through bank deposits and loans was losing its predominance. Thus, bonds and equities became the principal method for business finance in the second half of the 1980s (Goldstein et al., 1992: 60–61, Table A12).

Increasingly, the transnational banks were engaged in non-interest-earning activities such as the role of bookrunners and managers for bond issuing. The share of non-interest income in gross income was increasing in the 1980s; for example, from 31 per cent in 1981 to 38 per cent in 1990 in the case of large US commercial banks, and from 24 per cent in 1981 to 36 per cent in 1990 in the case of large Japanese commercial banks (Goldstein et al., 1992: 54, Table A6).

The financial service sector expanded as the world equity and bond market expanded. The major players in this market were the diversified financial service companies and banks from the core. According to the *Fortune Directory*, the world's top fifty diversified service companies recorded $19 billion profit in 1990, which was 70 per cent of the profit made by the world's top one hundred commercial banks, even though the assets of the former ($2,480 billion) were just one-quarter of those of the latter (*Fortune Directory*, 26 August 1991). In terms of the nationality composition of the world's largest diversified service companies, US companies dominated the list with nineteen in 1991, followed by Japan with twelve. The rest were all European companies (*Fortune Directory*, 24 August 1992: Table 14).

The world insurance market grew substantially from 1970 to 1983. Total life insurance increased by 4.5 times (to $180.1 billion); total non-life insurance increased by 3.8 times (to $263.3 billion); and total re-insurance increased 4.2 times (to $40 billion) (Nusbaumer, 1987: 131, Table 5-5). However, the international transaction of insurance services either through trade or FDI was still restricted by virtually all countries, and therefore the international transaction of insurance services was limited (Lanvin, 1993: 75; Nusbaumer, 1987: 130). As a result, insurance business tended to make higher profits. For example, according to the *Fortune Directory* for 1990, the world's top fifty life-insurance companies with combined assets of $1,907 billion made a net income of $43.7

billion, which was greater than the profits made by the world's top one hundred banks ($39.3 billion) with total assets of $13,927 billion (*Fortune Directory*, 26 August 1991).

In order to cover risks under such conditions, international reinsurance was increasing in importance with a concentrated market structure. Nusbaumer (1987: 133) states that, 'due to the size of risks involved in reinsuring business, the market tends to be dominated by a few large firms operating on a global scale.' The fifteen largest reinsurance companies in the world collected premiums that netted $12,354 million, which was 30.1 per cent of the total world reinsurance business (Nusbaumer, 1987: 134, Table 5–8).

In the advertising industry, there was a growing demand for the multinationalization of advertising firms so as to match the needs of advertisers who operated multinationally. From 1975 to 1985, the share of world advertising expenditures handled by advertising TNCs increased from 13 per cent to 20 per cent (Kakabadse, 1987: 47–8). The top ten advertising groups accounted for about 10 per cent of world advertising business in 1985 (based on data in Kakabadse, 1987: 49, Table 11).

The management-consultancy market was growing rapidly and advertising firms and accounting firms were the major players. The US market, which was the world's largest, had a revenue of about $4 billion in 1985. Arthur Andersen, the biggest accounting firm in the world, took $477 million of that market (Kakabadse, 1987: 50). Arthur Andersen expanded its offices outside the USA rapidly, from 19 in 1960, to 48 in 1974, and 105 in 1983 (Noyelle and Dutka, 1988: 30, Table 3–2). This is a good example of the expansion of business service TNCs.

Accounting firms also transnationalized their networks. Among the world's thirteen largest firms, there were 3,938 foreign offices in 1982 (Noyelle and Dutka, 1988: 31, Table 3–3). Law firms extended their foreign operation as well. Among the 100 largest US law firms, the number with foreign offices increased from 22 in 1965 to 46 in 1984. The number of foreign offices among these firms increased from 31 in 1965 to 105 in 1984.

Although the size of the business service sector was small compared to that of the industrial sector, it was an expanding and profitable sector in the 1980s. Kakabadse lists three forces that drove the expansion and concentration in this sector: (1) trans-border data flows and the existence of worldwide information networks; (2) the need of TNCs to expand their operations in order to be able to continue to service their clients, mainly other multinationals; and (3) the increasing capacity of a relatively small number of TNCs to offer a wide range of services in the world market (1987: 51).

The *Fortune Directory* list of the world's 100 largest diversified service companies has become dominated by the Japanese TNCs. Especially noteworthy was the fact that nine of the top ten largest companies were Japanese trading companies (*Sogo Shosha*) in 1990. The nationality breakdown of the top 50 and 100 reveals that East Asia, North America, and Europe took about one-third each in 1990, with a decline in the number of European firms in 1991 (from 32 to 28) and increase in East Asian firms (from 33 to 40) (*Fortune Directory*, 26 August 1991; 24 August 1992).

In spite of the predictions in the 1970s that TNCs would be taking over the world-economy in terms of asset and production shares, the growth of the top industrial TNCs in fact slowed down during the economic downturn (see Table 3.14). Prime opportunities for profit-making seem to have shifted to selected service sectors, and, because of the diverse characteristics of the service sectors, it seems as if many new business opportunities have been opened up in recent years. By taking advantage of such opportunities, some corporations have come to lead new billion-dollar industries in tourism, computer software, health information, and computer game programming. These fast-growing and profitable sectors, however, often relied on previously existing industries in some crucial aspects. For example, the growing tourism industry was providing many windows of opportunities for new business. But the most profitable segments – for example, production of airplanes for transportation, reservation information networks, and credit card and other services for travellers' convenience, were controlled by a small number of firms. Similarly, the booming diet industry has to rely on existing food-processing companies for the preparation of their products, and growing cosmetic companies depend on the giant chemical TNCs for the preparation of raw materials.

Together with high-technology industries, the business service sectors provided opportunities for further accumulation, and the contenders for these opportunities were the TNCs from the Triad.

US Hegemony and the World-Economy

The transformation of the world-economy and its agents of capital accumulation described above did not take place in a market free from government interventions. The core states have in fact been continuously negotiating the rules of the game for business enterprises bilaterally and multilaterally throughout the postwar period. The resulting principal elements of the postwar 'international economic order' – liberal trade and financial movement, and a fixed exchange-rate system with dollar–gold convertibility – were the result of such negotiations under the leadership of the USA as the hegemonic power of the world-system.

The liberalization of the movement of goods, services and capital has been a pillar of the postwar economic order (Bosworth, 1993: 89–90). The successive liberalizations under the US state's leadership, however, were utilized largely to create an environment favourable for US enterprises. The terms of agreement, of course, had to be acceptable to other states in the core zone, who had their own agenda to protect their enterprises. Still, the succession of intra-core liberalization measures were designed in ways that opened greater opportunities for US enterprises. These measures included the Marshall Plan (1940s and 1950s) which facilitated US exports to Europe, which otherwise lacked the necessary purchasing power; liberalization of merchandise trade (1950s and 1960s); liberalization of foreign direct investment (1960s); liberalization of international financial activities (1970s, 1980s); and the liberalization of trade in services, information and agriculture, which has been on the negotiation table in the 1980s and 1990s. Although these measures primarily helped US enterprises in the beginning, they were not to be the only beneficiaries of such measures. Based on strong state support and their historically-formulated organizational structures, European and Japanese enterprises eventually benefited from the liberal business environment as much as, if not more than, the US enterprises (see Maddison, 1989: 66).

The biggest shift in the international economic order during the postwar period was the termination of the fixed exchange rate system. Although the movement towards a floating exchange rate was a consequence of the relative decline of US hegemonic power, it constituted also a step toward further liberalization in the world-economy. When governments stopped intervening as directly in the foreign-exchange markets in the mid-1970s and further liberalized foreign-exchange transactions in the 1980s, the mechanism of setting up the most important price – that of money itself – was left to the self-regulating market.

Ironically, this was a result of successful policies on the part of states in the core zone to promote capitalist enterprises, which then grew rapidly to undermine these states' ability to control and intervene in foreign-exchange markets. By December 1973, 'the foreign assets of banks in OECD countries in foreign currencies amounted to $248 billion, compared with official reserves of $182 billion. By end 1987 these had risen to $3,056 billion compared with official reserves of $789 billion' (Maddison, 1989: 86).

The shift from the fixed exchange rate system to the floating exchange rate system, therefore, signalled the transition to a situation in which the financial strength of capitalist enterprises exceeded that of the states, since the direct cause of the end of fixed exchange rate was the massive speculation by the private investors in the foreign-exchange market. Once the West European and Japanese states stopped accepting depreciating US dollars at face value, the price of the dollar was left to be decided by the market, and the US economy as a whole was stripped of the privilege of running a trade deficit without accumulating debt. Thus, in the 1980s, the dollar's role in international finance changed from one of absolute dominance to one of merely relative primacy. For example, only 39.1 per cent of outstanding international bonds at the end of 1991 were issued in US dollars; and in terms of net issue, the dollar share was 30.0 per cent in 1990 and only 22.4 per cent in 1991 (BIS, 1992: 176).

Under the new conditions wherein the relative price of national currencies was determined by the overall economic standing of a given country in the world-economy, no single state, even the USA, could any longer make macroeconomic policy without taking into account the direct impact on its standing in the world-economy. The US state became subject to credit ratings by the private appraisers, beginning to find itself treated just like other states, supra-state agencies (for example, the World Bank), and TNCs in the globalized capital market.

As the financial markets became global and the enterprise networks became transnationalized, however, it became increasingly problematic to argue that what was good for a TNC was also necessarily good for the state in which its head office was located. A phenomenal rise in cross-border equity and bond transactions in the 1980s made the composition of capital increasingly 'multinational' for the major business enterprises. Given the increased ability of these enterprises to shift production sites across national boundaries, the interests of the enterprise and those of the workers of its home country were increasingly at odds with each other. Today what is good for General Motors (GM), one of the largest issuers of bonds in the Eurobond market, may be good for investors from all over the world as well as for some non-US workers employed by GM's parts/components suppliers outside the USA, but not at all necessarily good for US workers, who face potential layoffs in depressed Midwest towns. When the president of the USA sought to aid Detroit automobile executives in an effort to open Japanese markets, the principal beneficiaries were likely to have included Japanese institutional investors who were among the purchasers of GM's convertible bonds.

Yet, it remains true that states protect their corporations together with their farmers through subsidies and other measures (Teece, 1991: 43, 46). Although state protection may not by itself determine the success or failure of the enterprises in the promoted industry, there persists a widely accepted (and therefore politically influential) view that the living standards of a nation are determined by the degree to which it has technology-intensive, high-value-added industries that can compete in the world market (Cohen and Zysman, 1987: 59–61; Yoshitomi, 1991: 21). The states protect and promote high-technology industries through government policy on the premiss that, in consequence, their TNCs will keep the high-value-added activities, and therefore the high-wage jobs, within their boundaries. The competition among the core TNCs is fought primarily in terms of the development of technology. The US lead in technological development, as indicated by the proportion of R&D expenditure to GNP, eroded in the 1980s, as other major states (Japan, the Federal Republic of Germany, France, and the UK) increased their shares. In fact, in terms of non-defence R&D, Japan and the Federal Republic of Germany led other countries in the 1980s (Cohen and Noll, 1991: 28, Table 2-2).

What determines the success of an enterprise in high-technology industries is the accumulation of knowledge through learning-by-doing (Yoshitomi, 1991: 28) or the internal organization and management of the firm (Teece, 1991: 47). For this reason, the historical evolution of corporate structures in different countries (see Kogut, Shan and Walker, 1993: 78–81) matters for the outcome of high-technology competition and cooperation among the TNCs. What has been the performance of US TNCs in this regard? There has been increasing public concern in the USA that US TNCs have lost their competitive edge vis-à-vis Japanese TNCs in crucial high-technology areas such as electronics, semiconductors and semiconductor-manufacturing equipment (see Gover, 1993). The US market share in computers has also been thought to be at risk, and if this proves to be the case, the dominance in software may also be lost. If present trends continue, Gover argues, US-owned electronics manufacturers could be out of the domestic electronics business early in the twenty-first century.

Gover's concern is not unfounded. Yoshitomi (1991: 17) reports that more than 90 per cent of the bilateral imbalance between Japan and the USA is accounted for by only four categories of high-technology products: automobiles, computers, VCRs and semiconductors in descending order of the size of Japan's net surplus. Although some economists may insist that the US trade deficit and the Japanese trade surplus were basically caused by the difference in savings and investment in the two countries (see Bosworth, 1993), this presumed difference in macro-economic behaviour does not explain why the US trade deficit was concentrated in certain commodities.

On the other hand, it would be misleading to conclude that the US TNCs are losing in all industrial sectors In fact, despite the declining presence of the US TNCs in the *Fortune Directory*, they are still the top companies in many important industrial areas. Among twenty-six industrial categories used in the *Directory* in its 1991 listing, the top position was occupied by US companies in fourteen categories and by Japanese TNCs in only four categories (*Fortune Directory*, 27 July 1992). Even in the semiconductor industry, US firms regained top position in 1993 after eight years of Japanese domination in terms of market share, market size, and the amount of money spent on equipment investment (Shimura, 1994: 39). In addition, the network of collaborative agreement among the world's top TNCs has been continuously expanding in recent years. The research networks located in the universities and in the private and public laboratories maintain the role of the USA as one of the principal centres – still, no doubt, the leading centre – of basic research and technological innovation, and US TNCs remain its major beneficiaries.

Conclusion

The structure of accumulation in the 1945–73 period was based on steady economic expansion in the core zone realized by higher wages paid to selected workers in the core and the management of demand in the core zone, by the USA in particular. The periphery continued to serve primarily as the supplier of raw materials at low cost. Under the postwar structure, however, colonial markets were not the principal markets for the goods manufactured in the core; growing consumer, investment and government demand in the core itself provided the principal markets. The capital-rich US TNCs expanded their domestic markets and cultivated other markets through trade and FDI, thus making profits by expanding capital-intensive, vertically integrated production processes.

Successful expansion in the 1950s and 1960s resulted in rising costs of production. With the sudden shift in the distribution of purchasing power as a result of the oil price rise, the world-economy experienced stagflation, ending the rapid expansion of the postwar period. Although fall in demand in the 1970s was partially compensated for by the recirculation of petrodollars to states in the periphery which then were able to continue to purchase capital goods from the core, the tight money policy adopted by the USA to control inflation, together with recession caused by the second oil price hike, resulted in acute debt-service problems in the periphery and semiperiphery in the early 1980s.

While the US government deregulated banking and other financial sectors in the 1970s, non-US enterprises, especially Japanese, took advantage of cost-conscious and energy-conscious markets to compete successfully against the US TNCs. The capital-saving, energy-saving, flexible manufacturing network of the Japanese TNCs had originally been created in an environment of scarce capital and limited natural resources. Since the mid-1970s, however, the Japanese TNC networks have expanded to the semiperiphery and periphery through new forms of investment instead of via subsidiaries as a part of a cost-cutting strategy. In an environment of slow economic growth, financial surplus was circulated for speculation and the principal arena of competition shifted to business and consumer service industries as well as to high-technology production.

In terms of TNC activities and the structure of accumulation, the reproduction of the zonal structure continued with the usual geographical shifts of a Kondratieff-B period. The fact that some East Asian states have been able to enter the semiperiphery (or at least, so it seems at the moment) has been used to refurbish somewhat developmentalist hopes in a time of otherwise great disillusion, and has opened new peripheral zones as sources of cheap labour. The reincorporation of former socialist countries, especially China, into more intense participation in the com-modity chains of the world-economy has offered the potential of con-tributing to a major expansion of the world-economy in the beginning of the twenty-first century. The reduced state control over transnational corporate activities, however, accelerated intra-zonal and inter-zonal polarization. The role that the TNCs had created for themselves in the 1945–1967/73 period was jostled but not fundamentally changed in the 1967/73–1990 period.

Table 3.1 GDP share of country groups, 32 countries (1950, 1973, 1987)

	1950	*1973*	*1987*
OECD countries[1]	66.1	63.0	56.9
USA	(34.6)	(26.9)	(24.3)
Canada	(2.2)	(2.4)	(2.4)
Europe	(24.9)	(24.2)	(20.3)
Japan	(3.2)	(8.3)	(8.8)
Australia	(1.2)	(1.2)	(1.1)
Developing Asian countries[2]	14.4	15.5	23.5
China	(6.3)	(7.9)	(13.7)
Latin American countries[3]	5.7	6.9	7.2
USSR	13.8	14.6	12.4
Americas[4]	42.5	36.2	33.9
Europe[5]	38.7	38.8	32.7
East Asia[6]	12.2	19.7	27.5
South Asia[7]	5.4	4.1	4.8
Oceania[8]	1.2	1.2	1.1

Notes:

[1] Australia, Austria, Belgium, Canada, Denmark, Finland, France, Germany, Italy, Japan, the Netherlands, Norway, Sweden, Switzerland, the UK, and the USA.

[2] Bangladesh, China, India, Indonesia, Pakistan, the Philippines, South Korea, Taiwan, Thailand.

[3] Argentina, Brazil, Chile, Colombia, Mexico, Peru.

[4] The USA, Canada, and six Latin American countries.

[5] Austria, Belgium, Denmark, Finland, France, Germany, Italy, the Netherlands, Norway, Sweden, Switzerland, the UK and the USSR.

[6] Japan, China, Indonesia, the Philippines, South Korea, Taiwan, Thailand.

[7] Bangladesh, India, Pakistan.

[8] Australia.

Source: Maddison, 1989: 113, Table A-2.

Table 3.2 Absolute gap of per-capita GDP (in international $ at 1980 prices, and %)

	1950	1973	1987
$ gap from OECD average:			
Asian developing country average	3,048	6,791	8,254
Taiwan	3,027	5,765	5,461
South Korea	2,989	6,062	6,062
China	3,215	7,078	8,453
Latin American average	1,943	5,495	8,254
USSR	1,288	2,786	4,257
% of OECD average:			
Asian developing country average	14.2	13.5	19.1
Latin American average	45.3	35.1	29.7
USSR	63.7	64.5	58.3

Note: Country composition is the same as that indicated in the note to Table 3.1.
Source: Maddison, 1989: 19, Table 1.3.

Table 3.3 Total government expenditure as % of GDP for six OECD countries (France, Germany, Japan, the Netherlands, the UK, the USA)

1913	1929	1938	1950	1973	1986
11.7	17.8	27.7	26.7	37.4	46.3

Source: Madison, 1989: 71, Table 6.3.

Table 3.4 The role of government as the supplier of services and as the employer (selected countries)

	Government services as % of GDP	Government employment as % of total employment
UK[a]	14	22
France[a]	13	19
USA[a]	13	18
Germany (F.R.)[b]	12	16
Japan[a]	9	7

Notes: [a] 1983   [b] 1982

Source: Kakabadse, 1987: 10, Table 2.

Table 3.5 Annual growth rate of world trade

1948–60	*1960–73*	*1973–79*	*1980–88*
6.0	8.0	4.5	4.0

Source: Kenwood and Lougheed, 1992: 286.

Table 3.6 Export share of country groups, total 32 countries (1950, 1973, 1986)

	1950	*1973*	*1986*
OECD countries	79.2	86.4	82.4
Developing Asian countries	7.9	5.4	8.6
Latin American countries	8.8	3.4	3.3
USSR	4.0	4.7	5.7
Americas	38.7	25.2	21.2
Europe	47.7	59.0	56.6
East Asia	6.5	12.7	20.1
South Asia	3.4[a]	0.9	0.8
Oceania	3.7	2.1	1.3

Note: [a] The source data do not give consistent figures and this number is calculated by subtracting from the total.

Source: Source and country composition of each group as Table 1.

Table 3.7 Annual average FDI outflow and share of country and region (% and $ million for 1960–69; million SDR for the rest)

	1960–64	1965–69	1970–74	1975–79	1980–84	1985–88	1986	1987	1988
Industrial countries (%)	100.0	100.0	98.9	98.8	97.5	98.6	98.5	98.4	99.4
USA	65.9	66.6	51.7	45.7	13.2	24.1	27.8	30.2	11.9
Canada	1.9	2.2	2.9	4.9	9.7	4.2	3.1	3.4	4.9
Europe	30.5	29.3	37.0	41.6	63.2	50.8	49.9	48.1	55.2
UK	13.9	11.8	14.5	16.6	23.1	18.7	16.5	21.1	18.3
Germany (FR.)	4.8	5.6	8.3	8.6	8.8	7.7	10.3	6.3	7.0
France	5.4	3.1	3.6	4.5	7.1	6.7	5.4	6.2	9.8
Netherlands	2.9	3.9	5.1	6.7	11.3	4.5	4.5	6.0	2.4
Switzerland	n/a	n/a	n/a	n/a	5.2	3.3	1.5	0.9	5.0
Sweden	1.2	1.5	1.6	1.6	2.3	2.8	3.1	2.2	3.6
Italy	2.1	2.7	1.4	1.0	3.7	2.7	2.7	1.6	3.7
Belgium/Luxembourg	n/a	0.4	1.5	1.7	0.5	1.8	1.7	1.9	2.6
Other[a]	0.2	0.3	1.0	0.8	1.4	2.6	3.1	1.9	2.7
Japan	1.8	1.8	6.0	6.2	10.9	16.1	14.6	13.3	23.3
Other[b]	n/a	n/a	1.3	0.4	0.5	3.4	3.1	3.4	4.0
Developing countries (%)	n/a	n/a	1.0	1.3	2.5	1.4	1.5	1.6	0.6
Total (million $/SDR)	4,763	7,949	15,241	28,255	35,346	91,843	83,682	112,783	109,425

Note: [a] Austria, Norway, and Denmark for 1960–69. Norway, Spain, and Denmark for 1970–84. Austria, Finland, Iceland, Norway, Portugal, and Spain for 1985–88.
[b] Australia, New Zealand, and other European industrial countries for 1970–84. Australia and New Zealand for 1985–88, 1986, 1987 and 1988.

Source: Various issues of IMF, *Balance of Payments Yearbook.*

Table 3.8 Annual average FDI inflow and share of country and region (% and million SDR)

	1970–74	1975–79	1980–84	1985–88	1986	1987	1988
Industrial countries (%)	78.9	73.8	64.2	84.9	84.7	86.9	88.3
USA	14.7	23.8	33.1	43.1	44.8	42.9	43.6
Canada	6.1	3.6	0.1	1.9	1.8	3.9	2.9
Europe	49.4	40.5	28.9	35.7	33.5	36.3	38.0
UK	9.8	12.0	10.4	10.6	9.4	12.3	10.4
Germany (F.R.)	11.9	4.6	1.3	1.6	2.0	2.0	1.2
France	6.9	7.4	4.4	5.3	4.3	4.7	6.3
Netherlands	5.2	3.6	2.3	3.4	5.5	3.1	2.7
Switzerland	n/a	n/a	1.8	1.7	2.8	2.1	0.3
Sweden	0.6	0.3	0.3	0.6	1.1	0.3	0.7
Italy	6.2	2.2	1.8	3.1	-0.1	3.7	5.1
Belgium/Luxembourg	4.3	4.5	2.3	2.5	0.9	2.2	3.8
Other[a]	3.3	4.0	4.0	6.5	6.1	5.7	7.3
Japan	1.0	0.5	0.5	0.5	0.3	1.1	-0.4
Other[b]	7.7	5.5	1.6	3.8	4.3	2.6	0.2
Developing countries (%)	20.9	26.2	35.8	15.1	15.3	13.1	11.7
Latin America	11.4	14.1	10.1	5.8	4.8	5.0	5.8
Asia	5.6	7.4	8.3	6.0	6.2	6.4	3.4
Middle East	-4.0	-1.7	12.7	1.9	3.2	0.2	1.1
Africa	6.3	4.1	2.5	1.2	0.8	1.3	1.1
Europe (Cyprus, Malta)	1.6	2.3	2.2	0.3	0.3	0.2	0.3
Total (million SDR)	12,321	20,726	45,509	73,887	64,126	84,258	99,773

Notes: [a] Norway, Spain, and Denmark for 1970–84. Austria, Finland, Iceland, Norway, Portugal, Greece, and Spain for 1985–88.
[b] Australia, New Zealand, and other European industrial countries for 1970–84. Australia and New Zealand for 1985–88, 1986, 1987, and 1988.

Source: Various issues of IMF, *Balance of Payments Yearbook.*

Table 3.9 Share of average annual FDI inflow in gross domestic capital formation (%)

Country, region and economy	1980–82	1985–87
Developed market economies	2.9	3.4
United Kingdom	8.2	8.8
United States	3.5	4.5
Germany (F.R.)	0.3	0.6
Japan	0.1	0.1
Developing countries	6.0	6.1
Latin America and the Caribbean	6.0	5.0
Asia and the Pacific	5.9	6.8
Africa	6.1	9.0

Source: UNCTC, 1991: 8, Table 2.

Table 3.10 Nationality breakdown of the world top 50 industrial corporations

	1956	1960	1965	1970	1975	1980	1985	1990
North America	42	42	38	32	23	23	22	16
USA	42	42	38	32	23	23	21	16
Canada	1						1	
Europe	8	8	12	14	20	19	18	22
Germany (F.R.)	1	2	4	6	7	7	6	7
France					3	4	2	5
UK	4	2	3	3	4	2	2	2
Italy			1	2	2	2	3	3
UK/Netherlands	2	2	2	2	2	2	2	2
Switzerland	1	1	1		1	1	1	2
Netherlands		1	1	1	1	1	1	1
Austria							1	
East Asia				4	5	5	6	11
Japan				4	5	5	5	9
South Korea							1	2
Other					2	3	3	1
Brazil					1	1	1	
Mexico						1	1	
Kuwait							1	
Venezuela						1		1
Iran					1			

Note: The rankings are based on the total sales figures in respective years that were published in the following year.

Source: Various issues of *Fortune Directory*.

Table 3.11 Nationality breakdown of the world top 500 industrial corporations

	1975	1980	1985	1990
North America	**258**	**237**	**234**	**176**
USA	241	217	212	164
Canada	17	20	22	12
Europe	**168**	**168**	**148**	**168**
UK	49	51	48	43
Germany (F.R.)	38	38	33	30
France	29	29	23	30
Sweden	13	10	6	17
Switzerland	7	8	11	11
Italy	8	8	8	7
Finland	1	1	2	8
Netherlands	6	5	4	7
Spain	6	5	3	4
Belgium	5	5	3	4
UK/Netherlands	2	2	2	2
Norway		2	2	2
Luxembourg	1			1
Italy/Switzerland				
Austria	2	2	2	1
Portugal		1	1	
UK/Italy	1	1		
East Asia	**54**	**73**	**92**	**123**
Japan	54	66	82	111
South Korea		6	9	11
Taiwan		1	1	1
Other	**18**	**21**	**24**	**33**
Australia	3	2	5	9
India	2	2	4	6
Turkey	1	3	3	3
Brazil	1	1	2	3
South Africa	2	3	2	4
Netherlands Antilles	2	1	2	1
Mexico	1	2	1	1
Zambia	1	1	1	1
Venezuela		1	1	1
Chile	1	2		1
Kuwait		1	1	
New Zealand			1	1
Panama				1
Malaysia				1
Israel	1	1	1	
Argentina	1	1	1	
Indonesia	1		1	
Philippines		1		
Algeria	1			
Egypt	1			
Iran	1			

Note and Source: As Table 3.10.

Table 3.12 Nationality breakdown of the world top 50 banks

	1970	1975	1980	1985	1990
East Asia	**11**	**12**	**15**	**20**	**22**
Japan	11	12	14	19	20
Hong Kong			1	1	1
China					1
Europe	**19**	**23**	**24**	**18**	**25**
Germany (F.R.)	4	6	7	5	8
France	3	4	6	5	6
UK	5	4	4	4	4
Switzerland	3	2	2	2	3
Italy	4	4	2	1	2
Netherlands		3	3	1	1
North America	**19**	**14**	**10**	**11**	**3**
USA	15	10	7	8	2
Canada	4	4	3	3	1
Other	**1**	**1**	**1**	**1**	
Brazil	1	1	1	1	

Note and Source: As Table 3.10.

Table 3.13 The foreign manufacturing subsidiary networks of 315 largest transnational corporations in 1950 and 1970

No. of enterprises with subsidiary networks in:	US-based TNCs (180)		TNCs based in Europe (135)	
	1950	1970	1950	1970
Fewer than 6 countries	138	9	116	31
6–20 countries	43	128	16	75
More than 20 countries	0	44	3	29

Source: Vernon, 1979: 258, cited in Taylor and Thrift, 1982a: 1.

Table 3.14 World industrial concentration (selected industries)

Industry	Year	No. of top companies	World sales share (%)
Chemicals	1990	10	21.0
Pharmaceuticals	1989	15	29.5
Mainframe computers	1990	10	55.0
Personal computers	1989	11	63.8
Tyres	1991	5	76.9

Source: Market Share Reporter, 1992: 154, 178, 205, 250, 257.

Table 3.15 Direct foreign production as a percentage of home manufacturing, 1965–75

	USA	Japan	UK	Sweden	Germany (F.R.)	Average
1965	8.5	1.1	12.0	10.1	3.6	7.6
1970	11.8	2.0	19.1	13.2	10.2	10.6
1975	19.1	7.1	24.4	15.4	17.2	16.7

Source: Clegg, 1987: 58, Table 3.5.

Table 3.16 Production share of foreign-owned firms in total manufacturing sales, selected countries (%)

	Share	Year		Share	Year
Canada	51.1	1974	→	56.6	1977
UK	14.2	1971	→	21.2	1977
Germany (F.R.)	25.1	1972	→	21.7	1976
Japan	3.8	1972	→	4.2	1978

Source: Stopford and Dunning, 1983: 24–25, Table 2.2.

Table 3.17 Subsidiary/affiliate share in total corporate production and sales (%, selected industries, 1987)

Subsidiary production share in total corporate production	
Petroleum	49.6
Tobacco	46.3
Pharmaceuticals and consumer chemicals	42.4
Metal manufacture and products	19.7
Textile, apparel and leather goods	17.8
Aerospace	14.8
Foreign affiliate sales share in total corporate sales	
Petroleum	41.7
Tobacco	27.3
Engineering	23.9
Construction	23.6
Hotels	20.3
Motion pictures	20.0
Finance	16.3
Insurance	10.2

Source: Production: Stopford and Dunning, 1983: 66–7; Sales: Dunning, 1993: 81, Table 6.1.

Table 3.18 Subsidiary share of TNC production, selected countries (1981)

	No. of firms	Subsidiary share (%)
Small European countries		
Switzerland	10	79.2
UK/Netherlands	2	72.9
Belgium	4	69.0
Netherlands	7	58.4
Old TNC home countries		
UK	67	45.0
USA	242	32.0
France	20	32.6
Newcomers		
Germany (F.R.)	33	22.0
Italy	6	21.6
Japan	62	8.2

Source: Stopford and Dunning, 1983: 66–7, Table 4.6.

Table 3.19 Intra-firm trade share in total trade for the USA and Japan (%)

| | USA | | | | Japan | |
	1977	*1982*	*1985*		*1980*	*1983*
Exports	29.3	23.0	31.0		25.8	31.8
Imports	42.2	38.4	41.1		42.1	30.3

Source: UNCTC, 1988, cited in Sleuwaegen and Yamawaki, 1991: 146.

Table 3.20 FDI-related trade share in total merchandise trade (%)

	USA *(1986)*	Japan *(1983)*
Exports	55	41
Imports	52	57

Source: Julius, 1990: 74, Table 4.1.

Table 3.21 Average annual growth rate of manufacturing production

	1966–70	*1971–75*	*1976–80*	*1981–85*	*1986–90*
World	7.4	5.0	5.0	2.4	3.5
Developed countries	5.6	2.2	4.3`	1.9	3.1
Developing countries	6.7	8.0	5.6	4.2	8.2
North America	3.5	3.0	5.0	2.5	3.5
Caribbean, Central and South America	7.8	8.4	5.1	0.3	8.1
Asia	15.1	3.4	7.5	5.5	6.9
Asia excluding Japan and Israel	5.6	7.4	6.4	9.6	10.5
Western Europe	6.2	1.5	3.0	0.8	2.1
Eastern Europe and (former) USSR	11.3	10.6	6.5	3.6	1.7
Oceania	4.7	2.0	1.3	0.5	1.3

Source: UN, 1977; 1982; 1992.

Table 3.22 Automobiles produced (% share of world production, million units)

	1953	1960	1965	1970	1975	1980	1985	1989
Asia	0.1	1.3	3.6	14.2	18.1	24.3	25.1	28.6
Japan	0.1	1.3	3.6	14.0	18.0	24.0	23.9	25.7
NICs[1]			0.0	0.0	0.0	0.2	0.8	2.4
Other[2]			0.0	0.2	0.1	0.1	0.4	0.5
Americas	79.9	55.4	54.3	32.1	31.3	24.6	28.4	22.1
USA and Canada	79.9	55.4	52.4	32.1	31.3	24.6	28.4	22.1
NICs[3]			0.9	1.6	3.2	4.3	3.3	3.4
Other[4]			1.0	2.1	0.7	0.7	0.4	0.3
Europe	19.0	40.9	39.5	46.7	40.6	40.2	37.5	41.2
West[5]	18.8	39.8	37.4	42.8	35.0	33.3	30.6	33.4
South[6]			0.8	2.0	2.8	3.6	3.8	4.8
Other[7]	0.2	1.1	1.3	1.9	2.8	3.4	3.1	3.0
USSR	1.0	1.1	1.1	1.5	4.7	4.5	4.2	3.5
Total (*m. units*)	8	13	19	23	25	29	32	35

Notes:
[1] South Korea, Taiwan, Hong Kong, Singapore.
[2] Asia excluding Japan and NICs.
[3] Mexico, Brazil.
[4] Latin America excluding Mexico and Brazil.
[5] West Europe including the UK and Scandinavian countries.
[6] Spain, Portugal, Greece.
[7] East European countries.

Source: UN, 1976; 1981; 1991.

Table 3.23 Cotton woven fabrics produced (% share of world production, million square metres)

	1953	1960	1965	1970	1975	1980	1985	1989
Asia	10.6	12.8	34.1	30.4	49.4	57.3	64.2	66.6
Japan	10.6	12.6	6.4	4.9	4.0	3.6	2.8	2.3
NICs[1]			1.7	1.6	1.8	1.7	1.5	1.8
Other[2]		0.2	26.0	24.0	43.6	51.9	59.9	62.5
Americas	50.4	40.4	30.0	18.8	16.3	10.0	8.5	8.8
USA and Canada	50.4	40.4	22.0	12.9	8.9	6.2	4.4	4.7
NICs[3]			4.9	4.0	3.6	3.3	3.6	3.1
Other[4]			3.1	1.9	3.7	0.5	0.4	0.9
Europe	22.1	27.6	20.7	17.7	18.0	16.0	13.0	11.7
West[5]	13.9	17.5	12.3	9.7	8.8	7.6	6.3	5.4
South[6]			2.7	2.5	3.6	2.5	1.9	1.7
Other[7]	8.2	10.1	5.8	5.5	5.6	5.9	4.7	4.5
USSR	16.9	18.9	12.7	12.3	13.7	12.9	11.6	10.9
Total (*m. m²*)	22244	25547	47179	53891	52911	60329	73806	82067

Notes: 1–7: As Table 3.22. Estimated figures for Asia (1970, 1975), Japan (1989), Americas (1970, 1975), Canada (1975), South Europe (1989).

Source: As Table 3.22.

Table 3.24 Television receivers (% share of world production, million units)

	1953	1960	1965	1970	1975	1980	1985	1989
Asia	0.2	18.8	14.2	31.2	31.2	39.4	51.4	58.2
Japan	0.2	18.8	14.1	30.0	25.6	20.9	18.4	10.8
NICs[1]				0.3	2.5	12.2	10.8	17.1
Other[2]			0.1	0.8	3.1	6.4	22.2	30.3
Americas	84.0	31.4	37.2	23.0	22.2	22.0	18.2	16.4
USA and Canada	84.0	31.4	34.9	19.3	16.4	14.9	14.4	12.7
NICs[3]			1.7	2.5	4.1	5.8	2.9	3.0
Other[4]			0.6	1.1	1.8	1.2	1.0	0.8
Europe	14.8	39.1	34.5	29.5	30.4	25.7	18.4	16.1
West[5]	14.6	33.8	26.1	22.2	21.3	18.9	12.9	11.1
South[6]			1.9	1.8	2.3	1.9	1.9	1.9
Other[7]	0.2	5.3	6.5	5.5	6.9	4.8	3.6	3.2
USSR	1.0	9.1	12.2	14.6	14.1	10.4	9.7	8.3
Total (*m. units*)	9	19	30	46	49	72	96	120

Notes: 1–7: As Table 3.22. Estimated figures for Hong Kong (1985), Japan (1989), Canada (1985, 1989), South Europe (1989).

Source: As Table 3.22.

Table 3.25 Production of crude steel, ingots (% share of world production, million tonnes)

	1953	1960	1965	1970	1975	1980	1985	1989
Asia	2.9	5.6	14.3	20.7	23.0	25.5	27.8	29.7
Japan	2.9	5.6	9.0	15.8	16.1	15.6	14.9	14.1
NICs[1]			0.0	0.1	0.3	2.0	2.6	3.1
Other[2]			5.3	4.8	6.6	7.9	10.3	12.5
Americas	46.0	30.6	30.9	24.7	21.7	20.6	18.4	19.0
USA and Canada	46.0	30.6	28.6	22.4	18.9	16.6	13.3	13.5
NICs[3]			1.2	1.6	2.1	3.2	3.9	4.3
Other[4]			1.1	0.7	0.7	0.8	1.2	1.2
Europe	31.9	39.2	34.5	33.8	31.9	30.2	29.3	27.5
West[5]	28.5	34.5	27.0	25.4	21.5	19.4	18.2	17.7
South[6]			0.9	1.4	2.0	2.0	2.3	1.8
Other[7]	3.4	4.7	6.6	7.1	8.4	8.9	8.8	8.0
USSR	17.3	21.6	18.9	18.7	21.0	20.9	22.0	21.1
Total (*m.tonnes*)	158	216	448	581	629	706	702	759

Notes and Source: As Table 3.22.

Table 3.26 Growth of service sectors measured by the share in GDP (%)

	1970	1987
Developed countries	55	63
Developing countries	45	49

Source: Nicolaides, 1991: 51, Table 1.

The Age of Transition

Table 3.27 Share of service-sector FDI (%)

USA	1975	1980	1986
Outward FDI balance			
Trading	10.1	11.2	9.7
Banking	2.8	3.4	6.0
Financial and insurance	9.0	13.0	12.6
Inward FDI balance			
Trading	15.2[a]	18.3	20.1
Banking	4.4[a]	5.6	5.9
Financial and insurance	12.2[a]	16.3	19.0

Germany (F.R.)	1976	1980	1985
Outward FDI balance			
Trading	18.5	19.8	20.1
Banking	4.8	6.8	6.1
Financial and insurance	3.3	4.0	8.6
Inward FDI balance			
Trading	13.8	15.4	16.9
Banking	5.1	6.6	8.2
Financial and insurance	1.3	1.4	1.9

Japan	1970	1980	1986
Outward FDI balance			
Trading	10.6	14.8	13.7
Financial and insurance	8.9	6.6	17.1
Inward FDI balance			
Trading	4.8	12.2	11.6

Note: [a] 1973.

Source: Okumura. 1988a: 284–7, Tables B-1, B-2 (USA); 300–303, Tables D-1, D-2 (Federal Republic of Germany); 308–9, Tables E-1, E-3 (Japan).

Table 3.28 Service-sector share in total annual FDI outflow in the 1980s (%)

	1981–84	1985–89
Japan	61	73
Germany (F.R.)	55	64
USA	52	57
France	41	49
UK	35	38

Source: UNCTC, 1991: 10.

Table 3.29 Top 10 country shares in the service exports of the world (%)

USA	10.1
UK	10.0
Germany (F.R.)	9.1
France	8.9
Italy	6.4
Japan	5.2
Netherlands	5.0
Belgium	4.0
Spain	3.3
Australia	2.9
Subtotal	65.1

Source: Enderwick, 1989: 9, Table 1.2.

Table 3.30　Growth of the top 50 banks in the world

	1970	*1975*	*1980*	*1985*	*1990*
Total assets (*US$bn*)	500	1,292	3,056	4,269	10,129
Total assets of Japanese banks included in top 50	90	314	824	1,810	4,884
% of total assets	18	24	27	42	48
Total deposits (*US$bn*)	423	1,057	2,483	3,346	7,820
Total loans (*US$bn*)	298	866	2,030	2,831	6,540
Employees (*m.*)	0.97	1.30	1.55	1.60	1.62

Note and Source: As Table 3.10.

Table 3.31　Growth rate of assets held by top US corporations

	1957–60	*61–65*	*66–70*	*71–75*	*76–80*	*81–85*	*86–90*	*Av'ge*
Top 50 banks	5.0	9.7	12.1	4.4	3.5	6.1	4.5	6.5
Top 50 retail companies	7.4	10.3	8.7	0.4	4.6	15.3	18.9	9.4
Top 50 diversified service companies					13.0	12.3	16.0	13.8
Top 50 industrial corporations		8.1	10.1	−0.4	2.8	2.5	8.9	5.3

Source: Various issues of *Fortune Directory*.

4

The World Labour Force

Faruk Tabak

The process of industrialization of the world-economy after 1945, which was perhaps as extensive as that which had occurred in the several centuries before then, involved two spatial shifts.* First, previously modern industry had been primarily located in core zones; now it had become established in semiperipheral and peripheral zones as well. Second, while the inter-enterprise system's epicentre of capital accumulation was narrowly located in the USA from 1945 to 1967/73, it spread out to include Western Europe and Japan as well after 1967/73. The ensuing transformations in the structure of the world-economy's production system did not, however, 'unfetter' a concomitant and sustained increase in full-lifetime proletarianization. Instead, the rise in part-lifetime wage labour and households has come to govern, increasingly and worldwide, the organization of labour and production processes, particularly since 1967/73.[1]

This ongoing reorganization reflects and corroborates two tendencies reshaping the domain of work since 1945: a worldwide broadening of wage employment, albeit mostly part-lifetime; and a decrease in the

* Acknowledgements are due to Farshad Araghi and Sheila Pelizzon, both of the Fernand Braudel Center, whose working papers on rural and female labour contributed to the substance of this chapter. I am, of course, responsible for any errors of fact and interpretation.

1. By 'part-lifetime' or 'semiproletarian' households, I refer to those households that derive their income from a combination of wages (whether in cash or in kind), subsistence production, petty market operations, rents and transfer payments (including gifts). Full-lifetime proletarianization registers the fact that household units secure their income primarily and overwhelmingly from wages (see Smith, Wallerstein et al., 1992; also Wallerstein and Martin, 1979: 195–6; and Wallerstein et al., 1982).

share of the 'social' wage within aggregate household income, owing to a rise in 'incidental' or 'casual' wage labour. These developments mirror, in turn, a gradual enlargement in the realm of part-lifetime wage remuneration. From a long-term perspective, then, the postwar period can be said to have demonstrated, once again, how slow the pace of proletarianization of the world-economy has been, despite impressive economic growth rates, widespread and widening industrialization, and a continual and drastic contraction throughout the period under consideration in the relative share of the world rural labour force. The growth in part-lifetime waged work has thus come to fashion, directly or indirectly, the global realm of work since 1945, though it has become more pronounced and commanding since the beginning of the cyclical downturn in 1967/73. The pace of proletarianization on a global scale was slow, especially in view of the enormous boost given to it by the industrialization and employment programmes adhered to and implemented in the socialist world.

World-historically, however, even at the very height of the postwar boom, despite (or because of) profound transformations taking place within the domain of production and work, the sway and scope of full-lifetime proletarianization remained limited for two reasons. It was and is still located primarily in the core and the semiperiphery, but these zones enclose less than one-third of the world's labour forces, and this share is continually getting less. Furthermore, although the restructuring of world labour during the postwar upswing did extend the realm of full-lifetime proletarianization on an individual basis, it concomitantly diminished it on a household basis, sustaining what Hicks (1969: 135–7) calls a 'proletarian equilibrium'. This two-pronged movement has been best epitomized by the impressive rise in the core in the relative share of the female labour force, particularly in part-lifetime waged work, and by the remarkable growth in the semiperiphery (and the periphery) in 'the opaque and uncharted terrain' of production and work nurturing a plethora of semiproletarian households – the 'infra-economy' of Braudel (1981).[2] Preparing the setting for the proliferation in the number of semiproletarian households was the spectacular growth

---

2. Designed to highlight the two opaque zones between which the 'sunlit world of the market economy' is couched, Braudel's tripartite schema (1981: 22–3) depicts counterforces created in opposition to the market economy, both from above and from below. Lying below or alongside the market, which itself is presided over by the favoured and opaque domain of 'capitalism', is 'another, shadowy zone, often hard to see for lack of adequate historical documents: that is that elementary basic activity which went on everywhere and the volume of which is truly fantastic…. This infra-economy,

in rates of urbanization worldwide, the unyielding exodus from the countryside continually replenishing the global reserve army of labour. Within a span of merely four decades, as world population more than doubled to 5.2 billion in 1990, the rural population's share in it has shrunk to 57 per cent, down from 73 per cent in 1950 (Bairoch, 1988).

During the A-phase of economic expansion, proletarianization 'proper' was thus embedded in the countervailing mobilization of labour reserves which were potentially or actually comprised predominantly of part-lifetime wage-workers. It was indeed during the B-phase of economic expansion that the *largo tempo* of the increase in wage employment came to a halt, yet if there was a crescendo, it was reached owing to the growing proportion of 'intermittent' or 'irregular' wage employment. The period 1967–73 thus constitutes a moment marked by the sharp increase in the sweep and magnitude of one of the principal directional tendencies of historical capitalism, the non-universalization of proletarianization (Wallerstein, 1983; Broad, 1991).

Since 1945, wage labour as a proportion of the world's labour force has been steadily declining: the proportion of those remunerated with wages and salaries fell somewhat from 51 per cent to less than 40 per cent during the last forty years. These figures should be evaluated against the backdrop of a continual rise in the share of the world's potential labour forces by those under the age of 15, now comprising close to 40 per cent of the total population in most peripheral regions (45 per cent in Africa), an additional 20 per cent of the periphery's population falling within the 15–24 age group. The consequence is the incorporation into the work-force of growing segments that continue to expand the 'opaque terrain' of employment under conditions other than that of lifetime wage work.

To chart this continual enlargement in the realm of part-lifetime wage employment – that is, to anchor the trajectory of the world labour force in world-systemic trends since 1945 – I will trace the ramifications on the world's labour forces of the establishment, consolidation and decline of US hegemony. This vantage point, of course, does not allow one to take full stock of the panoply of productive activities that

---

the informal other half of economic activity, the world of self-sufficiency and barter of goods and services within a very small radius.' In employing this term for the post-1945 period, I refer not only to non-wage forms of employment, but also to those forms of wage employment remuneration which fall short of the 'social wage' – the 'direct wage', that is, which by definition is not inclusive of the so-called 'fringe and welfare benefits' and 'entitlements', not to mention 'intermittent' or 'casual' waged labour. I prefer to use the term 'infra-economy', primarily because, in Braudel's schema and usage, it is *of* the capitalist world-economy and thus an integral component of it rather than an 'incidental' outcome, as most theories of informal economy suggest.

provide livelihood to the overwhelming majority of the world's peoples. These modes of livelihood will be brought into our account only when they have a bearing on the overall trajectory of US hegemony in particular, and of the capitalist world-system in general.

Pax Americana and the Global Spread of Taylorism

The USA order furthered the organizing force and spatial stretch of the Taylorization of production in two ways. First, it widened the scope of the inter-enterprise system, which entailed the spread of the process of mass production. And, second, it facilitated and enforced the re-organization of production along Taylorist lines in the reconstruction of war-ravaged Europe and Japan, setting the stage thereafter for the inter-enterprise system to expand in earnest into these very locales.

Yet, in mapping the reconfiguration of the world-economy's labour forces in the immediate aftermath of the war, it should be noted that the increase in the pace of industrial and agrarian production during the war was anchored in the world-economic developments of the interwar period. The resumption of transnational expansion of US corporate capital after the war was contingent upon the reconstruction of war-devastated core zones as well as the sustenance of the economic momentum gathered in the non-core zones during the interwar period, especially in the Americas – that is, the 'Western hemisphere', the primary field of operation of US corporate capital until the 1950s. This momentum accelerated further with the expansive effects of the war (Gordon, 1988). It was within this setting that transnational corporations resumed their cross-border operations and reshaped the realm of manufacturing on a global scale, administratively integrating production and labour processes across select locales.

The tempo and mode of restructuring of the war-torn regions depended upon their place within corporate capital's compass before the war. Spatially, given the limited reach during the 1930s and 1940s of US corporate capital, state-mediated flows loomed large throughout the 1950s in the reconstruction, first and foremost, of Europe, which had been within the corporate compass until the early 1930s, and, only secondarily of Japan, which had not. From the early 1930s on, and up to the remaking of Europe, the Western hemisphere remained the primary *locus operandi* of the inter-enterprise system. Corporate economic flows came to supplant state-mediated flows in Europe in the late 1950s with the establishment of the European Economic Community (EEC), and in the Pacific Rim in the early 1960s with the end of PL480 and US aid missions.

These economic flows defined the contours of work on a global scale. For one, the spatial expansion of corporate structures of accumulation, via administratively and vertically integrated multi-unit organizational apparatuses, was built upon the Taylorization of production. So were state-mediated economic flows, for the installation of aid programmes demanded the purchase or transfer of capital goods that embodied technologies requiring or favouring Taylorization of production (Armstrong, Glyn and Harrison, 1984: ch. 4; Harvey, 1989: 132). Of significance within this context was the effect on the spread of Taylorism of wartime mobilization, which helped to ingrain it into the very fabric of manufacturing, both in Europe and Japan. Furthermore, the policies of import-substitution industrialization, which had been embryonic in the 1930s and then became the order of the day in most non-core locales in the aftermath of the war, were quite in tune with the organizational logic governing the transnational expansion of capital and the worldwide application of Taylorism. Extending further the global compass of Taylorism were modes of industrialization subscribed to in the USSR from the interwar period on, and from the 1950s in Eastern Europe.

Taylorization was not a smooth process, however. It dictated a new patterning within the realm of work, especially in the core zones where the war's end had brought the rise in the share of female employment to a sudden halt or had arrested it momentarily. The postwar 're-patriation' of the male labour force precipitated a decline in the number of 'gainfully employed' women. For example, between 1945 and 1960, in France, Norway and Belgium, the share of female labour declined from 38 per cent to 32 per cent, 22 per cent to 18 per cent, and 19 per cent to 16 per cent, respectively (Deldycke, Gelders and Limbor, 1968). The attendant restructuring of the female labour force, in consonance with the relative and temporary decline in its overall share, determined the pace and the character of the process of proletarianization in most core locales. On the one hand, the transitory decline in the relative size of the female labour force notwithstanding, the share of single women entering the workforce increased remarkably, at the expense of married women, serving to restore a household structured around the male breadwinner. In Europe, throughout the 1945–1967/73 period, the rates of growth for single women joining the labour force were just under those of men. In the USA the pattern was slightly different. Although single women did constitute the majority of the female labour force, the rate of participation of married women aged 45–49 increased relatively faster than the rates of both single women and young married women (20–24 years). In this instance again, postwar household formation patterns sanctioned the position of the male worker as the breadwinner in newly forming household units. It was in the 1960s that young married women began to enter the workforce once again, as a result of which by 1970, 31 per cent of married women in the USA worked for pay, up from 24 per cent in 1950 (Fox, 1984: 27).

On the other hand, the almost exclusive assignment to female labour of part-time work, steadily increasing in scope and significance (Darling, 1975: 73), secured permanent and 'full-time' work for the very same breadwinner. From the mid-1940s to the mid- or late 1950s, the female labour force grew intermittently, and notably less than its male counterpart. Moreover, the designation of part-time work as women's domain rendered the relative reduction in women's share particularly pronounced in manufacturing, given the tempo imposed by the Taylorization of production. The percentage of male labour in manufacturing increased constantly, across all locales, but most markedly in the core where it rose from 36 per cent in 1950 to 44 per cent in 1970, at the time that the share of manufacturing in total employment was growing in tandem, from 30 per cent to 37 per cent (ILO, 1986: V). Both the feminization of the labour force and the attribution of part-time work to female labour became common throughout the core zone, first in the USA in the 1960s, and then in Europe and Japan in the 1970s.

The so-called 'Fordist accord', reached in the USA during the 1930s and 1940s when corporate capital's global mobility was seriously hampered, prompted capital after the war to try to avoid its obligations by moving production beyond the suburbs and into small-town and rural America on the one hand, and to overseas locales on the other.[3] The search for labour reserves that enabled capital to bypass the Fordist accord served to swell the group of non-unionized wage workers, made up mostly of women and 'minorities' of all shades (Piore, 1979), as well as the number of semiproletarian households, at home and abroad. At home, the end of easy access in the late 1950s to existing labour reserves speeded up the inclusion of young married women in the labour force while it relocated much production offshore. Abroad, the influx of US capital led to the reconstitution of production and labour processes – most notably in Europe and Japan. With the unmaking of the *Lebensraum*

---

3. This accord was symbolized by the Wagner Act of 1933 which 'had given the unions power in the market place (with explicit recognition that collective bargaining rights were essential to the resolution of the effective demand problem) in return for sacrificing powers in the realm of production' (Harvey, 1989: 133); see also Arrighi and Silver, 1984: 187–9; and Burawoy, 1979. Here I use the term 'Fordism' primarily to refer to the predominance of 'social wage' arrangements, characterizing mostly if not exclusively the corporate sector, private and/or statal.

for the one and of the co-prosperity sphere for the other, male labour reserves in these locales were quickly depleted, and female (and 'imported') labour was needed to replenish the reserve army of labour.

The resumption in the late 1950s of the growth in the share of female labour, however, took place against a changed background. First and foremost, the rise in part-time employment became such an integral part of the reorganization of work in the postwar period that it became largely, and almost exclusively, a female phenomenon. For example, in Denmark and Sweden the proportion of women in the labour force was already around 40 per cent in the early 1970s and accelerated further with the onset of the crisis (Darling, 1975: 30). The percentage was relatively lower in the Western hemisphere, rising from 26 per cent in 1962 to 29 per cent in 1972 in the USA, and from 19 per cent to 25 per cent in Canada. At the beginning of the 1970s, in the European core (notably the Federal Republic of Germany, France, the Netherlands, Great Britain), 80–90 per cent of all part-time workers were women; in the USA, the share was lower – 65 per cent (ILO, 1984, I: 50). The assignment of part-time work to women should also be evaluated against the fact that during the A-phase the share of female labour in the labouring population of the core zones rose from 32.5 per cent to 35 per cent, whilst that of male labour declined from 61 per cent to 56 per cent. This decline occurred at a time when the percentage of rural labour in the core zone labour force dropped inexorably, inflating the number of urban labourers; as a result of the fast pace of emptying out of the rural areas, by 1970 rural labour was under 10 per cent (Singelmann, 1978: 1228–31).

Second, in synchrony with the above-mentioned trend, the proportion of female labour in manufacturing declined in most core locales. The period from 1950 to 1970 saw its portion decline from 25 per cent to 20 per cent in North America, and from 35 per cent to 28 per cent in Northern Europe (ILO, 1984, I: Table 3). Relocation of production from the core to the semiperipheral and peripheral zones, which generated a quick growth in the service and administrative sector in the core, encouraged increasing employment of female labour. Providing the infrastructural basis for the emigration of capital overseas, this sector's growth in the USA took off, as was to be expected, from the late 1950s, and in Europe from the late 1960s, to be amplified considerably during the 1970s. These service functions provided a climate hospitable to part-time work and hence to increasing employment of the non-beneficiaries of the Fordist accord, women and 'minorities'.

And third, the reservation of part-time work for female labour was complemented, from the late 1950s on, by the mobilization and subsumption of additional labour reserves by core capital to be employed primarily in manufacturing. Yet, the manner in which this mobilization was conducted in each core zone depended on the ongoing structuring of the Pax Americana. At the hegemonic epicentre, the transborder expansion of corporate capital was gaining pace, as attested to by the swift increase in the number of subsidiaries of US-based transnational corporations, primarily but not exclusively in Europe, and in the volume of US direct investments overseas (Vernon, 1979; Whichard, 1981).

In Europe, on the other hand, the combination in the production process of a reduced proportion of high-wage, skilled labour with a higher proportion of low-skilled or unskilled labour was rendered possible, thanks to the importation of immigrant labour from its semi-peripheral southern rim. This influx began in earnest in the latter half of the 1950s and went on unabated throughout the 1960s. For instance, the number of workers imported into the Federal Republic of Germany increased from 55,000 in 1958 to 250,000 by 1960. In most parts of Europe, the proportion of imported labour to that of the total labour force ranged from 10 to 15 per cent, at times reaching 30 per cent, as in Switzerland (Salt, 1981: 138–9). It should be mentioned that, though transborder expansion was of cardinal significance, labour inflows into the USA from Europe were also considerable during the 1960s (around 300,000 per year); this number is nonetheless small when compared with the huge influx of the 1970s and 1980s. In the Pacific Rim, corporate capital based in Japan found its mobility rather constrained in its erstwhile co-prosperity sphere because of the radical changes in the political landscape of the region. These changes prompted a Japanese policy of contracting out production rather than relocating production offshore via direct investments (Bunker and O'Hearn, 1993). In turn, the predominance of subcontracting created an environment not conducive to labour mobility.

. At the level of the world-system, these three seemingly divergent patterns were in fact conjointly framed by the transnational expansion of US-based corporate capital beyond the confines of the Western hemisphere beginning in the late 1950s. With the formation of the EEC, the meteoric rise in labour inflows to Europe spurred a parallel expansion in industrial activities, an expansion that deepened Taylorist productive organization and induced Europe-bound emigration of US corporate capital. In the Pacific Rim, too, the supplanting of US aid at the turn of the 1960s with corporate capital flows – originating both in the USA and in Japan – set in motion new developments in the region's labour markets. Japan's recovery took place within the confines of a productive structure largely formed at the turn of the 1950s. For one, the financial bottlenecks which surfaced after the war rendered idle a vast body of fixed capital. In addition, the Korean War boom was followed by fierce labour struggles, as exemplified in the case of the automobile industry. The imperative to sustain the turnover of the former by bypassing unionized labour led to the establishment of subcontracting of production as an integral and ever more crucial component of the principal organizational network (Smitka, 1991).

Owing to the gradual downgrading under growing competition of the textile/garment industries in the world-scale divisioning of labour, this organizational setting became the organizing framework for these industries in the early 1960s. They followed the tracks of cheap labour, and decentralized their centres of production, first to small towns and then to outlying jurisdictions such as Hong Kong and Singapore (Yoshihara, 1976: 117). This distinctive path was the outcome of three closely related factors which reflected the structure of regional labour markets during the 1950s and the earlier part of the 1960s: the highly rural character of the Japanese (and East Asian) female labour force; the relatively low rates of rural-to-urban migration; and the geographically dispersed nature of the then predominant textile and apparel industry.

The combination of these three factors favoured subcontracting of production, with emphasis on the use of a female labour force. Eventually, the full incorporation of female labour into the urban workforce in Japan had to await the transferral of such activities 'across-the-border', as well as the impact on rural labour of land reforms of the 1950s. The rapid expansion of agricultural production in the 1960s allowed a continual flow of rural-to-urban migration: the proportion of women working for pay in urban areas soared from 13 per cent in 1963 to 40 per cent in 1989 (Ogawa, Jones and Williamson, 1993).

Rather than marshalling labour into its centres of production, as in the case of Europe, or expanding its productive base worldwide via vertical integration, as in the case of US-based corporate capital, Japanese industry then contracted out and effectively orchestrated the integration of production processes spread over neighbouring territory. This complex and sprawling organizational hold of the region was consolidated by the replacement of US aid by corporate capital flows, especially in the former Japanese colonies of Taiwan and Korea, where these flows in effect strengthened the suppliers' end of the subcontracting nexus. As a result, in this second area under reconstruction, yet a different pattern of establishing the command of capital over labour emerged.

In broad outlines, then, subsumption of labour in the core zones dictated the mobilization of female labour on a part-time basis, a reserve

army supplemented later by immigrant labour from the semiperiphery
(Europe); by labour *in situ* in semiperipheral zones (US); or by mobilization of family labour via subcontracting of production (Japan). Instituted thanks to the steady and massive outflow of rural labour and/or
to the ability of capital to extend its organizational net outside and
beyond *intra muros* production, all these modes of labour control arrested
the full-lifetime proletarianization of households in the core. Emigration
of corporate capital produced a similar structuring in the semiperipheral
regions by mobilizing semiproletarianized labour reserves. Thus, the
deepening proletarianization of households in the core zones despite
the partial incorporation of female labour into wage employment was
complemented and counterbalanced by the growth of part-lifetime
proletarianized households in the semiperipheral and peripheral zones.

The Global Reach of Taylorism

A wide array of processes framing the division of labour in the world-
economy accelerated the burgeoning of infra-economies in the non-
core zones throughout the 1950s and 1960s – processes ranging from
rampant urbanization to mass migratory movements, from demographic
upheavals to the institution of new modes of labour control, not to
mention attempts by businesses to escape state regulation. By catering
to the protean infra-economy, these processes facilitated corporate
capital's foray into the vast field of part-lifetime waged work.

Given the wide spectrum of mechanisms underlying and reproducing
infra-economies in different quarters of the world-economy, a
substantivist reading of the development of a 'regulated' (that is,
Taylorist) realm in the post-1890s period has to account for the
modalities by which an enlargement in the 'unregulated' terrain has also
occurred (or rather recurred). The geographical distribution of these
wide-ranging trends was not random; the differences reflected the world-
historical structuring of productive activities. In what follows, I shall
dwell upon these modalities, and perforce operate through a score of
ideal-types of infra-economies which have hitherto served to secure the
non-universalization of proletarianization in the semiperipheral and
peripheral zones of the world-economy.

In certain quarters of the semiperipheral world, the momentum provided throughout the 1950s and 1960s by the speed and magnitude of
urban growth triggered a phenomenal surge in the number of part-
lifetime proletarian households. The expeditious emptying out of rural
areas, the salient feature of the postwar era, furnished the urban/
industrial/corporate sector with 'unlimited supplies of labour'. To be

sure, the rate of urbanization was sustained, if not instituted, by the extension of state machineries plus import-substitution industrialization and/or transnational expansion of capital. As a result, by the late 1960s the urban population in the semiperiphery in Eastern and Southern Europe had reached 55 per cent, and 65 per cent in the USSR and Latin America (UN, 1986; Jackson, 1987).

The statist framework governing the process of industrialization, an integral part of Pax Americana's interstate order, favoured growing rates of urbanization, for the most part particularly but not only the capital cities. The concentration of manufacturing and service activities in a rather limited number of cities in each national jurisdiction was the overarching factor in the organization of the post-1945 spatial order. Embodying this wave of industrialization in Latin America and Southern Europe, Mexico City, Santiago, São Paulo, Madrid, Barcelona, among others, exemplify the trend. In Latin America, at least 40–50 per cent of the GDP, manufacturing production, and services and employment were concentrated within sprawling metropolitan agglomerations. Soaring urbanization and spatial concentration of manufacturing activities in the semiperiphery were marked characteristics of the A-phase.

Where corporate capital monitored the ongoing division and integration of manufacturing processes, as in Latin America and the southern rim of Europe, the share of the urban labour force rose the most, and emigration from the rural areas was accordingly massive. The timing of corporate capital's transnational expansion and the nature of migration resulted in different modalities of semiperipheral development. In both regions, the integration into corporate structures of production extended the spread of Taylorization of production, promoting the employment of male labour on the shop floor. Yet, differences arising from the nature of available labour reserves, especially rural, found expression in differing modes of semiperipheral structuring. While agrarian structures in Latin America favoured plantation-like agricultural units, Southern Europe saw the reconstruction after the war of family-farm enterprises. The two paths of transformation created differing modes of income pooling.

In Latin America, migration was primarily to cities within the state, and female migration was not only part of it but actually its main component. The consequence was the expansion of an urban infra-economy that provided the livelihood of close to 30 per cent of the urban labour force, creating and catering to semiproletarianized households. It was just the opposite in Southern Europe, where migration was primarily emigration to the core zones, and almost exclusively male. In consequence, householding crossed state boundaries, spanning rural and urban areas, and hard currency remittances strengthened the hold of households over land.

In Latin America, it was the capital-intensive nature of agricultural production which drove large numbers of rural inhabitants, mostly women, to metropolitan conglomerates to be employed in the ever-expanding infra-economy. As the rate of rural population swiftly dropped, female labour's share of the total increase in employment jumped from 18 per cent in 1950 to 38 per cent in 1975, despite the fact that the increase in manufacturing employment was quite meagre. More often than not, women dropped out of the formal labour force after marriage, but they comprised the most substantial portion of the infra-economy, providing between 45 and 70 per cent of its labour. The concentration of population and manufacturing in a few urban centres where household members were engaged in a score of pecuniary pursuits enabled these units to increase that portion of their income accruing from part-lifetime employment (Boserup, 1970).

The changing face of agriculture was reflected in the decline not only of family farms but also in the size of their holdings. Between 1950 and 1970, the number of small farms in Latin America as a whole grew by an estimated 92 per cent, or 2.2 per cent a year; and the average size of smallholdings declined from 2.4 to 2.1 hectares in the same period, a contraction of −0.4 per cent a year (de Janvry et al., 1989). Non-farm employment in the rural areas shrank along with the contraction of the farm sector, and accounted for only one-third of rural labour, considerably lower than that in Asia or Africa (where the ratio is closer to two-thirds). The share of agricultural wage employment actually fell, due to the attendant contraction of family farms during the 1960s (Haggblade, Hazell and Brown, 1989: 1174–77; ILO, 1984).

Rural emigration in Latin America was so unyielding and continuous that the increase in the rural labour force failed to catch up with that in the agricultural labour force. The former, which grew by 0.6 per cent per annum during the 1950s and 1960s, was outstripped by the rise in the latter, which increased by 1 per cent in the 1950s and by 0.8 per cent in the following decade (Anderson and Leiserson, 1980: 220–21; Buttari, 1979). Also, the massive emigration from the rural areas has to be placed within the context of increasing intercontinental migration, the volume of which at the turn of the 1970s added up to approximately 3.5–4 million persons, mostly from peripheral zones to the semiperiphery (ILO, 1984). These developments also found their echo in the USSR and Eastern Europe, where the tempo of rural depopulation and urbanization rivalled those of other semiperipheral regions. The demographic loss of the Slavic republics during the war, now estimated to be 40 million, twice as high as previously believed, was only recovered in the early 1970s. It was due to the sheer size of this loss that the period beginning in the mid-1950s witnessed the relaxation of many of the controls on labour mobility in the USSR. Despite the passport system, close to 25 million people emigrated from the countryside between 1956 and 1970, leading to the enormous growth of Moscow, Leningrad, Kiev and Minsk (Helgeson, 1986: 148, 151–2).

In Southern Europe, the outflow of labour to the core zones and the inflow of remittances to the countryside implied a different agrarian structuring.[4] The growth of the labour force, which was about 0.3 per cent per annum during the 1950s, declined to 0.01 per cent in the 1960s due to the magnitude of core-bound migration. In Southern Europe, since it was largely males that migrated, the rate of growth of the male labour force fell drastically in the 1960s. In most cases it was negative: the rate went from 0.7 per cent to –0.2 per cent; in Italy from –0.05 per cent to –0.2 per cent in Greece; from 0.3 per cent to –0.9 per cent in Portugal, and from 0.5 per cent to 0.2 per cent in Spain (ILO, 1986, IV: 7–9). Rates of growth of female labour, on the other hand, increased region-wide, from 1 per cent in the 1950s to 1.3 per cent in the 1960s. The drop in agricultural employment in relation to total employment came much later than it did in Latin America, and was particularly marked between 1960 and 1973. The proportion of female labour in manufacturing rose impressively in Southern Europe (from 20 per cent in 1950 to 28 per cent of the female labour force in 1970), whereas in Latin America the share of female labour in manufacturing declined from 23 per cent to 20 per cent during the same period.

Along with a series of other 'invisible' exports, remittances made up a significant portion of the aggregate income of the households domiciled in Southern European countryside, and allowed them to provide corporate capital with part-time and casual workers, remunerated in part in 'traditional' wages (Keyder, 1985; Vergopoulos, 1979). This migratory pattern changed during the latter half of the 1960s. Labour outflows from these territories declined, or were overshadowed by the appearance on the global scene of a new family of migratory movements, emanating mostly from peripheral regions (Sassen, 1988).

---

4. For the impact of emigration on large-scale agriculture (for example, by raising rural wages), or on family-holdings (for example, by increasing households' ability to purchase land), or on patterns of land-use (for example, shifting from intensive cultivation [vegetable produce and industrial crops] to extensive [cereal] cultivation), see Filias, 1972 and de Oteyza, 1972.

The dissimilarity in the paths of rural transformation of these two semiperipheral regions is reflected in the expansion in Latin America of rural towns which emerged as increasingly important locations for new employment. Unlike Southern Europe, the rate of growth of the population of small towns in the 1960s was comparable with and often greater than the rate of growth of large metropolitan areas. In the light of the overwhelming predominance in Latin America of the infra-economic scaffolding, the fact that most studies trace its (conceptual) origins to *l'economia sommersa* in Italy is ironic. Even more, it neatly documents how restricted (and core-based) our points of reference are in trying to diagnose supposedly new social phenomena.[5]

Until the beginning of the cyclical downturn in 1967/73, it was thus primarily in the semiperipheral zones that the deepening/consolidation of stateness by means of formation/extension of a parastatal corporate sphere was accompanied by the relocation of labour-intensive manu-facturing processes under the aegis of transnational corporations. Subse-quently, wage employment in the 'formal'/'modern' industrial sector registered striking rates of growth, although the significance attached to full-time wage employment in this sector as a sign 'of 'development' certainly underestimated the sheer size and widespread nature of comple-mentary forms of employment by the corporate sector (parastatal or private). The growth in the labour force employed in the corporate sector, albeit considerable, was outstripped by that of the non-agricultural labour force. Conversely, the sheer size of the reserve army of labour permitted corporate capital to extend its operational domain by direct hiring on a casual basis and by subcontracting of production and marketing (see Portes and Benton, 1984: 596–7). Complementing this double movement was the new life given to 'traditional' wage (as opposed to 'social' wage) arrangements, and hence to the perennial infra-economy.

Whereas urbanization and migration, both resulting from and com-pounding the exodus from the countryside, furnished households – either through 'informal' activities or through remittances – in the Latin American and Southern and Eastern European semiperipheries with opportunities and means to widen their income mix, households in East Asia did not rely on either, due to the spatially dispersed nature of

---

5. Discussions of the 'third Italy' as the original site of 'nascent flexible produc-tion', argued to be radically and structurally dissimilar from 'third-world-like' informal economies, reflect a similar optic.

the predominant industries (textiles and food processing).[6] The well-knit network of secondary cities and the land reforms that altered the agrarian structure of the countryside prevented, at least until the 1960s, the kind of urban growth the other semiperipheral regions underwent (Durand, 1975: 149). In addition, subcontracting can be said to have discouraged labour migration in so far as *extra muros* production in the countryside was available. It was mostly during the B-phase that, given the fast pace of growth in the late 1960s and 1970s, the mobility of labour within and across the region became widespread.

Consequently, in stark contrast to other parts of the periphery, urban growth in East Asia was relatively low throughout the 1950s, reaching a mere 28 per cent in Korea in 1960. The peak of the population growth was reached during the latter half of the 1960s when it soared to 2.5 per cent per annum. The agricultural reforms of the 1950s had led to increased migration to the cities. Once employment on the farm became a thing of the past with the world-economic developments of the 1960s, the share of manufacturing in total employment went from 11 per cent in the 1960s to 21 per cent in the 1970s (van Ginneken and van der Hoeven, 1989). A big jump in female labour-force participation was also under way during the 1960–75 period, from 17 per cent to 33 per cent in South Korea, 22 per cent to 35 per cent in Hong Kong, and 14 per cent to 30 per cent in Singapore (Ogawa, Jones and Williamson, 1993: 52; Jones, 1984).

The confinement of transnational expansion of capital and the redistribution of productive activities to a few semiperipheral locales until the early 1970s left the state corporate sector in the periphery as the most sizeable source of wage employment. The expansion of the state corporate sector, however, precipitated similar processes of increasing rural-to-urban migration with consequent skyrocketing rates of urbanization, again to a few select centres, mostly to capital cities as bureaucratic seats of power. The coupling of urbanization with industrialization as a means of consolidation of nascent state structures was the particular mark of the 1950s and 1960s. Yet, the relatively limited size of this urban/corporate sector (employing less than 20 per cent in China and in certain parts of Africa less than 10 per cent of the population) set in motion a dynamic different from that in the semiperipheries (Doctor

---

6. For a typology of household migration patterns, and the ramifications on the mix of economic activities the households are engaged in, Boserup's seminal work, *Woman's Role in Economic Development* (1970), still stands out, despite all criticism levelled against it.

and Gallis, 1966). The need to diversify their sources of income compelled households to grow in scale, ushering in or reinforcing the demographic growth of the 1960s (Meillassoux, 1975). In the peripheral areas of the world-economy, it was thus the difficulty of reproducing the conditions of existence of infra-economies that accelerated population growth.

The predominance of an import-substitution ideology in much of the world, complemented by the need of US corporate capital to maintain protective barriers up to the late 1960s and by the absence of corporate flows to the periphery, fuelled autarchic industrialization policies that helped give an appearance of universality to the Taylorist élan of the era. The low ratio of exports to GDP in the core – the 1960s, the golden age of US hegemony, were an all-time low (Lipietz, 1987: 69) – was a key element in the postwar boom of the peripheral economies, but it was a precarious base.

From the vantage point of the world-economy, the growing ability of households to reallocate their labour supplies and to engage in multifarious economic activities provided the setting within which the process of proletarianization had been embedded. But in most (semi)peripheral locales, the expansion during the 1950s and 1960s in the infra-economy was intimately linked to the process of industrialization. The absolute annual growth during the 1950–80 period of wage employment in Latin America and Southern Europe, for instance, fell consistently below that of the non-agricultural labour force, and the share of agricultural wage employment actually decreased (ILO, 1984).

This proliferation in the range of non-wage-earning economic activities was hence more than merely a product of the B-phase, performing its usual counter-cyclical function. The widespread restructuring in the core zone of the structures of work in terms of Taylorism and Fordism during the A-phase created and relied heavily on the breadth and the protean nature of the infra-economies. On the one hand, the conspicuous absence in most parts of the periphery of transnational expansion of capital set limits on the extent of wage employment. From the vantage point of the periphery, despite major differences between the pre-1945 and post-1945 economic orders, two closely related systemic traits of the world-economy have exhibited a remarkable degree of continuity since the turn of this century: first, the inexorable boxing-in of capital flows within and among core and semiperipheral locales (and correspondingly, the dwindling share of the periphery in these flows), and second, the continuously growing share of manufactured goods within global merchandise flows. Both trends were consecrated in the Bretton Woods arrangements and even more by GATT.

On the other hand, the deepening of both interstateness and stateness, by promoting centrifugal tendencies, had a perverse effect on the restructuring of labour markets. The gradual expansion of state structures during the 1950s and 1960s stimulated attempts by enterprises to escape their reach and encouraged a proliferation in the number of non-state-administered enterprises (rather than, say, the increase of individual enterprises in size). This swelled the ranks of the infra-economy in the semiperiphery and the periphery. In the former, this centrifugal movement provided additional support to the widespread utilization of casual hiring and subcontracting. In the periphery, the broadening of the Taylorist realm had merely flowed from the consolidation of state apparatuses (via import-substitution industrialization) and attendant urbanization, notwithstanding the relatively limited presence of core capital.

Changing Modes of Expansion of Capital and Labour Control

What followed during the B-phase accelerated rather than reversed these tendencies. Part-time work, temporary employment and similar arrangements have in fact become indispensable elements of the reorganization of production in the core zones. And the 'informalization' of production and work in the semiperipheral and peripheral zones has reached colossal proportions. In Eastern Europe and the USSR, this took the form of the growing significance of piece-rate work (Haraszti, 1977). Since 1945, growing proletarianization in the core, comprising in the 1970s more than 80 per cent of the labour force (and unemployment ranging from 2 per cent to 3 per cent in Europe and 4 per cent to 7 per cent in the USA) has eventually increased the pace of the shift of labour-intensive manufacturing processes from the core to the semiperipheral and peripheral zones. Since 1967/73, the multiplication of the sites of provenance of capital emigration – adding Japan and Europe to the USA (Fröbel, Heinrichs and Kreye, 1980) – has in turn fostered both tendencies by increasing the share of temporary/part-time work and rates of unemployment (now reaching 11–12 per cent) in the core zones and the furthering of 'informalization' in the non-core zones.

Indeed, the relative share of wage labour in the world's labour forces climbed most notably not at the zenith of US hegemony but during the subsequent B-phase. The explanation, however, lies in the increase in part-time and 'casual' (part-lifetime) wage employment that accompanied the decline in full-lifetime wage arrangements. The rise in wage employment since the mid-1960s in the peripheral and semiperipheral zones of the world-economy is one consequence of this; although, of course, it is partially merely the reflection of the utilization by state agencies of new classificatory categories, designed to register newly added categories of wage employment rather than dwell exclusively upon the full-lifetime proletarian.) The B-phase thence became the locus of two closely related developments which altered the terrain on which post-1945 tendencies were founded.

First, in the 1970s there was a shift in the locus of the transnational expansion of capital, increasing significantly the amount invested in peripheral locations. Previously, capital flows were confined predominantly within and among core and semiperipheral locales. After the brief interlude of the 1970s, however, capital flows, triggered by the onset of the 'debt crisis' in 1981, once again moved mainly within the core. This did not restore, however, the post-1945 order. Rather, the extension in the territorial reach of capital during the 1970s had prepared the ground in the semiperiphery for the licensing and subcontracting of production. This 'outsourcing' served in part to compensate for the outflux of core capital as well as to render it 'more' mobile due to the low ratio of fixed capital in most subcontracting arrangements.

The global widening in corporate structures of accumulation signalled an important change within the inter-enterprise system. It incorporated (albeit at arm's length) a wide range of cascading units/firms. The increasing reliance within the corporate world on new modes of integration (such as subcontracting of production, licensing, and joint ventures) took place at the expense of the familiar web of subsidiaries and in-house operations (that is, vertical integration).[7] The impetus given in the late 1960s to the slowing down of vertical integration by corporate restructuring was supplemented in the 1980s by the momentum of the debt crisis. The deceleration in semiperipheral growth induced by the crisis led to the retrenchment of corporate capital at the core, and the decline in capital flows and direct investments favoured modes of integration other than that of vertical. Therefore, the scaling-down since the late 1960s of the TNCs and their subsidiaries nurtured a climate conducive to conducting a wide spectrum of productive activities, previously enclosed within corporate structures via Fordism and Taylorism, beyond the confines of these conglomerates (Harvey, 1989). This process has either grafted new groups of producers onto, or reassembled under, the organizational edifice of the TNCs certain fragments of the already existing reservoir of labour forces. Particularly in

---

7. On subcontracting and the hiving off of formerly internalized transactions, see Hirschman's discussion of 'hierarchies' versus 'markets' (1986: 85–7).

the Pacific Rim and its bordering regions, the widespread introduction of subcontracting attuned the world of work to its modes of functioning.

Second, the increasing condensation of trans-state relational networks woven by TNCs after 1967/73 provided additional impetus to inflate the opaque half of global economic activity. Prevailing state-subversive trends dealt a fatal blow in the periphery and semiperiphery to activities tied to the parastatal corporate sector and/or import-substitution industrialization. By default or by design, the waning capacity of state apparatuses to monitor and police 'social' wage arrangements – that is, employment covered by labour codes and legislation and regulated by the state – increased the amplitude of 'casualization' of work. As a result, trans-state processes, primarily originating from above in the transnational expansion of capital, were fortified from below by a widening in the latitude of the non-Fordist realm.

In the core zones, the massive emigration in the late 1960s and 1970s of capital 'overseas' was accompanied by the proliferation in the core of industrial home-work along with the ever-growing significance within the realm of employment of temporary and market-mediated work arrangements.[8] This reshuffling in the core helped to mobilize the reserve army of female and immigrant labour and scaled down the share of the traditional cadre of White male full-time wage workers. These intimately linked developments of the past two decades, colouring the changes in the place of production from factories to sweatshops, are attested to by the discussions surrounding 'flexible specialization', 'post-Fordism', and 'new forms of investment' (see, for example, Piore and Sabel, 1984; Williams et al., 1987). The transformations in structures of production and work, already under stress due to the wave of labour insurgency in the late 1960s, proved to be long-lived.

Stated briefly, then, the labour force formation patterns of the Kondratieff A-phase, which had laid the ground for a gradual yet progressive build-up of semiproletarian households, were given a vigorous boost by the developments of the B-phase (Fröbel, 1982). In the core, with the onset of the downswing, the employment of female labour reached new heights in the 1970s, and part-time and contract jobs became an indispensable part of the world of work in the 1980s. For example, in Great Britain, whereas the female labour force has risen by 3.1 million, that of male labour has increased by only 300,000. In fact,

---

8. In Europe, this tendency manifests itself in the diminution of employment protection by relaxing restrictions on the use of temporary workers and of fixed-term contracts, and by the reduction and organization of work time (see Osterman and Kochan, 1990; also Aglietta and Brender, 1984: 173–9).

by the end of 1994, the number of 'gainfully employed' women is expected to exceed that of men. Again in Great Britain, one worker in four is today outside permanent, full-time employment. When temporary staff and self-employed are added to the figures, then the percentage rises to 40 per cent (Beechey and Perkins, 1987: 37).

In addition, the world-scale centralization in the core of the tasks of servicing and monitoring the global productive apparatuses has proven compatible with, indeed has encouraged, the expansion of part-time employment (Sassen, 1991). In the USA it is primarily migrant labour that has been employed in this rapidly expanding sector of the 1980s, thus keeping part-time employment from being the sole preserve of female labour. In Europe, the assignment of migrant labour to manufacturing activities has made part-time female employment in the service sector relatively more secure. This partly explains why women have fared better in Europe in this recession than men: 5.6 per cent of women are currently unemployed, as opposed to 12–14 per cent of men. As a result of these developments, regulations in Europe monitoring part-time employment and contract jobs are being refashioned, in a piecemeal fashion, to conform to this emergent situation; whereas in the USA, where such regulations were never in effect, part-lifetime employment has boomed. The increase both in the volume of this kind of employment and in the number of persons ready to accept its non-Fordist package have resulted in falling wages instead of unemployment in the USA, in contrast to Europe.[9] The proliferation of contract-employment and self-employment, of piece-rate and home-based work, have involved the hiving-off of activities formerly internalized within corporate entities to separate enterprises, fortifying the foundations and development of non-Fordist employment patterns.

The overwhelming presence in the Pacific Rim of subcontracting of production has given the region its *sui generis* character. The regional latticework in the Pacific Rim mirrors in part the degree of multilateral dependencies woven under Japan's aegis. The territorial sway of subcontracting became the essential thread constituting the regional division of labour (Arrighi, Ikeda and Irwan, 1993; Cumings, 1984). An indispensable if not the central component of the organization choreographed by Japanese corporate capital, the continual growth in subcontracting of production, is evident in the structuring of the manu-

---

9. The nominal figures for Europe are relatively higher than the figures for the USA (around 11–12% as opposed to 6–7%), but the latter figure excludes 'discouraged job-seekers'.

facturing sector in Hong Kong: 57 per cent of its exports originate in local companies with fewer than fifty employees and marketed through 14,000 small import–export houses. This local weave has been corroborated by the character of migration in the region, which to date has been largely family migration. In sharp contrast with the trends colouring the rest of the world, urban households in the region have grown bigger in size than their rural counterparts elsewhere, and the difference between rural/agricultural families and their urban counterparts is the lowest in the world (1:1.5 against 2:4 in Latin America). The networks of subcontracting enveloping the Pacific Rim within corporate structures of accumulation thus cast a radically different setting for labour flows than the one provided by the vertical integration of production by the TNCs.

Regional integration in the Pacific Rim has gone on unabated in spite of the massive outflux from the region of Japanese corporate capital during the last two decades to other core locales. Though capital flows have of late resumed their overwhelmingly interregional character, the networks in place are no longer exclusively dependent on capital movements originating in Japan; they now stem from other parts of the region as well (via Hong Kong and Taiwan). Along with recent changes taking place in former Soviet Asia and China, it seems likely that these multilateral networks woven by Japanese corporate capital, originally involving only the so-called four dragons (South Korea, Taiwan, Hong Kong and Singapore), will undergo further modification. The opening up of new territories is rendered obligatory by the strengthening of labour in the four dragons. Subcontracting networks, previously almost exclusively enclosing the four dragons, are in the process of extending their spread to parts of Southeast Asia (for example, Indonesia, Thailand, Malaysia) (Singh and Kelles-Viitanen, 1987) as well as to southern China.

These seemingly divergent yet complementary developments signal that the longevity of these subcontracting networks is not necessarily bound up with the present downturn. Subcontracting of production has been more than a countervailing force deployed against the vagaries of the downturn. The acceleration during the last two decades in subcontracting has either added a new array of producers to, or reassembled under, the organizational edifice of the TNCs certain fragments of the existent reservoir of labour forces. For example, in Indonesia, 75–80 per cent of the manufacturing workforce is and remains in rural areas – in manufacturing hamlets, so to speak. Economic flows emanating from the core and channelled through networks enveloped within the gargantuan 'general trading companies' (*sogo shosha*) have effectively discouraged core-bound labour flows. Whatever mobility there is, mostly from the peripheral regions of the Pacific Rim, is channelled towards the Persian Gulf, and from the semiperiphery to the USA. The passing of huge sums in remittances back home without the interme-diation of banking institutions or state agencies has in effect helped to reproduce the (financial) conditions of existence of the units/firms at the outer perimeters of the subcontracting networks, hence strengthen-ing the existing pattern.

This structuring has delimited the sphere of circulation of migratory movements to the shifting margins of the Pacific Rim, to some degree insulating the Japanese epicentre from labour inflows. Despite the rapid growth during the past two decades in the region, the magnitude of labour flows has been relatively unimpressive. Of the 3.5 million people who have migrated so far, only 1.2 million have done so within the region; most of the rest emigrating to the Persian Gulf (Stahl, 1986). Prospects of an expansion in the hinterland (for example, by the uni-fication of the Koreas or the further opening up of Guangdong via Hong Kong) are likely to reproduce the conditions of existence of these networks on a larger scale. These ever-growing concentric circles may in the near future continue to generate relatively low levels of labour mobility within the region.

In harmony with the ebbs and flows of Japanese corporate capital, the highest rates of urban growth in the outlying regions were reached in the 1970s, up from 4.2 per cent in the 1960s to 5.2 per cent; they have since fallen to 4.5 per cent. And the highest growth rates since the 1970s have been reached in the category of cities with populations less than a million (Douglass, 1988). That the urban artery in Asia has a relatively well-developed ancillary of secondary cities has helped this phenomenon take a firm grip in the region. In 1975, in East Asia less than one-fifth, and in South Asia less than one-third, of the urban population lived in secondary cities (Rondinelli, 1983: 53–7). This also explains the fact that, in South Asia, the fastest growth took place in cities with populations less than 2 million while the rate of growth of the primate cities declined considerably. The present trends in urbani-zation strengthened the existing fabric of production in the region.

Though similar organizational readjustments within other core zones have been the order of the day since the late 1960s, the extent of this renovation has been comparatively modest. The relocation of production abroad via subsidiaries and the continuing force of the USA rendered the liquidation or renovation of this existing corporate network extremely difficult. The relatively limited extent of transnational expansion of European corporate capital until the late 1960s and its subsequent reliance on the import of migrant labour were, of course, limitations on its ability to resort to subcontracting of production. Even though its latecomer status has absolved it from the necessity of liquidating (part of) its corporate network, the full integration of Southern Europe (the former frontier of the Community, now placed on a par with the rest), and to a limited extent of Eastern Europe, have imposed serious limits on the extension and widespread employment of this other mode of integration. Indeed, recent developments in Eastern Europe, where subcontracting for European – mostly German – firms had become a frequent phenomenon in the 1970s and 1980s (van der Wee, 1986: 397) have rendered it an increasingly arduous undertaking. The 'economic labour collectives', which leased state-owned plants and machinery outside working hours, have virtually disappeared in consequence of the recent industrial privatizations.

The Expanding Dominion of Semiproletarian Households

The broadening of the non-Fordist sector in the core has been accompanied by a swift expansion in the number of semiproletarian households in the semiperipheral zones as well. It was triggered by a decline in the state's capacity to control and regulate economic flows and labour markets, because of both transformations in the interstate system and the 'footloose' expansion strategies employed by corporate capital. The processes underlying the reproduction of semiproletarian households during the A-phase – urbanization, migration and demographic growth – lost their force as a result of the changes in the interstate and inter-enterprise systems. In fact, all three have become, during the past two decades, attributes of peripheral rather than of semiperipheral regions.

For one thing, during the 1970s, the urban 'bias' inscribed in import-substitution industrialization came to a sharp halt, tilting the balance at the expense of the biggest conurbations. Seen from this angle, the fast pace of urban growth experienced before the debt crisis started to subside revealed that it was basically the extraordinary growth of lesser cities (and, at times, of towns) which has kept the overall rates of urban growth high since the 1970s.

This decline is fully consonant with the world-economic developments characterizing the post-1967/73 period. Having radically altered the balances established during the 1950s and 1960s which favoured urban concentration and deruralization, these recent developments per-force dictated a new spatial patterning on a world scale. By downplaying the urban geography of the former period, the reversal of the 'enclosure' movement which had concentrated (agrarian and industrial) production predominantly within the inter-enterprise and interstate networks triggered secondary urbanization, facilitated 'ruralization' of manufacturing activities, and refashioned the agrarian landscape. In short, it called into question the rural–urban nexus of the post-1945 period.

With the downturn, the withering away of import-substitution industrialization and the burgeoning of commercial agriculture and husbandry unleashed centrifugal tendencies, reducing the growth rate of the primate cities. The change in capital flows during the 1970s favouring the periphery made these changes visible first in the semiperiphery. But the debt crisis and the ensuing movement of capital toward the core in the 1980s ensured that the full impact of the downturn would be felt in peripheral and semiperipheral areas alike, with however some nuances for the semiperiphery, given the pivotal role they played during the A-phase.

The concentration of industrial production in metropolitan areas slowed down. For example, in Chile, Santiago's proportion decreased from 49 per cent to 38 per cent between 1973 and 1980 (Gwynne, 1985: 82–131, 234). Subsequently, the rate of metropolitan growth decelerated. In São Paulo, secondary cities of the state with a population of over 100,000 increased, at an annual rate of 5.3 per cent, faster than the 4.6 per cent of the metropolitan area itself (Townroe and Keen, 1984). It was during the 1970s that the cities with populations between 0.5 and 4.0 million had the lowest growth rates. Those with populations between 100,000 and 500,000 were growing at an average of about 3.9 per cent annually, whereas the rate declined to 3.1–3.2 per cent in those with populations ranging from 0.5 to 4.0 million (Preston, 1988).

Between 1965 and 1975, even though the total population in cities over four million in peripheral and semiperipheral regions grew from 55.9 to 120.6 million – that is, at a phenomenal rate of 7.7 per cent – almost half of this growth resulted from an absolute growth in the number of cities in this group, from nine to seventeen. If calculations are somehow 'corrected' on this basis, then 32 million should be added to the former group. In other words, the urban growth rate 'through graduation' would be in excess of 3 per cent. That the absolute increase in the number of megalopolises needs to be taken stock of in tracing trends in urbanization goes without saying. However, it should not inflate the growth rate attributed to metropolitan conglomerations. One cannot claim the end of the predominance of primate cities. The centralization of industrial pursuits is still with us, although signs of its abatement are also evident and abundant (Storper, 1991). The corporate restructuring, flowing from the renovation in the informational infrastructure, has inaugurated the supersession, if you will, of the importance of physical concentrations by a network of information and economic flows orchestrated 'from without'.

The decline in rates of urban growth has followed different modalities in different parts of the semiperiphery. In highly urbanized Latin America, the change is exemplified in the deceleration of rates of urban growth: down from 4.5 per cent in the 1960s to 4.2 per cent in the 1970s, and to 3.7 per cent in the 1980s. The highest rate of growth in the 1980s was in the category of cities with less than 2 million inhabitants, while the primate cities also grew fast. Equally, the populations of secondary cities grew about 8 per cent faster than the total population of the largest cities. In the Pacific Rim, where a considerable influx during the A-phase of US corporate capital favoured primate cities, the outlying cities (for example, in the Philippines, provinces adjacent to Manila; or in Malaysia, Penang) were as affected as the metropolitan provinces during the drastic contraction in property markets in 1992 (*Far Eastern Economic Review*, 30 April 1992: 37–48).

As parastatal corporate entities encountered formidable difficulties because of the retrenchment of capital to the core in the 1980s, the infra-economy serving as an adjunct to this economic realm contracted too. The contraction in employment was accompanied by attendant declines in informal earnings, partly due to the rapid rise in labour reserves in the infra-economy and, more importantly, because of the parallel decline in demand by a shrinking corporate sector due to the drop in urban wages. With the share of urban population in the Latin American semiperiphery now reaching 80 per cent of the total population, the contraction in the state/corporate sector and the very slow tempo of industrialization were translated as incessant growth in the realm of the infra-economy.

This is partly why, despite the fact that 'formal' sector (corporate or parastatal) has either been auctioned off or has downsized considerably, employment in the 'marginal' sector has not shown any corresponding quantum leap. Rates of urban unemployment in metropolitan agglomerations in Latin America as well as in Southern Europe have skyrocketed and have persistently been higher than overall 'national' rates of unemployment. Here again, the Latin American semiperiphery exhibited a path different than that of the Southern European semiperiphery. In the latter, where female employment in manufacturing has been relatively higher, unemployment of women, more so than that of men, has also been the order of the day. In the former, by contrast, where the feminization of the labour force employed in the infra-economy reached significant proportions, owing to the gradual slackening in this sector in concert with the transformations in the corporate sector, female-headed households mushroomed (Schmink, 1986; Schultz, 1990).

Hence, centripetal forces shaping urbanization patterns during the A-phase, at variance with recent historical developments, have of late lost their spatially organizing force. The reversal is signalled by a deceleration in the growth of primary cities and a complementary rise in that of secondary cities at the semiperiphery, and in the loss of the agglomerative power of the metropolitan conglomerations at the core. At the same time, natural increase became a more important factor in the growth of the urban areas, at times accounting for more than 70 per cent (Roberts, 1978: 105). There was also a metamorphosis in migratory flows, which have become more intra-urban in character, within or across national boundaries (Roberts, 1990).

In sharp contrast to the A-phase, during the B-phase the relatively limited size of the agricultural labour force in the semiperiphery, the closely intertwined nature of urban and rural labour markets, and the high levels of urban unemployment acted in harmony to bring down the rate of demographic growth. The trends sustaining secondary urbanization played a role in this. The commercialization of non-cereal agriculture, and the growing importance of exports of more lucrative non-food crops, used to replenish foreign-exchange reserves rather than to subsidize the corporate/urban sector, have opened up new areas of temporary employment. The mobilization of this agrarian reserve army by labour contractors in relatively centralized small-town labour markets has fuelled the development and growth of such towns. These largely pendular and periodic sojourns in small towns rendered the recruitment on a temporary basis of these town-based workers by landowners easier for their own needs or those of rental farms. The agricultural labour force has become more and more urbanized, mainly based in small towns.

Hence, the difficulties encountered by rural producers in competing with these relatively well-organized labour supplies have placed additional checks on the tendency of households to expand via demographic growth. Besides, land concentration and the resulting increase in landlessness have accelerated rural out-migration since the late 1970s. Yet, the change in the structure of agrarian production and falling urban incomes have altered the character of labour flows. The out-migration is not primarily catering to urban labour markets. Rather, as discussed above, landless workers now have a tendency to cluster in the neighbourhoods of adjacent small rural towns (with populations of less than 100,000). Rural producers increasingly dependent on non-farm sources of income but unable to find sufficient employment opportunities to migrate and abandon the agricultural sector, depend on seasonal, temporary work, for two reasons. On the one hand, the deterioration in employment opportunities in urban areas has led people to look for additional work in agriculture. The labour-intensive character of new lines of specialization (horticulture and livestock farming as opposed to grain cultivation) meant that the demand for labour had increased, albeit minimally, on the other.

These processes augur a fertility decline and a deceleration in migration originating in the semiperiphery. It is not the processes of urbanization and migration, supported by precipitous population growth, which have refurbished the infra-economy, but changing modes of corporate expansion and a weakening in statizing trends. The sub-contracting armature knitting together the Pacific Rim has proved to be better equipped to weather the economic downturn, has increased the competitive pressure on the successful semiperipheries of the 1960s, and has quickened the dissolution of the Taylorist sector.

The belief in the developmentalist paradigm that the reach of Taylorism was all-encompassing has been belied by its relatively swift decline. In fact its reach was to a large extent coterminous with that of the semiperiphery. The post-1945 trajectory of the semiperipheries – that is, their impressive rise in the late 1950s and 1960s and their relapse thereafter – paralleled that of Fordism/Taylorism. The bypassing of the semiperiphery by core capital in the 1970s, and the favouring of peripheral locales in its search to reduce labour costs was compounded in the 1980s by the debt crisis. Therefore, the continual growth since 1945 of infra-economies, at first somewhat eclipsed by the strong performance before 1967/73 of the semiperipheries (and the concomitant growth of their 'corporate' sphere), has since captured the attention of social scientists.

The reversal at the periphery in statizing trends and hence the downsizing of the parastatal sector precipitated processes quite divergent from those characterizing the semiperiphery. The waning of the parastatal corporate sector and the growing intra-core and inter-core integration revealed the limits within the realm of work of the organizational edifice of the A-phase. Stated briefly, new trends fostered demographic and urban growth as well as migratory outflux to keep pace with its growing marginalization.

Given that high population densities and the predominantly labour-intensive agricultural systems dominate the agrarian landscape of southern Asia, and that cultivator holdings are usually small or middle-sized, cultivators with large families and smallholdings either cultivate the land very intensively or rent additional land from non-cultivating owners. In sparsely populated areas, as in sub-Saharan Africa, large families can put into use more land than small ones. In both cases, child labour has been widely used, which in the long run does not restrict household size. Also, the fact that women in sub-Saharan Africa and South Asia, where higher proportions of males were forced to work in urban areas, have been relegated largely to the (subsistence) agricultural sector in rural areas provided additional incentive for bigger households and demographic growth (Meillassoux, 1994; Boserup, 1990). The importance of being populous was mirrored in the growth in the number of household members during the 1980s in many a peripheral region, but mostly in Africa and in South and Southeast Asia.

The need to diversify their sources of income along the rural–urban nexus still kept internal migration and urbanization rates high (UN Center for Human Settlements, 1987). Migration in Africa, for instance, has remained at high levels – over 6 per cent since 1965. In Southeast Asia, 62 per cent of Bombay's and 71 per cent of Dhaka's increase in population during the 1970s and early 1980s was attributed to net migration. In the case of the latter, the percentage was up from 63 per cent in the 1960s. The scenario held true for Manila and Bangkok as well, among many others. The social structuring brought about by these migratory flows ·was different in the various quarters of the periphery. Where male populations were perennially adrift, as in Africa, over 40 per cent of households came to be headed by women, 85–95 per cent of whom were employed in agriculture. In Asia, where family migration overshadowed the rest, the percentage was down to 16–20 per cent (UN, 1989: 190).

The rise in overall wage employment notwithstanding, a combination of falling/stagnating real wages and declining 'regular' wage employment has significantly reduced the full-time wage component of household income since the late 1960s. Of total household income in the periphery in the late 1980s, 10–20 per cent came from full-time wage employment, income from 'formal and subsistence' and 'informal and subsistence' each contributing 30–40 per cent (Evers, 1989; ILO, 1984).

Even though the transnational expansion of capital during the first two decades was generative of labour flows catering primarily to urban centres, its extension in the 1970s to new and mostly peripheral localities induced a sea change in the character of labour flows streaming into the core, as exemplified by the changing composition of imported labour both in Europe and in the USA. In the former, the provenance of labour flows now widened from Southern Europe to the Mediterranean basin at large, and in the latter, from Europe to Asia and the Caribbean.

As a result, core-ward migratory movements came to dominate global labour flows, reaching 75 million per annum in the 1990s (Golini and Bonifazi, 1987: 123; Barnet and Cavanagh, 1994: 296). Accompanying and underlying these inflows was the redistribution within the corporate world of production functions worldwide, and condensation of service functions at core locales – hence the literature on global cities.

As a result, the sheer reach of the capitalist world-economy vis-à-vis households has been modified by processes furthering, first, the almost-ceaseless growth of the infra-economy in the semiperiphery, stemming from the waning of the state sector and new modes of corporate expansion, furnishing labour with alternatives to wage labour. In the periphery, these two tendencies were complemented by demographic expansion. Second, the transformation of world agriculture, which has rendered grain production the preserve of core zones, has impelled rural producers in non-core locales to specialize in the production of export crops (Tabak and Kasaba, 1994). The relative decline in the periphery in the share of grain cultivation, which, in the course of the last thirty years, had come under the jurisdiction of a female labour force, mostly as a result of high rates of male out-migration from rural areas, is in the process of restructuring: the newly gained dominance in agrarian production in the periphery by non-grain export crops is in the process of rendering it an almost exclusive province of male occupational activity. This has the potential for downscaling the share of the female workforce in agriculture in the periphery and semiperiphery. Third, the waning of the parastatal corporate sector, or its shrinkage under financial austerity programmes, has increased the tendency to shift services back into the domain of communities and households. Mention should also be made of the fact that in China, starting from 1978, household production responsibility or the household contract system, which came to replace the commune system, similarly replicated, though in a different fashion, the trends characterizing the rest of the periphery. By the end of 1984, about 95 per cent of rural households were involved in the contract system (Rawski, 1979).

The perverse effects of the swift expansion in part-lifetime proletarian households worldwide underline the benefits to capital of a continual shrinkage in full-lifetime proletarianization. The growth during the B-phase in contracting out of production is, to be sure, a reflection of the periodic 'ruralization' of manufacturing activities. In the highly urban setting of the post-1945 period and the perpetually narrowing urban/rural divide, the description 'rural' needs to be interpreted to include the slums and 'temporary' quarters of major conurbations housing contingent workers and day labourers, not to mention secondary and lesser cities and towns. This rhythmic occurrence has characterized the modern world-economy since its inception. In the short run, the present restructuring is not at variance with the pattern of cyclical rhythms of the world-economy and does not in itself register any systemic turning point.

In the long run, however, it may prove to be a secular trend. In the core zones, households of one or two person(s) have come to account for some 50 per cent of the total number of households (Sweet, 1984); this limits the array of householding strategies. Concomitantly, between one-fifth and one-third of all household income now derives from 'public revenue' (Therborn, 1984: 27), which renders the bypassing by corporate capital of social wage arrangements more than likely. Consequently, emigration of corporate capital to non-core locales in its search for semiproletarian labour and household preserves may prove to be a secular trend. That is, the B-phase starting with 1967/73 might represent, within the sphere of production and work, a break with the patterns of the past, both recent and distant.

5

World Human Welfare

*Sheila Pelizzon and John Casparis**

The expansion of welfare on a world scale was a central feature of the
ideological debates of the Cold War. The USA as the hegemonic power
was committed in theory to this expansion – not only at home and for
its European allies but also for the Third World as part of the concept
of the development of underdeveloped countries. This principle was
sometimes given the special name of human development. The USSR
was equally committed to this principle, asserting however that socialist
development was much more efficacious in providing such welfare, and
often pointing to non-European areas of the USSR as evidence of the
benefits of socialist development for peripheral areas. Thus, during the
Cold War, world human welfare was a realm of rhetorical debate, with
both sides alleging that the primary objective of their aid and assistance
to other nations was to advance human welfare.

Welfare provisions in the modern world are pre-eminently a state-level
function. State agencies provide welfare services to people in their jurisdictions. Most states in Western Europe, North America and Australasia
had already developed national welfare structures before 1945 (as had
the USSR), but the postwar period saw a quite sharp acceleration and
expansion of these programmes. In addition, since 1945 this process has
been extended geographically, although its provisions generally remained
less extensive in non-core regions of the world. The United Nations has
developed global programmes both directly and through its specialized
agencies. Each of the three major dimensions of welfare has its own

---

* The sections on health and food were primarily the responsibility of
Sheila Pelizzon; the sections on education were primarily the responsibility of John
Casparis.

specialized agency: WHO for health, UNESCO for education, and FAO for food.

We seek to assess the degree to which human welfare has been realized, and the growth or decline of equality in its realization on a world scale. We shall take as the constituents of welfare adequate health provisions – both public health measures (such as sewage, abundant clean water, disposal of refuse of various kinds) and access to modern medicine (both prevention and cure); adequate social income – old-age pensions, unemployment benefits, and health insurance; the extent and quality of educational facilities; perhaps most crucially, adequate nutritional levels and housing; and finally, the general quality of the environment, which has more recently been added as a social concern.

There has been a long-term trend within the modern world-system, at least since the nineteenth century and in the core zones, of increasing the state's role in ensuring increased human welfare. We commonly refer to this trend precisely as the development of the welfare state. The high-water mark of such an increase in welfare-statism was in fact reached circa 1967/73, after which world human welfare levels began to recede. The major argument used to justify this recent downward shift politically was the presumed fiscal inability of governments to afford the growing levels of social expenditure. This shift seemed to entail almost immediately a visible increase in inequality. It is, however, perhaps the case that the degree of (social, political and economic) inequality had in fact already been increasing during the previous phase of world economic expansion, but had remained hidden or masked behind the cloak of increasing official welfare-statism on the one hand, and the rhetoric of rising levels of living on the other (which was no doubt true for selected portions of the world population). In the phase of world economic contraction, this cloak of welfare-statism has been partially stripped away, and therefore the inequities now stood more starkly revealed in a period of increasingly austere levels of living for the majority of the world's people.

From 1945 to 1967/73: The Apogee of the Welfare State

After 1945, there was general acceptance in the states of the core zone of the idea that the 'concept of citizenship involved not merely a right to participate in political decision-making, but also a right to share in the general welfare of society' (Ambrosius and Hubbard, 1989: 127). The concept of the welfare state had been quite controversial before 1945. The reasons for the increased commitment to its implementation at this point were several. The 1930s had been characterized by waves of labour unrest in Western Europe. It was believed that a renewal of such unrest would make it difficult to maintain the wartime recovery from the depression of the 1930s. It followed that a *modus vivendi* between capital and labour was necessary. But, at just this time, labour was in a relatively strong position. The war against fascism had just been won, and the union movement was relatively strong throughout the core zone. Consequently, the labour movement was able to impose on the states the obligation to maintain full and stable employment, the public provision of a range of universal and personal services, and a 'safety net' of services to alleviate poverty (Mishra, 1990: 18–19). Though all these commitments involved, in effect, some reallocation of global surplus, the welfare state was seen by governments and employers as a necessary ingredient of world economic growth.

The exemplary document was the Beveridge Report of 1942, officially implemented by the British Labour government at the end of the Second World War. The measures adopted included democratization of educational policy; old-age pensions; the creation of a 'safety net' against hardship due to poverty, accident, and unemployment; family allowances, which varied according to the number of children in the family; and, most notably, a national health service (Ambrosius and Hubbard, 1989: 127). Over the following ten years, similar types of social policies were adopted in most other states in the core zone. There were, of course, local variations in social coverage and rate of adoption. For example, it was not until 1960 that agricultural workers were included in the French national health care scheme, and not until 1965 in the case of the self-employed (Kimberly and Rodwin, 1984: 258). In the Federal Republic of Germany, the mandatory national health insurance plan was not adopted until 1955, and it covered only 90 per cent of the population (Oppl and von Kardoff, 1990: 43). Sweden introduced national insurance into the health care system in 1955, Norway in 1956, Finland in 1963, and Denmark in 1971. In terms of national variations, Switzerland and the Netherlands were the only countries to follow state welfare models in terms of old-age pensions, while in the Federal Republic of Germany separate insurance funds were set up for different social strata and occupational groups (Ambrosius and Hubbard, 1989: 128). Nonetheless, in all these countries the underlying principles of the new welfare programmes were the universal participation of all citizens, equality of contribution, and comprehensive coverage.

Full employment was easy to arrange, given the strong economic growth of core economies in the 1950s and 1960s, which also favoured and supported these extensions of welfare provision (Ambrosius and

Hubbard, 1989: 129). Of course, the full employment policies affected primarily men. Most women were still defined as housewives, and as such could not claim unemployment insurance or other benefits relating to employment. However, European welfare-statism was augmented in the 1950s and 1960s in the direction of child and maternity supports, such as maternity leave and allowances, and day care.

The USA was the only state in the core zone where welfare-statism made little pretence at universality. What there was, with the exception of social security (old-age pensions), was fragmented, primarily aimed at assisting the elderly or the very poor, and intended to be palliative rather than preventative. Programmes of general relief and aid to families with dependent children had been established in the 1930s. The principal new welfare measure enacted immediately after the Second World War was the GI Bill of Rights, providing funds for higher education and home ownership. It was geared more to enhancing the opportunity for self-advancement than to extending economic rights as an attribute of citizenship.

The provision of food subsidies to the poor through the Federal Food Stamp Program was adopted primarily in order to keep agricultural prices high and to reduce food surpluses (Kutzner, 1991: 69). There was some increase in state-provided (fragmentary, non-universal) welfare measures in the 1960s. Medicare and Medicaid gave the elderly and poor access to medical services (Kimberly and Rodwin, 1984: 258). This was partly in reaction to agitation from the bottom up. The riots by African-Americans in the northern ghettos were a great impetus to the social commitments made by the Johnson administration. They drew attention to the fact that, while the establishment of maternal and child health clinics had cut the rate of African-American maternal mortality, more than ten million African-Americans were still suffering from chronic malnutrition (Beardsley, 1987: 276, 291).

Semiperipheral states also enacted a range of welfare measures, some of them similar to but less extensive than those enacted in the core zone after 1945. Portugal, Spain and Greece had national health insurance programmes by 1975, but they covered only 70 per cent of the economically active population. Italy arrived at universal coverage only by 1978. Eastern Europe was even more varied: the USSR had had state-supported health insurance since the 1930s and East Central Europe since the postwar period. However, health insurance tended to be geared towards workers in the industrial sector. The self-employed and peasants, except in the German Democratic Republic and Czechoslovakia, were left out of social insurance until the 1960s and 1970s. Old-age pensions tended to be set at a relatively low level – one-quarter of former salary, although the benefits improved by the 1970s (Ambrosius and Hubbard, 1989: 129–31).

Generally, the standard of living as measured by per-capita real-income levels and levels of consumption rose at this time in states in the core zone (and in the semiperiphery) due precisely to full employment and welfare-statism. The share of household expenditure on basic needs – food, clothing, housing, heating – fell from over 75 per cent before the 1950s to about 50 per cent by 1960. This resulted in a convergence of consumption patterns of consumer durables between upper and lower strata, and enabled an increase in the variety and quality of food consumption.

1. *Health*

All governments of the core zone throughout this period subsidized health institutions. The improvement of health care was, however, directed more to cure rather than to prevention. Government funds provided for building and consolidating hospitals and establishing co-operative arrangements between medical schools, research facilities and hospitals had the effect of consolidating the position of high-technology medicine (Kimberly and Rodwin, 1984: 259). The success of the US pharmaceutical industry in the patenting of the production methods of penicillin in 1945, and the subsequent development of various antibiotics (Wainwright, 1990: 64), led to the development of a complex of expensive new technologies, fuelled by infusions of government money both in the USA and in Western Europe. Patient care, diagnosis and treatment involved increasingly considerable spending on tests and technological interventions (Hollingsworth, Hage and Hanneman, 1990: 33). To be sure, the development of vaccines and antibiotics did mean that many previously life-threatening diseases – tuberculosis, pneumonia, bronchitis, streptococcus infections, most childhood diseases – were no longer fatal. This was reflected in the increased longevity and decreased infant mortality of core populations (Ambrosius and Hubbard, 1989: 14–15, 76, 246).

The bulk of the population in the core and those in the European semiperiphery benefited in the period 1945–1967/73. The majority of people now had security of income, food, housing and employment. Government-sponsored health insurance allowed access to medical care for those who previously might not have received it. In the USA demand for more medical care was linked to economic growth and the rise in the numbers of people occupying white-collar jobs as well as to the increase of real per-capita income of 76 per cent between 1950 and

1973 (Kervasdoué and Rodwin, 1984: 5, 7). The bleaker side of this was that the costs of medical care doubled in the 1950s and again in the 1960s. This meant that those without insurance had diminished access to medical services. Comparison of France, Great Britain, Sweden and the USA showed that this happened regardless of whether or not prices and personnel were controlled by the state (Hollingsworth, Hage and Hanneman, 1990: 39–40).

The prime function of the World Health Organization (WHO), set up early in the postwar period, was to improve the delivery of health care to peripheral populations. WHO defined health quite broadly: 'a state of complete physical, mental, and social well-being and not merely the absence of disease' (UN, 1952: 22). In practice, the organization gave priority to curing tropical diseases, which were conceptualized as 'the jungle undergrowth ... which had to be cleared before a country has a fair chance at development'. Health provision took the form primarily of vertical projects – the eradication of malaria with mass sprayings of DDT, the curing of yaws by administering penicillin in mass injection programmes – activities which were seen to be immediately useful in terms of raising the productivity of workers and land (UN, 1952: 25). Vertical projects, however, often had limited efficacy in improving general health conditions. Some progress was made. By 1958, WHO had shown that leprosy could be cured with drugs, and that antibiotics were effective against tuberculosis without hospitalization (WHO, 1988a: 18). On the other hand, by 1955 it was clear that malaria eradication was doomed to failure as anopheles mosquito resistance to DDT had already surfaced (UN, 1957: 32). Reported malaria cases increased from 1962 to 1975 (UNEP, 1987: 349; Bull, 1982: 30).

2. *Education*

Since 1945 the trajectory of education has been one of expansion, improving access, and compelling more students to stay at school. To understand what has happened in the provision of education, we have taken World Bank and UNESCO data, and regrouped them according to the three zones of the world-economy, using the classificatory decisions found in the study by Arrighi and Drangel (1986). Adult literacy rates indicate the educational base from which each zone developed its schools. The periphery began with the greatest obstacles: less than one-quarter of its adults were literate in 1950. By 1975 adult literacy was still only 36 per cent. The semiperiphery made very rapid changes. From an adult literacy rate of 68 per cent in 1950, the states there achieved close to universal primary-school enrolment by 1960, and by 1975 the adult literacy was 87 per cent. In the core zone, almost all adults were literate and all children in school before 1945.

School enrolment expanded throughout the world and at all levels of education. More children went to school and stayed there longer. As the world moved in the direction of universal primary education, access to schooling became more equal among countries at lower educational levels, although to be sure there was still inequity in the quality of education offered to different segments of the national and world population. Simultaneously, however, it became less equal at the tertiary level. The number of students enrolled at universities in the core zone far outweighed the number elsewhere. Enrolment fluctuations in the core and the semiperiphery from 1960 to 1988 reflected primarily demographic changes. Birth rates in the core were close to replacement levels. Migrants, who grew in number in the period, were younger on average than the population they entered, and hence fed more children into the schools of the core. But the demographic effect was modest; the age distribution of the core was such that about the same number of children were fed into the schools from year to year. This is shown in Table 5.1. In the semiperiphery the demographics were moving in the same direction but remained more volatile. Total enrolments escalated within a 15 million range over the twenty-eight years. The population of the states of the semiperiphery remained youthful. Birth rates were declining but from a higher level than in the core. Pockets of high fertility remained in the countryside and among displaced agricultural workers in the cities. Further reductions in infant mortality and increased migration from the periphery also contributed to growth in population and school enrolment.

In marked contrast were the trends in states of the periphery. The doubling of enrolment was an immense achievement, and yet, as of 1988, still one-quarter of all the children in states of the periphery were without any schooling. With rapidly falling death rates and high birth rates, the populations have tended to have accelerating growth rates throughout much of the period, although population-control programmes in some countries – for example, in China and Indonesia (Lutz, 1994) – have lowered the growth rates in recent years. The very young age composition of the periphery meant nevertheless that, even with declining fertility levels, primary-school enrolments would continue to increase. The states of the periphery thus had population burdens that were not shared by those of the semiperiphery or core, placing them at a distinct disadvantage. Not only was primary school far from universally available but, in addition, throughout the period fewer girls than boys went to school. Furthermore, the share of national income that states of the periphery had to devote to their primary schools was much greater than elsewhere.

In this period, the model of a unified high-school system with a general curriculum for all students (as opposed to a two-tier system) that had been developed in the USA spread to many other countries. The United Kingdom created so-called comprehensive schools (Reynolds, Sullivan and Murgatroy, 1987). The continental European secondary schools also made their schools more accessible, diversified the curricula, but kept a majority of students in vocationally specific tracks that combined schooling with apprentice-work experience (Schneider, 1982: 207–26). Although access improved in all systems, minorities everywhere have had to fight for such access and they still remain disadvantaged. Thus, in the USA, educational discrimination was legally abolished in 1954, but African-Americans have continually found it necessary to seek access through the courts. In any case, discrimination in housing restricted access to better schools. In core states with a heavy influx of foreign migrant workers, there was unequal access and discrimination (Fibbi and de Rham, 1988). In openly racist states such as South Africa two separate and unequal school systems existed. Female students felt the pressure of vocational channelling once they reached the secondary system, and in many states had, in addition, less access than male students.

As shown in Table 5.2, by 1988 almost all children of secondary-school age went to school if they lived in the states of the core; in the semiperiphery two-thirds did so; but in the periphery only one-quarter were enrolled. Although the opportunity to go to secondary school lagged in the periphery, the numbers enrolling were accelerating. By 1988 the secondary schools of the states in the periphery were enrolling 144 million of the world's 221 million secondary pupils. Enrolments in the core remained stable, given the stabilization of fertility rates in these states. In the semiperiphery the expansion continued to be driven by the growing number of young people. Part of the expansion in secondary education was due to the declining importance, worldwide, of agricultural labour. Secondary-school graduates mostly entered the urban labour market. In the two largest states of the periphery, the proportion of the population classified as urban rose: in China from 18 per cent in 1965 to 53 per cent in 1989, and in India from 19 per cent to 27 per cent in the same time period.

After 1945, secondary education expanded throughout Western Europe, to include more members of the working classes and rural people. This had the consequence of raising economic and social expectations (King, 1969: 48). Especially after 1960, changes in the structure of the job market (Ambrosius and Hubbard, 1989: 108) brought about increased demand for education, in particular at the tertiary level. In the USA as well, increased access to higher education gave working- and lower-middle-class people a means of improving their social and economic status, made them less willing to engage in menial or routine jobs, and legitimated the increased role of the state in securing human welfare (Darknell, 1980: 291).

Governments sought to meet this demand by founding new universities, and reducing or abolishing fees through state support. At the same time, university admissions were expanded as were the numbers of universities in Great Britain (Peterson, 1965: 161), in the Federal Republic of Germany (Merritt, Flerlage and Merrit, 1971: 127), and in France (Tournier, 1973: 114). Government funding of universities in the USA served further to enhance enrolment. In the context of the Cold War, this was intended to 'mobilize and direct the resources of [the United States in order to] ... compete with the mobilized, determined, aggressive society from the other side of the Iron Curtain...' (Clark, 1964: 98).

Enrolments at the university level, the age group 20–24 shown in Table 5.3, were the least driven by demographics. No state mandated university attendance. The core was home to about 20 per cent of the world's people, but over 40 per cent of the world's students attend universities in the core. The large core universities were the principal centres of world knowledge production, transmission and dominance (Galtung, 1971: 92–4). While the period after the Second World War saw a major expansion of university institutions in the periphery, nonetheless the institutions located in the core retained their dominant role through funding for research and their ability to attract worldwide talent (Arnove, 1980).

A large number of the universities in the periphery had been founded as core-dependent institutions – by missionaries and as extensions of core universities. In postwar but still colonial British Africa, for example, the universities did not set their own examinations nor grant independent degrees. Independence meant finding resources in meagre state budgets and setting new moral agendas. The paucity of national resources meant that there continued to be a major flow of graduate students to the universities of the core and the semiperiphery.

The popular conception of education is that it has been unremittingly beneficial. Since the nineteenth century, education has been considered an avenue for individuals, if not groups, to rise through the social ranks. But in practice this has implied a crystallization and legitimation of the ranking system, even in the popular perception. The increase in educational opportunity in this period served, to be sure, for some individuals as a mode of income improvement. But it also served as a counterweight to the right of all to economic well-being. Expansion of educational achievement validated inequalities of placement and rewards in the job market. The educational system thus performed an exclusionary function as well as one of individual advancement (see Bowles and Gintis, 1976, for the USA; and Carnoy, 1974, for Africa).

Women's access to the university system has remained seriously limited. In France, for example, the great state universities have rarely accepted women candidates for appointments to chairs, and in general have offered women only mediocre careers (Tournier, 1973: 114). In the USA, the GI Bill of Rights had increased working-class enrolment at tertiary institutions, and kept returning veterans off the unemployment rolls (Gittell, 1991: 32), but of course this primarily benefited young men. In addition, although the amount of schooling may have increased, the class structure has tended to remain more or less what it has always been. Children brought their backgrounds with them to school. Teachers shaped the culture of the classroom and injected their own biases into their treatment of students. Assessments of ability, such as 'objective' testing, favoured the dominant culture. As Collins (1988: 175) noted: 'although there has been a massive expansion of schooling in virtually every society (and especially in the United States, where 75 per cent of the population now graduates from high school and nearly half attends college), the overall amount of social mobility in society has remained constant throughout this century.'

3. *Food*

The most fundamental issue in welfare is of course food, the production and distribution of which has been consistently a major political issue since 1945. Immediately prior to the Second World War, the principal grain-producing states had stocks of unsellable surpluses resulting from increased productivity due to technical inputs, and from the depression. This problem was most acute in the USA and Canada. The war brought only temporary relief to this problem. Immediately following the war, some further solution to the problem was found in providing both Europe and East Asia with war relief (Morgan, 1979: 93).

By 1949 the USA had taken the lead in working out trading rules regarding grain sales with other key importers and exporters. Because of the ideological constraints imposed by the Cold War, China, the USSR and Eastern Europe were unacceptable as clients of the USA; these countries therefore regularly bought wheat from Canada (Puchala and Hopkins, 1980: 80). The most formal expression of this were the International Wheat Agreements of 1949, which permitted Canada and the USA to dominate the international wheat markets and to function as an informal duopoly (Puchala and Hopkins, 1982: 261, 265).

At this time, the US government, because of its internal subsidies to farmers, was developing a large grain reserve. By the early 1950s, the US government was running into difficulties disposing of its reserve supplies. The Europeans had absorbed all the grain they were capable of absorbing. US companies, farmers and the government found themselves confronted with a glut of grain and associated storage and management costs (Antle, 1988: 85). Attempts to find new markets were only partly successful. The practice of fattening cattle on grain proved to be only a partial solution. The USA became the principal source of the corn/soybean feed mix on which the industry relied (Morgan, 1979: 100). One outgrowth of this practice was the development of the broiler chicken industry, but attempts to create a market in the Federal Republic of Germany for US chicken failed. The Germans liked the chickens, but started their own broiler industry. Another method used for creating markets for stocks of surplus US wheat was the creation of a taste for bread among the Japanese. This was done through the Japanese school-lunch programme to which the USA contributed as part of its programme of rehabilitation of Japan (Morgan, 1979: 104). This did not, however, go far to solving the problem of surplus grain stocks.

By the early 1950s government and agribusiness in the USA could find no outlet for surplus food (more specifically, grain stocks) in Europe or at home, and since China, the USSR and Eastern Europe remained politically out of bounds, new outlets for surpluses were sought (or rather created) through food aid to the newly decolonized states. A certain public-relations groundwork had to be laid in order to explain to both the US public and the governments in the peripheral zone why food aid was needed.

In 1954, the imagery of the 'population bomb' or 'explosion' was inserted into the public dialogue via a pamphlet published by the Hugh Moore Fund. It was this image more than anything else which validated the public dumping of surplus grain stocks via concessionary sales in the programme known as Food for Peace (Public Law 480), which was established as a feature of US government policy in 1954. This was followed by a programme set up by the UN in 1960: the World Food Program (Kutzner, 1991: 68–9). In fact there appears to be very little hard evidence that food aid was needed, or that in general there was any more of a chronic food shortage in peripheral states than there had been in the preceding fifty years. While it is true that world population, which had been rising for several hundred years, began to rise even more swiftly after 1945, and there had been some spectacular famines, it seems that in the 1950s, Africa, Asia and Latin America were still self-sufficient in food (Brown, 1988: 13; Grigg, 1983: 305). Indeed, prior to 1945 many Third World areas had exported grain, averaging 13 million tons per year (National Research Council, 1975: 13; see also Table 5.4 below). Nor had the need for food aid been increased during the period under study. It seems that food production outstripped population growth everywhere in the 1950s and 1960s, except in Africa. Yet famines occurred in India during the 1950s and 1960s where, although population grew by 55 per cent, rice production had increased by 60 per cent (Kutzner, 1991: 25; cf. Table 5.5 below).

Considering the rationales of the Food for Peace Program, it becomes quite clear that feeding hungry people was not the most important objective of the programme. In a listing of the aims of the programme, combating world hunger and malnutrition is only the fourth purpose listed. The first three relate to disposing of agricultural surpluses, developing export markets for US agricultural commodities, and expansion of international trade, all of which relate to the economic motivations of the US government and business in passing PL480 (Kutzner, 1991: 69).

The setting of the rules concerning international flows of food was assumed to be the prerogative of the governments of supplying countries. The free market was deemed the best way to allocate food-stuffs globally. Extra-market channels of food distribution were accept-able only as long as income derived from trade was not dramatically reduced. To this end food-aid recipients were required to import com-mercially an amount equal to their average imports of the preceding five years in order to be eligible to receive shipments of food aid. It is noteworthy that Japan in terms of rice-pricing policies, the EEC in terms of its so-called Common Agricultural Policy, and at times the USA itself have honoured these free-trade stipulations more in the breach than otherwise (Puchala and Hopkins, 1982: 263–5). In effect, it has only been Third World countries that have been required to abide by these rules.

There is no denying the efficacy of PL480 as a dumping mechanism. From 1954 to 1964 food aid accounted for 34 per cent of total US grain exports and for 57 per cent of Third World imports of grain (Raikes, 1986: 165). While it is doubtful whether food aid ever did much to feed or even cheapen food for the poorest strata of the popu-lation, there is a good deal of evidence to suggest that these policies were actually harmful to the national or local agriculture of certain recipient states, particularly African ones. African governments came to rely on imports of wheat and rice to feed their urban populations. These replaced traditional staples. Government commitment to providing cheap food for urban dwellers meant that famines, such as those experienced by rural people, did not generally occur in urban areas. But this policy meant a shift towards a less varied diet, and, unless income was high enough, towards a less nutritious one as well. Furthermore, part of the price of the purchased diet to the consumer included packaging (Bryceson, 1989: 435). This type of staple-import policy also deprived rural people of a market for the crops they did produce (Raikes, 1986: 161; Selwyn and Drobnick, 1978: 19).

Governments were not unaware of the disjuncture this caused. But these import policies were kept up for fear of urban food riots (Raikes, 1986: 174). There was also a preference, on the part of government officials, for dealing with agribusiness or other governments rather than with a host of small producers. While Africa may be an extreme example of the detriment to both nutrition and the structure of local economies wrought by PL480, it is not the only case. Around 1968, implementation of PL480 concessional sales of wheat succeeded in turning South Koreans from a nation that ate rice only as a staple to one that became partially wheat-eating, which incidentally made them dependent on the USA for food imports. Cargill and Purina were also able to set up feed-grain imports in South Korea under the aegis of PL480. Similar processes were implemented in such areas as Taiwan, Colombia, Bolivia and Guatemala (Lappé and Collins, 1977: 371–8).

If the world, or rather the USA, was suffering from a grain glut, what explains the promotion of the Green revolution, which, at least theoretically, was supposed to increase grain output even more? Would it not ruin markets for PL480 grain? It must be remembered that PL480 was undertaken to promote the agenda of the US government. That agenda was only in part concerned with economic issues. Agribusiness multinationals were principally concerned with securing markets. If markets could not be found for agricultural outputs, then markets had to be found for agricultural inputs. The Green revolution involved inputs that included not only new high-yielding variety (HYV) seeds, but a whole range of other inputs: fertilizers and pesticides, irrigation equipment, tractors – to name only the most obvious ones. Those who supplied these inputs profited from the Green revolution. According to Lester Brown: 'Only agribusiness firms can supply these new inputs.... [T]he multinational corporation has a vested interest in the agricultural revolution' (Brown, quoted in George, 1977: 90). Furthermore, recipient states were frequently under constraint to buy the agricultural inputs for the Green revolution from the US agribusiness multinationals. For example, in 1965 while in the midst of a drought-induced famine, India was forced to buy supplies of US-made fertilizer under threat of having PL480 shipments discontinued, despite the fact that there was an adequate fertilizer industry in India (George, 1977: 91).

A certain type of conventional wisdom has hailed the Green revolution as having increased the involvement of agriculture in peripheral regions in world markets: 'Agriculture became more closely integrated in the overall economy. Within countries a rising share of production becomes marketed, more off-farm inputs purchased, more institutional credit used and more off-farm income earned by rural households' (Alexandratos, 1988: 4). In short, since the 1950s it has forced rural people to work harder without necessarily increasing their standards of living. As the Green revolution was implemented, it became clear that a technocratic approach was leaving certain side-effects unaddressed, notably the displacement of small peasants and rural poor and the consequent swelling of the ranks of urban poor (Dahlberg, 1979: 73; George, 1977: 102). Although productivity rose for India such that grain was then exported from that nation (Kutzner, 1991: 25), this simply meant that the government used the increased productivity to offset dependence on foreign grain rather than to increase food consumption among the poor (Wolf, 1986: 18). Therefore it is probable that levels of malnutrition and outright starvation have remained at the level of the 1960s if they have not actually increased (Raikes, 1986: 161).

The HYV grains themselves were of a less nutritious quality, and their cultivation has added to malnutrition. They tended to be starchier and hold a lower protein content than do older varieties (George, 1977: 101). Furthermore, the cultivation of the new varieties often displaced the growing of more nutritious crops such as the pulses in India that local populations had previously grown for subsistence (Dahlberg, 1979: 53). While evidence varies, most studies have shown declines in nutrition levels associated with switching from subsistence farming to cash-crop production; this had already been noted in the Andean region of Peru in the 1950s, preceding the Green revolution. A study undertaken in Tabasco, Mexico, showed that the diets of cash-cropping peasants who purchased their foodstuffs were nutritionally inferior to the diets of nearby subsistence-farming peasants. In this case the food budgets of individual families had to compete with allocations of cash for agricultural inputs. The same was noted in the Cuaca Valley in Colombia where cash-crop production impinged upon the labour time available for the cultivation of subsistence crops (Dewey, 1989: 414–17). The implication of . this is that cash-crop production involved lowered standards of living for rural people, whether or not that cash crop production was undertaken in connection with the Green revolution.

The period 1945–1967/73 saw an increase in the flow of basic food-stuffs from core to periphery. In one sense this represented a change in direction of the usual historical trade patterns of the modern world-system. On the other hand, in those parts of the world where wheat and rice have not formed part of the traditional staples, these may then take on the character of luxury imports.

The overall picture in this period, then, was one of genuine progress in the core in terms of giving people security of income, housing, food, medical care, and opportunity for self-advancement through education. Arguably, the advantages bestowed by full employment policies and welfare-statism were not only to narrow the gap between rich and poor in terms of certain types of consumption, but also to give labour a more equal bargaining position vis-à-vis employers. However, clearly not all the groups among the core population shared equally in these benefits. The benefits were less for non-Whites, immigrants, the disabled and women, among others. Immigrants and non-Whites were utilized as cheap labour forces in all parts of the core. To the extent that in Western Europe 'minorities' were purposely created out of non-nationals, the schools serving as a major locus of such social definition, the expression of racism may be said to have increased quantitatively. To the extent that migrants were expected to bear the brunt of industrial or agri-cultural job losses, they faced increasing discrimination. Therefore racism increased qualitatively as well. The agenda for women, while never precisely defined, presumed the model of the male breadwinner: 'fiscal legislation, social security provisions, and employment policies treated married women as ... dependent on their employed husbands, penalized as taxpayers, and entitled to only limited sickness and unemployment benefits' (Balbo, 1987: 209).

In the periphery, however, the results of 'development' were less sanguine. There was more medical care; people lived longer because some diseases such as malaria, tuberculosis, yaws and leprosy had been controlled (not eradicated) because of the existence of DDT, and the (limited) availability of antibiotics and vaccines. There were greater levels of basic literacy because of the introduction of mass primary schooling. There was more food production, and food aid, but it was unlikely that any of this reached, or even indirectly benefited, the poor. The Green revolution expanded wheat production in some areas and involved peasants in national and international markets, but it undercut subsistence and deepened dependency. Such industrializing semiperipheral countries as Chile, Brazil and Mexico found that their internal income gaps widened between 1960 and 1970 (Müller, 1979: 161–2).

From 1967/73 to 1990: The Welfare State under Attack

Between the mid-1960s and the end of the 1970s, social spending as a proportion of national product rose in the core zone despite (indeed, because of) the beginning of the economic downturn. In Western Europe, it went on average from 13.4 per cent of GNP in 1965 (only 9.4 per cent in 1950) to 22.4 per cent in 1977. The increase in spending on benefits is also observable measured as a percentage of net national disposable income in Belgium, Denmark, the Federal Republic of Germany, France, Italy, the Netherlands, and the UK (UN, 1978: 28).

The major part of this was health-care expenditure, which doubled its share of the national product. There were three major reasons for this expansion. One was the ageing of the population, which meant that an increasingly higher proportion of the population were drawing pensions and demanding medical treatment (Ambrosius and Hubbard, 1989: 129, 132). At the same time, new problems in health care arose, with previous successes generating rising expectations and rising costs (Kervasdoué and Rodwin, 1984: 3–4).

A second source of increased expenditures on welfare were the unemployment benefits necessitated by the economic downturn as the various states, especially in the core zone, sought to protect the incomes of the unemployed. Levels of unemployment in OECD member states increased from 2 per cent to 5 per cent of the labour force between 1970 and 1975. Between 1960 and 1976 the rate of unemployment benefit per day increased three times in Italy, four times in France. Unemployment benefit amounted in 1976 to 60 per cent of the earnings of unskilled workers in Belgium, 68 per cent of net earnings in the Federal Republic of Germany, and 80 per cent in Luxembourg (UN, 1978: 13, 17). Further measures included job creation in the public sector, monetary compensation for early retirement, and subsidies to private firms to increase employment (UN, 1978: 16). These last measures were in part welfare for the rich (Frank, 1980, I: 44).

As unemployment rose and economic stagnation intensified, Western European governments became increasingly hostile toward immigrants. Overt racism increased, taking various forms: anti-immigrant media campaigns which fuelled fears of 'swamping', physical attacks on the persons and property of immigrants, the rise of neo-Nazi groups, and a deliberate emphasis on the problem of migrants in the policies of major political parties, and the rise of new parties whose major plank seemed to be mobilization against migrants. Immigrants provided governments and employers with a convenient scapegoat on which to blame the social problems of poverty, crime and pollution (Castles, Booth and Wallace, 1984: 5). In addition, the line between illegal immigrants and citizens of colour (for example, Hispanics in the USA, Antillais or Beurs in France, 'Pakis' in the UK) was often blurred in public discussion.

The third reason for the expansion of welfare benefits was in response to popular agitation as well as to pressure within the service bureaucracies. In the USA race riots dramatized the problems of poverty among African-American urban immigrants in northern cities. Student revolts highlighted the discontent within higher education, which had become accessible to working-class children. Workers' strikes in Europe coincided with student unrest, and generated concern among the elites and the impetus for welfare reform (De Swaan, 1988: 227).

Among the complaints of protesters were that states had failed to promote welfare and equality. For example, there were political movements to eliminate private beds in hospitals in the expectation of increasing equality in health care. This happened in Sweden in 1968, in Great Britain in 1974, in France and Spain in 1982 (Starr and Immergut, 1987: 237–8). In the USA, the welfare-rights movement informed the poor of their 'right to welfare [transfer payments], encouraged [them] to apply for it and helped [them] to obtain it' (Piven and Cloward, 1977: 272). When the welfare-rights movement showed signs of faltering, it blended with the African-American movement protesting against structural unemployment and African-American poverty in northern cities (Piven and Cloward, 1977: 331). It was noted that African-Americans received 50 per cent fewer Medicaid benefits than Whites, and that Medicaid missed about 40 per cent of the potentially eligible poor (Hollingsworth, Hage and Hanneman, 1990: 160). The outcome of these revelations was the extension of welfare. The Food Stamp Program was made more accessible, and urban African-American incomes in the south were raised to 75 per cent of those of northern urban African-Americans (Beardsley, 1987: 296). In northern cities, community health centres were started to provide poor people with a health service in a personalized (that is, non-clinic) setting (Ehrenreich and Ehrenreich, 1978: 66).

The civil-rights movement in the South, whatever its failings, did have the result that terror ceased to be used as a quasi-official method of social control against southern African-Americans (Piven and Cloward, 1977: 256). Furthermore, the widespread belief that race

correlated with mental ability was undermined, and the ideology of individual advancement appeared to be reaffirmed. African-Americans, in particular those who had been activists or leaders in the anti-poverty or civil-rights movements, found their way into electoral politics, federally financed jobs, and higher-ranking jobs in business and the professions, while institutions of higher education revised their admission policies to admit more minorities. However, this signified cooptation as well as gains (Piven and Cloward, 1977: 255). The same process could be seen with regard to women.

The protests in core and semiperipheral states between 1968 and 1973 politicized the questions of welfare and social equality. The concern of authorities was to contain these movements, especially as the economic downturn deepened. To that end, the very methods of the social movements of the time were used to reassert the status quo ante, and indeed to reduce equality as much as possible. What antisystemic social protest had done was to repoliticize issues of medical care, poverty and welfare in general, issues that had become relatively depoliticized after the Second World War. Policy issues had become less the provenance of (assertedly neutral) civil servants and professionals, and more that of politicians or openly politicized bureaucrats. At the same time, the very act of politicization became an instrument of control, containment and reversal by those of the 'new right' persuasion wherever they could control the state (Starr and Immergut, 1987: 240).

The enormous economic expansion of the A-phase had made possible a significant increase in welfare expenditures. The economic contraction of the B-phase, however, led everywhere to fiscal crises of the states, of varying severity. Thus, after the last spurt upward of expenditures in the early 1970s, this led in most countries to important cutbacks in human welfare expenditures. One response to fiscal crisis has been to make the provision of human welfare less a concern of the state and one more dependent upon the market. Other sources of finance for human welfare provisions – kinship networks, religious institutions, philanthropic and other non-governmental organizations – expanded their role in the downturn but were able to take up only some of the slack. They did not seek, in any case, to replace the states and the market as the basic providers, but only to serve in a supplementary role.

Despite, therefore, the remarkable expansion in provisions for human welfare, the world-system was not structured to provide world welfare services at a level that met the requirements laid out in the UN Declaration of Human Rights. Since, however, states have increasingly secured their legitimacy by the human welfare services they provide, their increased inadequacies in this regard, beginning in the mid-1970s, especially coming after their improved performance in the preceding twenty-five years, put a serious strain on the credibility and hence stability of the state structures. By the end of the 1970s, with the failure of Keynesian policies to solve deteriorating economic conditions, 'general confidence in the mixed economy and the welfare state evaporated' (Mishra, 1990: 1).

The neo-conservative position, which was gaining increasing strength in the core zone at this time, was hostile to taxation in general, in particular for welfare-state expenses (Mishra, 1990: 13–14). What was known as 'welfare backlash' (Piven and Cloward, 1977: 331) had its earliest (and perhaps strongest) manifestations in the USA. The result was economic retrenchment at the level of federal government funding of social programmes. In particular, various facilities such as the community health centres in northern cities were immediately targeted for elimination of funding as they were viewed as places for the airing of, and organization around, wider social issues than the treatment of health problems (Ehrenreich and Ehrenreich, 1978: 66). The rollback of welfare benefits was sometimes dressed up in progressive language (for example, Nixon's Family Assistance Plan), but in general welfare reduction became a key right-wing issue (Piven and Cloward, 1977: 307–41).

In Europe, the political reaction varied. Just as Great Britain had set the pace for welfare-statism in Europe after 1945, Thatcher set the pace for its dismantling. An alternative was the intensification of social-democratic corporatism adopted by Sweden, which finally led to their ousting from power in the 1980s after fifty years of continuous control of the government. In 1981, the French socialist government under Mitterrand initially went in a direction which strengthened the welfare state, but, in the face of world recession, the French government soon found itself retreating (Mishra, 1990: 14). Nonetheless, both France and the Federal Republic of Germany, even under conservative governments, were more cautious about cutting welfare-state provisions than the UK or the USA.

Neo-conservatives retrenched social programmes geared to the poorer sections of the population or to groups that had historically suffered discrimination, but treated social programmes with universal application – such as government-supported medical care, old-age pensions, or funding for education – somewhat differently. What has been particularly under attack are those policies and programmes which tended to equalize conditions between workers and employers, and/or cause some portion of aggregate income to accrue to labour rather than capital: full-employment policies, services to the poor, public housing, unemployment compensation benefits (especially supplementary ones), as well as those institutions which tended to exert upward pressures on wages: unions, Wage Councils in Great Britain, Food Stamps and Aid to Families with Dependent Children in the USA (Mishra, 1990: 14, 24, 26–7). In almost all states, there was a slower rate of growth of income transfer in the 1980s than in the 1970s, especially in temporary sickness benefits, old-age and veteran pensions, and maternity benefits. Per-capita unemployment benefits in real terms declined, as the criteria for claiming them were tightened while the numbers of claimants increased (UN, 1993: 111–12).

Unemployment has been particularly acute for youth, older workers, and women. On the one hand, the unemployment of youth has increased pressure on older workers to retire; on the other hand, it has stimulated reappraisal of educational institutions. Women, while showing slightly lower unemployment than these other two groups, have been disproportionately located in low-paid jobs in the service sector and part-time employment (UN, 1985: 68–9, 71). The result has been a deepening and widening poverty gap. The population in poverty in the USA went from 12.6 per cent in 1970 to 15.2 per cent in 1983. In Great Britain in 1983 the numbers of people in poverty were estimated at 13.5 per cent of the total population, a 55 per cent increase since 1979 (Mishra, 1990: 27, 29). Anywhere from 250,000 to 3 million people are homeless in the USA, while 250,000 public-housing units and 10.3 million dwellings stand empty (UN, 1993: 61–2). Similar developments have taken place in Great Britain, where rents for council housing, which housed manual workers and other low-income households, have doubled and 15 per cent of council housing was sold at a discount to sitting tenants (Mishra, 1990: 24).

During the 1970s, the numbers of women living in poverty increased by 100,000 a year. Cutbacks in welfare disproportionately affected women and children, which has resulted in the 'feminization of poverty' (Stallard, Ehrenreich and Sklar, 1983: 5, 17, 46). The differential in infant mortality rates between African-Americans and Whites narrowed slightly between 1969 and 1974 (from 83.1 to 81.1 per cent). Since then, however, the gap has consistently widened, reaching 108.1 per cent in 1987 (Reed, 1993: 16–17). In Europe, the poorer half of the population in general, and women, migrants, the young and the old in particular, have been especially hard hit by cutbacks. In Great Britain, the Black Report published in 1980 noted that, while differentials in mortality and morbidity that favoured the higher social-economic classes had existed since the 1950s, this differential increased in the 1980s (Smith, Bartley and Blane, 1991: 373). In Sweden, it has been noted that hectic and monotonous work, unemployment and smoking are important factors in cardiovascular disease and early death. Recently, it has been noted that inequalities appear to be increasing in general, and that immigrants are particularly at risk (Didericksen, 1990: 366).

The socialist states were not immune from generally deteriorating conditions. In Eastern Europe, the world-economic crisis and the crises of the states resulted in declines in general welfare. In Poland the death rate rose above 0.95 per cent in 1970 and remained at this level. This increase has been particularly marked in terms of female mortality (Duch and Sokolowska, 1990: 343). Infant mortality increased from 22.9 per 1,000 live births in 1971 to 37.1 per 1,000 over the course of the 1970s. The increase in pollutants is believed to be responsible for an increase of cancer deaths (Wnuk-Lipinski, 1990: 862, 869).

Most recently, the dismantling of the Communist regimes in the former USSR and Eastern Europe has led to considerable social dislocation, inasmuch as social-service spending played an important part in the standard of living. This has been particularly acute in the fields of medical care and housing. Unemployment has skyrocketed, and there is a widening gap between rich and poor (UN, 1993: 63, 98, 112). In much of the periphery, welfare-statism, to the extent it ever existed, was replaced by direct repression and accompanied by economic austerity mediated by the World Bank and the IMF (Frank, 1981: 188–229).

1. *Health*

If one takes standard health statistics as appropriate indicators, then health conditions may be said to have generally improved: life expectancy at birth rose in the peripheral zone from 57.4 years in 1975–80 to 61.4 years in 1985–90; infant mortality rates declined in the peripheral zone from 97 per 1,000 live births in 1975–80 to 78 per 1,000 in 1985–90. It is believed that, in the peripheral zone, maternal mortality rates have also declined (UN, 1993: 34–5). However, a comparative study of maternal mortality rates in five countries showed that, while maternal mortality rates had fallen in all of them, the gap between the maternal mortality rates in the states in the peripheral zone (Mauritius, Venezuela and Thailand) and the two in the core zone (England and Wales, and the Netherlands) had actually grown between 1970 and the late 1980s, whereas in the previous period the gap had narrowed (Kwast, 1989: 56).

In addition to the 'traditional' diseases of the peripheral zone, more 'modern' ones, such as cancer and heart disease, have increased rapidly. Half of the world's cancer patients now live in developing countries

(WHO, 1988a: 32). This increase is only partially explainable by the fact that the population is living to a greater age (Vainio, Parkin and Tomatis 1990: 165–7). Many of the previously controlled diseases such as malaria have made a comeback. While immunization has decreased many childhood diseases, adult tropical diseases have 'gone on a rampage' (*World Health*, May–June, 1993: 4). The expanding slums suffer from inadequate housing, water provision and sewage-disposal arrangements, aggravated by declines in public-health expenditure, poor allocation of resources, poverty and malnutrition, and the processes involved in modernization itself (Abel-Smith, 1990: 62; Cooper Weil et al., 1990: vii). To this list may be added the dumping of various toxic substances and the siting of unsafe industries in the periphery by core-based TNCs. As usual, poor people, women, children and adolescents have been disproportionately affected. Overall, the gap in the growth of GNP between core and periphery did not close in the 1970s (UN, 1978: 18). A study comparing the GNP of newly industrialized states with that of states in the core zone found that the gap had actually widened, although the GNP of all rose (Arrighi and Drangel, 1986).

Water projects of various kind have been favourite development projects. The World Bank has financed construction of over 11,000 large dams between 1951 and 1982, almost one-third of the 35,000 large dams in existence (not counting China). These projects, while often providing flood control and hydroelectric power, have however been the focal point of a number of environmental problems, including involuntary displacement of rural populations (for example, the Narmada Sagar Dam Project in India that is displacing 95,000 people), sedimentation and erosion, salinization and waterlogging of soils (with detrimental effect on crop yields), adverse effects on fish populations, and various negative health consequences (Dixon, Talbot and LeMoigne, 1989: 4, 26, 59–63). The worsened health effects have been listed as housing difficulties, overcrowding, rising costs of living, prostitution, and the introduction of new diseases into a local area during the immediate period of dam construction. Post-development problems associated with dam or irrigation projects included increased incidence of malaria and schistosomiasis. Data from the Akosombo Dam in Ghana demonstrated that the pre-dam prevalence of schistosomiasis in children stood at 5–10 per cent, while post-dam the prevalence was in excess of 90 per cent. These results have been paralleled elsewhere in varying degrees in Asia, Africa and Latin America (Hunter, Rey and Scott, 1982: 1127–9).

In 1978, in a move reflecting contracting contributions from member states, WHO and UNICEF endorsed a Health for All Policy, based on preventive and primary care (WHO, 1988a: 23). This actually represented a retreat from the broad aims of the 1950s, which were now seen as unlikely to be met, given the tendency to reduce international welfare spending in the light of the fiscal crises of the states and the rising costs of medical care (Abel-Smith, 1990: 62–3). The more limited preventive programme was afforded legitimation and inspiration by the successful campaign to eradicate smallpox which took place between 1968 and 1977 (WHO, 1988a: 14). The emergence of the primary health care approach changed the organization and management of maternal and child health (among other things). Health care was to be provided in an 'integrated manner' at the community level. Specialists were to provide backup at a higher level (WHO, 1980: 134). But if Health for All was a way to enable Third World governments to provide increasing amounts of health care cheaply, without relying on international welfare transfers, it was at first a failure. What the WHO did was to implement primarily the maternal and child health portion of this programme. In practice, this boiled down to dispensing birth-control pills and other forms of chemical contraceptive. This effort was especially strong during the early 1980s. While it was true that in peripheral areas there has been a much higher maternal death rate than in the core (WHO, 1988a: 30), there is no evidence that it has been improved by contraception. The contraception campaign was motivated by the fact that US feminists had begun to raise concerns about the long-term health effects of the pill, which led to its declining usage (Hartmann, 1987: 178). This represented a threat to sales (Chetley, 1990: 29).

Fears that world population was outstripping food supply were re-awakened in the late 1970s. In fact this particular 'food crisis' was a temporary phenomenon, brought about by drought in India and the Sahel, rises in the world prices of grain due to the US–Soviet grain deal, and a rise in fertilizer prices due to OPEC's increase in petroleum prices (Raikes, 1986: 165). The result was the stepped-up effort on the part of USAID, the World Bank, WHO, and various population control groups to encourage the use of birth control on the part of poor (and especially rural) women in the Third World by any means possible, including coercion. Scant attention was paid to the issues of the health and safety of the individual women involved (Hartmann, 1987: 132). This effort at population control was paralleled in China with the initiation of the one-child policy. While it might be argued from an environmental standpoint that there has been excess population, this must be set in context. In the Third World, children have been necessary additions to household labour forces. The effects of modernization have been to deprive households of male subsistence labour. This has necessitated longer working hours for women in order to make ends meet. The commercial cutting of forests has made the collecting of fodder for cattle, the collection of firewood, and provision of water more difficult (Jacobsen, 1993: 75). In this context additional children continued to be an asset. Yet as population swelled, peasants tended to expand their plots onto unsuitable terrain. The forest was further depleted and more time had to be spent gathering fuel and fodder (Durning, 1989: 43).

Environmental degradation thus spiralled. Industrial emissions of air pollutants such as nitrogen oxide, carbon monoxide, ozone, lead and sulphur dioxide were reduced in OECD countries between 1970 and the late 1980s. Industrial flight to the periphery brought with it, however, this very pollution that had been reduced in OECD countries (Ives, 1985: 172–86). But there was no reduction in various microtoxins, including but not limited to PCBs (polychlorinated biphenals), benzene, cadmium and arsenic, which are hazardous to the human central nervous system, carcinogenic and tetragenic. These were connected to specific industries, and were not well regulated or systematically controlled (OECD, 1991: 36). Apart from direct exposure of workers to microtoxins, these pollutants, carried in the air and the food chain, affected the population at large. There is growing evidence that such industrial/agricultural pollution has been a causative factor in such diseases as cancers, which are now the second largest cause of death in the core and parts of the semiperiphery (UNEP, 1991: 240–41). Furthermore, nitrates, caused by fertilizer runoff, appeared in the drinking water of populations in OECD states, a phenomenon deemed especially injurious to the health of infants (OECD, 1991: 182). However, the biggest growth in the amount of pesticide and fertilizer residues appearing in human tissue was found in the populations of the periphery (UNEP, 1987: 118–19).

2. *Education*

The United States led the core in the continued expansion of tertiary education. Although no single model emerged, what was created was the 'mass university', with all its opportunities but also with all its social stresses and upheavals (Schneider, 1982: 219–21). About one-third of all young adults in the core were enrolled at university. By the 1990s, the extended period of child dependency, for which we invented in the twentieth century the term 'adolescent', had been extended well beyond the age of twenty into a new dependent category, that of 'student'.

However, despite all the years of pushing education as a development strategy worldwide, educational profiles remained unequal, particularly at the university level. The secular, linear expansion of schooling remained unbroken from 1945 to 1990. The B-phase, however, marked a shift from celebrating the expansion to criticizing it: laments over poor quality, and consequently calls for revision of the curriculum, tightening of standards, elimination of frills, and going back to basics (Meulemann, 1982). Much of this translated into restricting access by reasserting the class-based discipline of education. There probably has been a deterioration of standards, as measured by teacher/student ratios, class sizes, and availability of educational materials. But the fiscal justification has served primarily to shift the burden of schooling costs from the state onto the market and the family, and to place the blame for the school system's inability to ensure job access on the students.

In decline, the United States found its model of mass, general education under attack. The United States high school has been unfavourably compared to secondary schools in Japan and the Federal Republic of Germany (Cremin, 1990). Core states that had liberalized access to the university during the A-phase found themselves overrun with students. The Federal Republic of Germany restricted enrolment to its medical schools. The United States raised the cost of tuition steeply at its public universities. More students therefore turned to enrolment in community colleges or to part-time enrolment. Enrolment of African-American male college students actually declined during the 1980s in the United States (National Center for Education Statistics, 1989: 159–61). The B.A. degree itself no longer served as a creditable credential for entry into a lifetime career. The young were cautioned that education would be endless and that one should expect to change careers. Thus, while the university had become more accessible, the market for its graduates did not necessarily improve.

The burden of the B-phase fell most heavily on zones outside the core. Demands for elementary schooling continued to grow even as the other sectors wrestled with outmoded structures. The most serious drain was that of emigration. At all skill levels the brain drain continued (Rehsche, 1981). The core was the greatest beneficiary since it drew on two zones. The educational system of the periphery had the highest expenses whilst its ability to pay was the lowest. Each national system of education helped to reproduce the class structure; and class, in turn, structured the school. At the world level, schooling helped to maintain the zonal division of the world economy. With the universalizing of primary and secondary education the maintenance of the core's unequal advantage became lodged in the universities.

Expansion of educational opportunities did not mitigate the

unevenness of the relative disadvantages acquired by those persons most badly affected by the destruction of welfare-statism and world-economic downturn. While the numbers of women enrollees in the university rose in most core and semiperipheral states in the 1970s, some of this increase represented primarily the incorporation of teacher training and nursing instruction within the university framework. Only in the USA at the Master's level have women reached equality in numbers with regards to higher degrees in general (Sutherland, 1991: 132).

Changes in the world-economy brought about changes in the notion of what constituted higher education. The B-phase saw a return to vocationalism, aggressive tracking, and cutbacks in liberal arts university programmes (Carnoy and Levin, 1985: 259–67). No country's educational system has resolved the problems of having too many students and too few jobs. Employers objected to the skills and attitudes university graduates offered (UN, 1985: 36), preferring people with technical skills and attitudes commensurate with those of good employees. The increasing so-called overeducation and unemployment of university graduates has caused governments in both the core and the European semiperiphery to respond by redefining higher education as existing to serve the economic needs of society. This has led to a redefining of tertiary education to include anything from vocational training to doctorate work in physics (Sutherland, 1991: 131). This trend was paralleled in the USSR and Eastern Europe in the 1980s (UN, 1985: 34).

In this situation women were as disadvantaged as ever, either clustered in humanities programmes which had little market value – this has been true in places as diverse as France, Sweden and Poland (see UN, 1991: 53) – or relegated to those educational and training programmes which reflect conventional women's job-market positions: at the lower end of the pay/status hierarchy in such fields as textiles, sales, domestic science, art, welfare work, administrative and clerical work, nursing, hairdressing, and food technology (Wilson, 1991: 207). The tendency in a number of countries to replace government grants with student loans has also worked against female students, as, even with comparable qualifications, women continued to earn less than men (Sutherland, 1991: 133).

The expansion of education in the core and semiperiphery has been paralleled in the periphery, even down to the gender gaps. But financial constraints have put a brake on quality: there were shortages of books and other supplies; teachers were not always well-trained. However, as the school-entering age cohort has continued to increase, pressure for continued spending on schooling has come from below. At the same time, governments have been reluctant to exert pressure at the top to expand educational institutions at the secondary and post-secondary level (UN, 1985: 34, 41). The absolute number of women who were illiterate was increasing (WHO 1988b: 21). In China the egalitarian aims of education that were advocated during the Cultural Revolution were abandoned in favour of the renewal of a more elitist system (UN, 1985: 34). This has included the exclusion of women (Mak, 1991: 44).

3. Food

The Green revolution accentuated regional disparities in wealth inasmuch as it was initially pursued in areas where irrigation already existed, such as the Punjab, coastal regions of Turkey, and the central lowlands of Thailand. Labour migrated to these areas, drawn by the initially higher wages at harvest times. This meant that less favoured regions were deprived of labour. As time went on, machinery replaced labour in Green revolution areas, and rural labour was displaced (Cleaver, 1979: 228–9; Kutzner, 1991: 68–9). The package of manufactured inputs that constituted the Green revolution required outlays of cash, requiring credit, which was generally available only to the relatively well-off (Bull, 1982: 83–4). At the same time, the Green revolution and large-scale commercial agriculture became avenues for the sale of pesticides which had been banned in the core zone: DDT, endrin, chlordane, heptachlor. The first cases of widespread poisoning and adverse environmental effects began to show up in the early 1970s in Karnataka, the Philippines, Bangladesh, and parts of East Africa. In these locales, pesticides entered the human system through the food chain – the poisoning of fish in rice paddies or the poisoning of fruit trees. The first human victims of this poisoning were the rural labourers (Bull, 1982: 63–79).

The agricultural strategies of low-income countries adversely affected women. While it was formerly assumed that poverty was shared equally by household members, this was now demonstrably no longer the case. Resources tended to be allocated in ways which favoured men and boys. This occurred as governments promoted privatization of property in favour of male heads of households. This was particularly true in Africa. In Asia, village 'commons' were allocated to government agencies and large landowners. In both these locations women formerly had in most cases had access to land through lineage heads and kinship ties. Access to credit, agricultural technologies, improved seed, and access to agricultural extension services often depended on land ownership. This barred women from competing in cash-crop schemes. At the same time there was little research and development of subsistence food crops (Jacobsen, 1993: 70–72). It is not surprising that the 'new varieties' reduced women's share in income, or that 'in few locations have [the new varieties] been women's crops' (Lipton, 1989: 190, 238).

All this is partially a reflection of the fact that there is an in-built gender bias in development policies that is shared by all, from development experts down to local peasants (and even their wives), the belief that women and the work they do are inherently unproductive. The ideology of the male breadwinner bringing home a valuable cash earning has become universal. Yet empirically the work of women – growing food for household consumption (80 per cent of it in Africa, 70–80 per cent of it in India, about 50 per cent of it in the Caribbean), drawing wood, fetching water – consumes 12–18 hours per day, and enhances the value of cash income by 30–60 per cent. In all regions about 50 per cent of cash-crop cultivation was done by women, although men tended to claim the profits (Jacobsen, 1993: 63–8).

This resulted in a gender bias in nutrition in that the proportion of food allocated to women and children by a household depended on their status, prospects and power in a socioeconomic context. Small girls in poor households were fed less than small boys, and their risk of death was therefore higher (Lipton, 1989: 236–7). Yet women, children and adolescents constitute three-quarters of the population of the periphery, and are the people most in need of good nutrition. Malnutrition of women before and during pregnancy, and of all children during the first five years of life, constitutes the single most important cause of health problems carried to later life (Nightingale, Hamburg and Mortimer, 1990: 116–72). Further, while it has been noted that the children of educated mothers enjoy better health (Nightingale, Hamburg and Mortimer, 1990: 125), it has been suggested that the relative disadvantage of daughters in terms of receiving food and medical care may actually be greater among better-educated mothers who deploy their nurturing skills selectively (Cleland and van Ginneken, 1989: 28). Studies based in India have shown that these types of gender gaps have widened since 1980. Similar patterns of discrimination have been found in Bangladesh, Nepal, Pakistan, and throughout the Middle East and North Africa (Jacobsen, 1993: 65).

As is now recognized even by official publications, malnutrition is more a function of income than of population growth (UN, 1993: 28). While real per-capita income rose by 53 per cent in the 'developing' states between 1960 and 1973, and by 66 per cent in the 'developed' ones (National Research Council, 1975: 4), poverty appeared to have increased or maintained previous levels in Africa, Asia and Latin America (Griffin, 1987: 7). The reasons for this have been listed as poorly paid or irregular employment (Frank, 1980, I: 13–14), growing rural landlessness (WHO, 1988b: 33), inappropriate development schemes, and ignoring the role of women in agriculture (Kutzner, 1991: 15, 27, 31; Griffin, 1987: 8–9, 18). Whatever the cause it seems likely that, given the growth of poverty and the rise in the prices of basic foodstuffs, malnutrition increased or, at the very least, stayed the same. In turn this suggests a deterioration in health. Malnutrition has been linked to acute and chronic infections such as malaria, hepatitis, tuberculosis, and low maternal and child health status (WHO, 1980: 128; Uyanga, 1990: 653).

A significant reversal in the downward trend of the provision of human welfare is dependent on the ability of states to overcome their so-called fiscal crises. But the biggest single source of the fiscal crises (in the context of a world-system in which states will not cut significantly their military expenditures) has been the increasing expenditure of governments on equalizing access to human welfare. It seems a vicious circle, difficult to dismantle.

Table 5.1 Adult literacy, 1950–75, and enrolment in primary school of 6–11 year-olds, 1960–88, by zones of the world-economy

	1950	*1960*	*1965*	*1975*	*1985*	*1988*
Percentage of adults who are literate						
Periphery	22	22		36		
Semiperiphery	68	76		87		
Core	98	98		98		
Primary-school pupils (million)						
Periphery		161	210	283	316	324
Semiperiphery		59	73	64	73	74
Core		47	50	47	39	41
Proportion of 6–11 year-olds enrolled						
Periphery total		42	50	59	73	73
Periphery females		31	38	49	64	64
Semiperiphery		95	98	99	100	99
Core		98	96	99	99	99

Source: UNESCO and World Bank yearbooks.

Table 5.2 Enrolment in secondary school of 12–17 year-olds, 1960–88, by zones of the world-economy

	1960	1965	1975	1985	1988
Secondary-school pupils (million)					
Periphery	19	36	88	132	144
Semiperiphery	9	16	40	47	49
Core	20	29	33	32	28
Percentage of 12–17 year-olds enrolled					
Periphery	6	9	16	25	26
Semiperiphery	31	38	57	67	71
Core	58	63	77	91	94

Source: UNESCO and World Bank yearbooks.

Table 5.3 Enrolment in tertiary school of 20–24 year-olds, 1960–88, by zones of the world-economy

	1960	1965	1975	1985	1988
Tertiary-school students (million)					
Periphery	1	3	7	12	13
Semiperiphery	3	5	8	11	11
Core	5	7	15	17	19
Percentage of 20–24 year-olds enrolled					
Periphery	1	1	2	5	5
Semiperiphery	6	9	15	21	23
Core	12	17	25	35	36

Source: UNESCO and World Bank yearbooks.

Table 5.4 The changing pattern of world grain trade, 1950–88 (million tonnes)

	1950	1960	1970	1980	1988
North America	+23	+39	+56	+131	+119
Latin America	+1	0	+4	–10	–11
Western Europe	–22	–25	–30	–16	+22
Eastern Europe/USSR	0	0	0	–46	–27
Africa	0	–2	–5	–15	–28
Asia	–6	–17	–37	–63	–89
Australia and New Zealand	+3	+6	+12	+19	+14

Note: Plus sign indicates net exports; minus sign, net imports.

Sources: FAO, *Production Yearbook*; US Department of Agriculture, 1988; Brown et al., 1989: 45.

Table 5.5 Annual percentage growth in world grain production, in world population, and in world grain production per capita, 1950–73 and 1973–86

Period	Grain output	Population	Per-capita output
A-phase, 1950–73	3.1	1.9	1.2
B-phase, 1973–86	2.1	1.7	0.4

Source: Brown et al., 1987: 133.

6

The Social Cohesion of the States

Georgi M. Derlugian

From 1945 to 1967/73: The Time of Universal Deliverance

The unprecedented economic expansion of the world-economy of this period was accompanied by an equally unprecedented expansion of the effectiveness and orderliness of the state structures in the world-system, including its 'actually existing socialist' zones.[*] It was also the time when the national liberation project in the Third World, expressed by the symbolic word 'Bandung', seemed to come to fruition. Various religious institutions, beleaguered by both the modern state and antisystemic movements, seemed to have reconciled themselves to the auxiliary role triumphant secularism had conceded to them, and began to see their common future in social work, the preaching of tolerance, and ecumenic dialogue.

The systemic disorders of the interwar period were suddenly over, although to many observers prior to 1945 the system had seemed damaged beyond repair. In short, paradoxically, in the 1950s and 1960s almost everyone appeared to feel that they could rightfully claim they were in the process of reaping success from the trials and tribulations of previous decades. This was true of the antisystemic movements (a term we define broadly to mean all those groups that pursue social change in ways that will fundamentally restrict or impede capital accumulation, the principal underlying process of the capitalist world-system). But it was even more true of the defenders of capitalism. It was true

---

[*] I am grateful to my friends and colleagues José Mota Lopes and Shuji Hisaeda for their materials on antisystemic movements and environmental degradation used in writing this chapter, and to Dieter Rucht for his meticulous editing.

not only of religious leaders (now almost universally speaking a language of *aggiornamento*), but even more so of the secularists. It was true not only of national liberation forces in the Third World, but even more so of the colonial powers that were seeking to dismantle their colonial systems in ways that would guarantee global order.

Around the world, the states had emerged from the disorders of 1914–45 enormously reinforced, especially in the core zones of the world-system. These core states as well as many semiperipheral states had already been expanding their domain since the latter third of the nineteenth century into what had previously been defined as 'non-state' spheres of social activity, advancing in five separate directions: (1) the public sector, by the nationalization of previously private capitalist enterprises; (2) macroeconomic management, or the use of taxing and spending powers of the state for the regulation of the macroeconomic situation, largely in accordance with Keynesian ideas; (3) regulation of economic and social activity through a panoply of specialized agencies with powers to set standards in many diverse fields, from airfares and telephone rates to the safety of drugs and children's toys; (4) social engineering aimed at eradicating politically determined 'social evils' (poverty, racism, sexism, drug abuse, adolescent delinquency, and so on); (5) welfare provision in its strict sense, with the state posing as guarantor of a certain minimal standard of living (King, 1983: 8–9).

These welfare-state tendencies have a continuous history from the Factory Acts of Great Britain in the 1840s, Napoleon III's social state, and Bismarck's policies in Germany, to Lloyd George's liberal reforms in Great Britain and those of Giolitti in Italy at the turn of the twentieth century. The most pronounced push towards the actively interventionist state, however, was the result of the enormous strain of the First World War and the ensuing phase of worldwide economic depression of 1929–39, which set the stage for the post-1945 welfare state.

The newest Leviathan was variously conceptualized. Marxists derided it as 'state monopoly capitalism', yet virtually praised it as the 'organized capitalism', 'ultra-capitalism' or, in the case of the Communists, as the 'last and the final stage, the eve of socialism'. The ultra-right theorists and the fascist or numerous para-fascist practitioners of the 1920s and 1930s claimed it as their 'new state' corporativism. It took a while for the liberal centrists to rid themselves of the verbal constraints of nineteenth-century 'Manchester' dogmas. But, by the 1930s, they had an openly statist agenda of their own. With the defeat of the fascist model, the liberal statist (Keynesian) vision would eventually become the prevalent agenda of the post-1945 period and serve as the ideological foundation of US hegemony. The process of cooptation of the antisystemic

Communist and revolutionary nationalist regimes in the periphery and
semiperiphery at the interstate level (Yalta and the tightly controlled
Cold War, but also the recognition of the legitimacy of the non-alignment
stance) turned the Soviet model of national-bounded, developmentalist
anticapitalism into what might be called the subhegemonic paradigm.
Needless to say, it was statist in the extreme, or, as Stalin put it, 'the
state in the USSR withers away not as a result of slackening of its
functions, as Marx and Engels supposed, but as a result of its maximal
strengthening' (*Problems of Leninism*, cited in Fursov, 1991: 87–8).

This more qualitative statist tendency was coupled with the quantitative expansion in the sheer number of sovereign states in the interstate
system. (Consider merely the multiplication in the number of embassies
and general staffs!) The vision of a sovereign state conforming to certain
'norms of stateness', a vision bred originally in the core but now applied
in full to the periphery and semiperiphery, was actively pushed by both
the new hegemonic power and its subhegemonic partner, the USSR.
Despite the intrinsically world-imperial character of the first and
foremost Communist state and the internationalist rhetoric which was
central to its Marxist legacy, it is significant that the Bolsheviks and
Stalin on two separate occasions felt obliged to conform to the norm
of self-determination of nations: first, in the early 1920s, by creating the
set of formally sovereign republics to be federated within the USSR, as
well as formally recognizing the independence of Mongolia and Tannu
Tuva; and again in the late 1940s, discarding the idea of the Comintern's
original vision of the USSR as an alliance open to any would-be socialist
state in the world. (Bulgaria did not become just a 'Bulgarian SSR', as
Lithuania did in 1940, even though it is said the Bulgarian Communists
were interested in this possibility.)

The national self-determination programme proclaimed simultaneously by Woodrow Wilson and Lenin in 1917 seemed to have
triumphed in the post-1945 abolition of colonialism and the vast increase
in the number of formally sovereign state entities, with modern – that
is, capitalist – bureaucracies either modelled on or directly trained by
the core 'capitalist' states or their semiperipheral Communist counterparts. To be sure, all too many of these newly independent or reborn
peripheral states of the 1950s and 1960s proved their newness/weak-
ness by creating formidable systems of police surveillance and mechanisms to extinguish internal opponents. The incontestable truth is that
it 'has become evident that the phenomenon [of state-organized terror]
has more global roots than [local cultures] and is tied to the increasingly
sophisticated and continuously expanding bureaucratic and technical
capabilities of states everywhere for violence and repression' (Bushnell

et al., 1991: 3). Gulags and Gestapos became, perhaps, the quintessential attribute of twentieth-century stateness, especially outside the infallibly lucky core zone.

Inside Western countries, the post-1945 accelerated economic growth and liberal sociopolitical arrangements resulted in an unprecedented degree of class peace. The situation in the world-system's peripheries, where dictatorial regimes prevailed, might better be described as relatively undisturbed stability. The main condition, and simultaneously the result, of this postwar phenomenon was the emergence of the full-blown welfare state in the core and the statist developmentalist model elsewhere. The median size of public expenditure in the core reached 29.6 per cent in 1962, grew to 32.7 per cent in 1970, and continued its unprecedented expansion up to 1980 when it reached 40.2 per cent. Comparable and even faster growth in public expenditure could be observed in most of the non-Communist states outside the core, though the composition of the budget was different there – fewer welfare payments, more investment in infrastructure and also in armaments (UN 1985: 89–90).

In what then seemed to be a major historical change, both Communist and social-democratic parties registered an unprecedented increase in their political influence and, at least apparently, in their capability of systemic transformation, either coming to power directly or serving as the principal and legitimated opposition. Soviet participation in the defeat of Nazism, and the Chinese Revolution in the Far East, seemed to make this tendency unstoppable. The 'world socialist movement' appeared to be strongly on the rise, with its Communist component registering its great strength in the 'camp of socialist countries' from the Elbe to the Yalu, but also elsewhere, notably in France, Italy and Indonesia. The social democrats were increasingly influential in Great Britain, in the smaller countries of Western Europe, and in the erstwhile British dominions. There was growing radicalization in the rest of the periphery, inspired by the achievements in China, seen as the right kind of foundation for a strong socialist movement in the Third World (Sweezy, 1949: 14). Maurice Dobb, for instance, writing in 1947 what was to become a classic of scholarly Marxism, had no hesitancy in asserting that,

> In the contemporary world property-rights divorced from social activity are universally despised and are on the defensive; whereas the working class has everywhere emerged stronger, more conscious of its strength and more purposeful than was ever the case before. The vision of a future rich in promise ... has begun to fire minds with a new faith and new hopes. (Dobb, 1964: 386)

In retrospect, however, these apparent successes of the anticapitalist movements appear rather to be a form of cooptation, after the first moment of potential revolutionary breakthrough. The antisystemic movements of the core and its immediate semiperiphery, in the form they took in the 1917–45 period (the 'old left'), were largely neutralized (or, learned the limit to which they could push without jeopardizing themselves and the system in which they existed). Most remarkably, this was achieved through 'statization' rather than outright repression, with the subsequent possibility of securing a share of the material advances of the post-1945 order and prosperity. Cold War geopolitics allowed the ruling Communist parties to remain in charge of the states they had already controlled, while offering to the Western Communist parties (which seemed to be on the verge of taking power in France, Italy and Greece) the lure of becoming an established opposition, with actual control over many local governments (notably in Italy and France). Social democrats in the 1950s were shedding their last relics of Marxism and generally 'Red' rhetoric and historical symbols prompted by their growing proximity to taking state power. The highly symbolic event was the adoption of the Bad-Godesberg programme by the German Social-Democratic Party in 1959 which marked the final takeover of the place of the old Liberal parties on the West European political gameboard by the direct ideological descendants of Eduard Bernstein's revisionists of the 1890s.

Civic movements were certainly rarer in the 1950s than after or before, but they also appeared much stronger in terms of numerical strength, organization, and accorded prestige. Both the relative rarity and the strength of civic movements were due to their affiliation with the established political parties, sometimes more than one at the same time, like the peace and anti-nuclear movement that drew support from the Communists, Social Democrats, left Catholics, and even some moderate conservatives. This pattern of multilateral cooptation helps to explain how such a universally popular and seemingly powerful movement of the time could be subservient to the Cold War geopolitics and ultimately so ineffective.

This created a formidable stability in the voting patterns in the Western countries, which showed no major change until the mid-1980s (see Figure 6.1). It is worth noting that, just as in the crime rates (Figure 6.2), the stabilization of the trend clearly predates the advent of the Kondratieff-A, being clearly pronounced since the 1920s and probably since the *belle époque* at the turn of the century. This seems to present graphic proof of the overall argument that the post-1945 order and prosperity were not merely the effect of the conjunctural

(Kondratieff) economic cycle or the end of the long world war of 1914–45 (the struggle for succession to British hegemony), but rather the cumulative result of several secular trends and cyclical rhythms.

Spreading from the new hegemonic country, the American model of labour relations (that is, management of class conflict) became the pattern first in Western Europe, then in Japan, and later on even within the broader semiperiphery. From the perspective of the labour movement in the core zone, this was arguably the right model in the late 1940s, more adequate to a situation characterized by the beginning of an economic expansion based on mass production, domination of the world-economy by US corporations, and a Cold War conception of global security. The project of global economic expansion was based on the re-creation of markets and growing levels of productivity, demand and consumption. It thus required the institution of increased wages, social security benefits, the distribution of bonuses, and expanded leisure time – the so-called Fordist 'regime of accumulation', as described by the authors belonging to the 'Regulation School' in political economy (see Aglietta, 1979).

In Europe as in the United States since the Depression, this model informed the type of relations between labour and capital that the Keynesian (or *dirigiste*) welfare state simultaneously made possible and required. As the expansion continued, it led to full employment; industrial wages more than doubled in the USA and did almost as well in Western Europe. These processes effectively eliminated earlier labour radicalism as well. In countries with historically strong Communist and trade-union organizations, large sections of the population (not necessarily, however, industrial labour) tended to support the left at local and national elections. This, however, became a conscious popular tactic of exerting pressure on the state and capitalist groups in order to obtain/preserve concessions and was certainly not a strategy of seeking the revolutionary overthrow of the regime.

From the perspective of capital the institution of the welfare state had started as an alternative to the political stagnation of conservatism, which gave rise to the insecurity of potential revolution. It became, however, also a central factor in the stability, economic growth, and sustainable high rates of net profit that the world-economy was able to attain throughout the 1950s and 1960s. It was not before 1967–73, when the expansion began to slip into depression, that the limits of the Fordist model became clear. On the side of capital, high wages and social benefits came to be seen as increasingly burdensome, given falling profits and the consequent acute competition that ensued; while, to the working classes, the previous incorporation of their organizations into the labour-management schemes led to the loss of bargaining capabilities that translated into steady decreases in real earnings over the following two decades.

Ecumenicism was the most overt expression of modernity's impact on the historical religions. Its intellectual underpinning was the idea of ideological pluralism, one of the quintessential ideas of modern liberalism. Ecumenicism was the product mainly of Western liberal Protestantism, other religious organizations participating in the dialogue for quite secular, even prosaic, reasons. For the Roman Catholic Church, the pinnacle of its accommodation to modernity became, undoubtedly, the council of 1962–64, usually known simply as Vatican II, and the pontificates of Popes John XXIII and Paul VI. Jews underwent sweeping secularization both by being progressively concentrated and integrated into the booming 'melting pots' of the USA and the USSR, and by accepting Zionism, *par excellence* a secularizing doctrine in that it made stateness a necessary fulfilment of Judaism.

Secularism was even more triumphant in its impact on the religions situated in the zones that became the Third World. Secularism became the *conditio sine qua non* for international and internal recognition of developmentalist credentials, the main venue of legitimation for the recently created/reconstructed states. The various religions located in these countries struggled defensively to maintain their position, with different degrees of resoluteness and zeal, be it Shinto in postwar Japan, Chinese popular cults after the Communist victory of 1949, the Hindu caste system under pressure from the Indian state and Congress nationalism, or Islam pushed aside by both the Shah in Iran and various Arab socialist parties (Ba'ath, the Nasserists).

However, there were, after 1945, fewer frontal assaults from the secularist movements coming to state power (with the notable exception of Albania) than had been the case in the 1920s in the USSR and Mongolia, Mexico and Turkey. Once having assumed an enlightened outlook and accepted a separation from the state, mainstream religious hierarchies enjoyed relative prosperity not only in the West but even in most of the Communist East.

Christianity and Islam continued their missionary advances in Africa, whilst Africans, under the conditions of decolonization, began to take control over the local state-bound religious institutions. Soon they would become aware of their growing worldwide numerical advantage over their co-religionists in the North and demand to be taken seriously in terms of institutional power (among Roman Catholics most notably, but also in many Protestant churches and Islamic Sufi orders) (Whaling, 1987: 84). In the 1950s, Southern 'reformulations' of Christianity and

Islam in terms of their nativist attitudes began to be socially and politically significant: the sprawling Afro-Christian 'Zion' churches in Africa, as well as in the Caribbean (Rastafarians, Afro-Brazilianists, and so on); Cao Dai, Hoa Hao, and other syncretist cults in Southeast Asia. These hotbeds of religious dissent were the direct prologue to the explosion of non-secular movements of protest in the 1960s among the non-White communities of the 'Northern' zone, most notably in the USA, Great Britain and South Africa.

The glory of the post-1945 state is best measured, perhaps, by its ability to contain and monopolize violence. As Gurr notes in his historical survey, crime in the Western societies was then at its 'all-time historic low' (1989, I: 43). Charles Tilly adds that, 'all parts of Europe moved in the same direction.... [B]reaking and seizing by civilians played a smaller part in European contention, while agents of national states became more and more heavily involved in such collective violence as occurred' (see Figure 6.2). With wars increasingly more frequent and regular since 1480, especially in the twentieth century, and tremendously more destructive, 'the sphere of state [has become] more and more violent, while civilian life has turned relatively peaceful' (1989: 93–4).

The explanation provided by Arlacchi for the secular downturn in crime rates in Italy appears similar to that of Tilly: the state effectively had monopolized violence and neutralized/absorbed its perpetrators. He says that, during the post-1945 years, 'the power of the Mafia lost not only its legitimacy, but also its autonomy and sovereignty through the State's reclaiming control over public order.... [The mafiosi's] integration into the State's administrative apparatus, through their appointment to the newly-formed public agencies, helped in many ways to neutralize the element of lawlessness and violence that the mafiosi had embodied' (1986: 79). The low was attained in 1962 with only a single Mafia-related registered murder in Italy.

Criminal and vigilante violence also dramatically decreased in the United States. By all accounts there was a precipitous decline in the numbers of vigilante gangs and instances of lynching since the late nineteenth century. After the infamous and overromanticized gangster wars of the Prohibition epoch, US gangsterism entered a period of business prosperity and relative orderliness. The Kefauver Committee's conclusion, reached in the early 1950s, that the criminals of the prewar period had 'entered the legitimate areas of business enterprise in approximately 50 areas' seems correct and provides an interesting contrast to the more bureaucratic Italian mode of integrating the mafiosi (see Nelli, 1987: 25–7).

The unprecedented mid-century extension of the functions of the state was expensive, and this was reflected in the growing levels of taxation and the increasing share of state budgets in the GNP. The report on the long-term trends in tax revenues of the OECD countries sums it up this way:

Though variations between countries are considerable, the main trends over the period from 1955 to 1980 were:

- — an increase in the ratio of total tax receipts to GDP;
- — a decreased reliance on consumption taxes and an increased reliance on income tax and social security contributions;
- — a large increase in the share of tax receipts from individual income taxes and employers' social security contributions with a smaller increase in the share of receipts from general consumption taxes and employees' social security contributions;
- — a large decrease in the share of receipts from taxes on particular goods and services (mostly excises) with a smaller decrease in the share of receipts from corporation income taxes and property and wealth taxes (OECD 1981: 2).

The same report states that in 1955, 'the unweighed average ratio [of tax levels to GDP] for the countries participating in the study was 24.7 per cent and 36.6 per cent in 1980, an average increase of around 0.5 percentage points per year, though during the second half of the 1960s the average annual increase reached nearly one percentage point.' But *nota bene*: 'Most of these trends have slowed down since 1975 and come completely to an end by 1977: tax levels and tax structures in 1980 were almost identical to those in 1977.'

This highest level of taxation in the 'developed market economies' was reached by UN estimates in the 1970s: 'around 43% of the GNP, with 67% for Sweden and 64% for Netherlands to 38% in the United States and 30% in Switzerland, as compared to 15% in the developing countries' (UN, 1985: 92). Estimates for the share of tax evasion and the 'shadow' economy in the core countries are patchy and conflicting. Nevertheless, authors of such estimates without exception agree on one point: from 1950 to 1970 it was negligible, or at least significantly less than the levels of the two following decades (see Pyle, 1989: 53; OECD, 1987).

We may observe similar trends toward consolidation of state structures all over the world in the same period. In large areas of the globe, statehood was crystallized for the first time, or after a long period of anarchy and localized non-state power relations. Latin American *coroneis* and *caudillos* disappeared along with traditional bandits, often integrated into state agencies as rural police, elected offices, or members of national party hierarchies. The Arab states of the Middle East passed from semicolonial dependency and tribal patrimoniality to more 'modern' independent states, through either republican revolutions or updating their monarchies, making them more compatible with the functioning of the modern world-system.

The guerrilla phenomenon that spread throughout the periphery in this period did indeed pose a challenge to the existing state order, but in the name of an alternative state order, a 'people's' state order. Vietnamese, Algerian, Angolan, Mozambican, Namibian, and most Latin American guerrillas fought with the explicit programme either of creating new states or of taking state power and using it as a tool for radically transforming the social order.

The Communist bloc that came into existence after 1945 included a good number of states that had previously been locales of internal troubles. The new Communist regimes first froze, then reformulated a series of endemic conflicts that had considerably hampered the functioning of the pre-Communist regimes in these areas. The endemic conflicts previously found virtually everywhere in these states, from the Balkans to central Asia to southern China, seemed to be buried under the weight of the Communist order, newly established through revolutions.

After an initial period characterized by extreme violence, the Communist states entered a period of relatively peaceful evolution. State and party bureaucracies, having rid themselves of the deadly dangerous instability of 'Stalinism with Stalin', expanded and flourished, being able finally to reap the fruits of their position and to enjoy them in peace and security. All Communist systems underwent decentralizations and horizontal expansions of their state agencies.

At the interstate level, especially in the core and adjacent zones, one of the most important consequences of the catastrophic experience brought by the two world wars of the twentieth century was arguably the delegitimation of war, if not its elimination. This served as some protection, if not for state regimes then at least for state frontiers. Significantly, since 1945 there have been hardly any declarations of war by one state upon another. Rather, there occurred (rather numerous) 'interventions', either by a country on behalf of a more or less artificial internal ally of the intervening power, or by the world community embodied in the United Nations. In all cases, it was assumed that the boundaries of the state would remain intact. In the core, the imagery of atomic extermination so vividly diffused in the 1950s and 1960s served as an unparalleled device for imbuing both political decision-making and mass consciousness with blocs of strong anti-war sentiment.

Of course, open military as well as 'covert action' interventions in intrastate and interstate conflicts were regularly undertaken by the superpower rivals or their allies, and in most instances were an integral part of the Cold War policing inside the two blocs. Such interventions tended to stabilize existing regimes. Interventions in the Third World, where shifting seams existed between the geopolitical blocs, were even more frequent. Such interventions were usually fairly efficacious (for example, Lebanon, 1958; Congo, 1961–64; Dominican Republic, 1965). There were very few attempted or successful conquests after the Second World War. India's forcible decolonization of the Portuguese enclaves of Goa, Damão, and Diu in 1962 is now a totally forgotten incident. Israel's expansion in the wars of 1948 and 1967 was widely discussed, precisely because of its exceptional nature. Yet these were almost negligible acts of conquest and annexation by the standards of previous epochs, and amazingly rare occurrences on a world scale.

Parallel to what had been previously observed in Europe, moments of mass violent upheaval in the periphery tended to be short, though far bloodier, with the state usually able to repress them. Outbreaks of mass violence that accompanied major political upheavals in some countries (India, 1950, 1956, and 1961; Tunisia, 1952; Iran, 1951–53; German Democratic Republic, 1953; Morocco, 1952–56; Hungary, 1956; Haiti, 1957; Laos, 1954 and 1960; Southern Rhodesia and South Africa, 1960; Uganda, 1963; Kenya, 1963) appear as mere blips in the pattern (Taylor and Hudson, 1972: 94–102).

The political independence of the new states of Africa and Asia was accompanied by a spectacular bloating of civil bureaucracies and military personnel. Creation of bureaucratic and military positions as a means of recompense to the activists of the pro-independence movements and of consolidating the social base of the post-colonial regimes was certainly commonplace, sometimes reaching exorbitant proportions.

The growth of national armies in the periphery was deliberate, and even hailed as a way of securing the newly acquired developmentalist statehood; very soon, it came to be seen as the last resort in managing and preserving it. Particularly extensive were the military build-ups of post-revolutionary regimes (Cuba, Vietnam, Iraq). Even more spectacular was the proliferation of modern intelligence services in the semiperiphery. Previously the exclusive privilege of the 'imperialist' core states before 1945, sophisticated intelligence agencies emerged all over Asia, from China and Korea to Iraq and Israel, and in Latin America (Cuba). The very notion of a Cuban or Pakistani spy network would have seemed a ridiculous oxymoron in 1917 or even 1950, but no longer in 1970.

In short, the data seem quite straightforward and unequivocal. In the period of 1945–1967/73 we observe the state everywhere expanded, expansive, and in all its glory. The long-term process of state formation and state expansion appeared to culminate in an unprecedented triumph. The whole globe was covered with sovereign states, and these appeared to be working in a quite satisfactory manner. For the first time there were almost no merely 'nominal governments' that could rule outside the capital cities only thanks to the support of local non-state and parastatal authorities (warlords, strongmen, sheikhs, tribal chiefs). There were certainly exceptions, such as the Colombian *violencia* of 1946–66, but they were indeed exceptional, often rather 'play-offs' of earlier struggles (Bergquist, Penaranda and Sanchez, 1992: 7–8).

Criminal and political popular violence was generally at an exceptionally low level and contained/absorbed by the state, which in its turn in most cases was able to (re)assert its monopoly of coercion. The various liberation and guerrilla movements in this period almost invariably were expressly statist in their outlook and they consciously reproduced typical state functions and attributes whenever and wherever possible (liberated zones, external missions, and so on). It should not be forgotten, furthermore, that the various national liberation fronts and peasant insurgencies effectively channelled popular violence and a great deal of criminality, reincorporating and reordering them in the framework of counter-state 'liberating coercion' and revolutionary violence. This function was explicitly noted and vaunted by one famous theorist of these movements, Frantz Fanon, who propounded the desirable role of the lumpenproletariat in a national liberation movement (1963: 119–64). The net gainer, of course, was the universal state order.

State bureaucracies grew worldwide, not only in the core, where they seemed to provide the necessary basis for sociopolitical stability, but also and especially in the newly independent states in the periphery and semiperiphery. Post-1945 geopolitical arrangements explicitly reasserted the principle of sovereign states and implemented it in practice in the tremendous expansion of the number of independent states (more than threefold, judging by UN membership). Three glorious decades indeed.

From 1967/73 to 1990: The Time of Undoing

Most of the trends discussed previously underwent dramatic change in the period following 1967, when the earliest signs of reverse began to appear, or after 1973, when troubles became obvious and general. Numerical patterns overwhelmingly show that 'something was happening'. For instance, the number of armed attacks jumped in 1967 to 3,400 from the median of 1,600 in the previous decade (Taylor and Hudson, 1972: 103–9). The incidence of mass protest and violence in the USA reached such levels that it put the hegemonic power far beyond the average of the rest of the core states and prompted one analyst to suggest that 'the decade of 1960 was perhaps the most tumultuous in American history' (Gurr, 1989: II, 109). We have in this period in the USA such singular events as the assassinations of both John and Robert Kennedy, Martin Luther King, and Malcolm X, as well as the urban riots, the Kent State University shooting, and the Wounded Knee rebellion, although the rate of fatalities tended to be much lower in the hegemonic country than in any Third World country. The new anti-racist, student and anti-war movements that swept the USA in the 1960s emerged largely despite the previous existence of orderly structured movements and organizations. Their untamed nature and very newness was their greatest source of disruptive power and therefore their greatest strength. Even though often addressing old issues, the rhetoric and tactics for a time regained full antisystemic flavour.

There was always a lag between the USA and the rest of the core. Western Europe and Australia, which had reached their historical lows of non-state violence and disorder already in the 1920s and 1930s, remained relatively peaceful through most of the 1960s, although crime rates had been slowly growing there, too. France and Italy of 1968 appear low in violence as compared to the tumults of the 1900s, the 1930s, and the late 1940s in France, or the 1920s and the 1940s in Italy (Tilly, 1989: 67–75). For Europe and Japan the years of most intense challenge to state authority were the 1970s, which were marked dramatically by terrorism (extremist national movements in Italy, the Federal Republic of Germany, Japan, France and Greece; but also separatist movements in Spain, the United Kingdom and France). By incidence of terrorist attacks these countries surpassed even Latin America, which the media proposed as the leading zone of terrorism of the 1960s.

Mafia-type criminal organizations expanded tremendously in the core countries, and at the same time their power declined (see Figure 6.2). This is not as paradoxical as it may seem. Crime became more dis-organized because of the growing competition between the mafia clans and the entrance of new criminal syndicates. Furthermore, organized crime simply sank into the ocean of popular, mostly teenager, crime and violence (Reuter, 1983 *passim*). Adolescent criminality became a typical mark of the sprawling deindustrialized areas throughout the North Atlantic core zones (Western Europe and the USA) and the East European Communist semiperiphery. Those might be simply street gangs, or the new, younger and meaner, variety of fan clubs in sports and rock music, or politically tinted groups, such as neo-fascist skinheads in the West and neo-Soviet 'Liubery' in Russia. Street gangs certainly lacked international connections and possibilities to conduct substantial criminal business. These functions were being overtaken in the late 1960s and 1970s by so-called large-scale crime, which in fact means essentially criminal multinational corporations (Arlacchi, 1986: 214–15). They were concentrated in the international trade in drugs and weaponry, but also in the illegal movement of labour, contraband conventional goods, and money transfers. Most experts agree that the creation of the Eurodollar market in the 1950s and the expansion of petrodollars in the 1970s offered unheard-of opportunities for organized crime, both in illegal transactions and in money laundering. The drug market remained the most profitable, the most violent, and the most inter-nationalized. The share of seizures of drugs by state authorities rapidly expanded in the period 1970–90, doubtless reflecting an ever-growing volume of the illicit drug trade (see Table 6.1).

This rapidly growing phenomenon is intimately linked with the expansion of non-controlled international finance markets, which is the locus where most of the criminal profits can 'go legit'. A good indicator of such activity seems to be the growth of investment in 'tax haven' countries, whose number increased between 1945 and 1980 almost tenfold. International organizations like the OECD have become increasingly worried about this mass tax evasion and the effects that it brings (see OECD, 1987). Talk about the necessity of creating an inter-national tax police has become persistent (see OECD, 1987: Preface). The scandal of the early 1990s concerning the Bank of Commerce and Credit International (BCCI) deepened the concern and may serve as a stimulant to more direct action.

Taxation had posed serious problems to virtually all states in the 1970s and 1980s. Historically, the levels of taxation have been growing over the whole period of the capitalist world-system (for the better-documented 'classical' case of France, see Figure 6.3). In the USA in 1887 federal receipts were about 3 per cent of GNP, driven largely by custom tariffs, given the non-existence of a federal income tax (not introduced before 1913). In 1937, US federal receipts reached 5.5 per cent of GNP, jumping to nearly 20 per cent after 1945 (Stein, 1988: x).

The year of 1969 was marked in the USA by an avalanche of press criticism aimed at the welfare state, which was then taken up in virtually all Western countries. Popular attitudes towards high government expenditures (which was a euphemism for distrust in the ability of the state to manage society) changed dramatically in the late 1960s and

1970s. The percentage of those critical in the USA and Great Britain jumped from around 50 per cent in the mid-1960s to nearly 80 per cent in the 1970s. All OECD countries faced a revolt of taxpayers in that period (beyond the fringe movements that always exist) in one or another form. The high-tax issues were taken up either by old conservative and populist parties, or by new anti-government movements, particularly in Western Europe (serving for the decade of the 1970s as the main component of the category 'other' parties, in Figure 6.1) (Peters, 1991: 157–9, 172–4).

Considerable tax reductions and rearrangements have been introduced through governmental reforms since the early 1980s by virtually all OECD members (or at least a rhetoric of thrift and competitiveness), as well as by such important semiperipheral countries as Mexico, Colombia, Indonesia and China (the list may easily be expanded). On the other hand, taxation has nearly disappeared in several dozen Third World countries due to the lack of state enforcement of the tax and tariff policies and their own personnel's 'endemic' corruption, as this pattern of individual accumulation through corporate elite control of the state agencies is usually called. In the 1980s an average civil servant's salary was providing for basic living expenses only for between one and twelve days a month in virtually all countries of tropical Africa, which clearly shows that the motivation for joining the bureaucracies must have been other than the direct salary (MacGaffey, 1991: 15). As a result, foreign aid became the main source of revenue for a sizeable group of peripheral states, while some were actually being run at one or another level by various international or local non-statal agencies (see Brodersohn, 1988: 118–24; for the Kurdish phenomenon, see van Bruinessen, 1992: 33–67).

Problems with collecting and legitimizing state revenues were directly related to the general trend towards relieving the state of many welfare and economic functions. The last significant nationalizations in the world took place in the mid-1970s and were connected to the victories of socialist-oriented regimes in the former Portuguese colonies, Ethiopia, Indochina, and some smaller Third World states. The French socialists nationalized some banks in 1980–81, but then launched 'decentralization' a few years later. In the 1980s the whole trend was dramatically reversed. Policies based on monetarism and neo-conservative tax reforms swept over the West and began to be the new dogma in the debt-stricken South, enforced by the IMF and creditor clubs. Extensive denationalization programmes have been undertaken in Great Britain, France, the Federal Republic of Germany, Italy, Sweden and Japan; and in the Third World in Bangladesh, Benin, Brazil, Chile, Dominican Republic, Ecuador,

Jamaica, Côte d'Ivoire, Kenya, Mexico, Pakistan, Peru, Portugal, the Philippines, South Korea and Zaire (UN, 1985: 97). After 1990, this list was dramatically expanded by sweeping privatizations in the ex-Communist countries.

Even in prospering Japan, a country in which the role of the state in the economy had been central throughout the modern era and in which state service was prestigious, 'the number of applicants for the civil service examination has been decreasing since 1979' (Sakamoto, 1991: 109). This phenomenon is attributed to the growth in prominence of the private corporate bureaucracies. The *UN Report on the World Social Situation* argues that:

> Renewed interest has emerged in recent years concerning potential roles for the private economy in providing public services – fire and police protection, supply of day-care, old-age home facilities, ambulance services, and even construction and management of privately owned prisons. The USA resorted to such services more than any other country – $66.8 billion had been spent only in 1980 at the state and local levels.... Both developed and developing countries increasingly recur to private sector for the supply of utilities services – electricity, gas, water. (UN, 1985: 93–4)

In many countries such typically public services as the postal service, telecommunications, and even jails and police have been increasingly privatized. By the estimates of the *US News and World Report* (12 November 1990: 12), in the USA every third security guard is private, hired by either communities or corporations. It is estimated that by the year 2000 the share of private guards in the overall police force will reach one-half. Analogous processes in the former Communist countries are even more dramatic. In Russia alone by the beginning of 1992 there were more than 100,000 registered private detectives and guards, and a thriving market for security devices and trained dogs (*Nezavisimaya gazeta*, 9 May 1992: 6).

This is exactly the marketization of previously state-exclusive functions so much discussed and often praised during the 1980s. Although the functional effectiveness of such public-to-private transfers may be reasonably satisfactory in some cases, the overall result is to undermine further the institutional pillars of modernity without offering any obviously better alternative. In a nutshell, public good – the most fundamental one in the case of law and order – becomes private or corporate privilege.

Territoriality and sovereignty, the two central intertwined principles of the interstate system, are coming increasingly into question. Western European integration was the main empirical argument for most authors.

In a famous description given by Peter Katzenstein (1987), the Federal Republic of Germany was termed 'a semi-sovereign state', deeply penetrated simultaneously by the NATO structures from above and by the federal *Länder* from below.

There were, however, considerable theoretical difficulties in conceptualizing the processes of globalization and regionalization, construed as 'overcoming the state'. The idea emerged from empirical observations that led various authors to conclude that a global authority was either very desirable in the 'interdependent and more complex' world (for instance, Walker and Mendlovitz, 1990), or as something already in the making (see Gilpin, 1975; Keohane, 1989; Camilleri and Falk, 1992). Concerning the state and globalization/regionalization, called by some authors the 'new federalism' (see D'Amico and Piccone, 1991: 2–12), there is a slightly different agenda organized around the concept of postmodernity. It was quite rapidly assimilated into the political science mainstream, itself a sign of conceptual crisis (see Apter, 1987; Ruggie, 1993).

There appears to be major confusion or evasion about the crucial question of why the current transformation of 'the state-based organization of power is happening. Most of the argument is reducible essentially to a snapshot of reality not grounded in coherent theory. This is exactly what Ruggie captures by saying: 'Prevailing perspectives have difficulty describing and explaining the process ..., but none suggests that it is not occurring' (Ruggie, 1993: 141). Shall Minerva's owl fly at dusk again? There is even more confusion about the antisystemic movements, the major source arguably being the residual political and ideological commitments of observers. As pointed out by Andrei Fursov:

> one of the main, if not the main, failures of the left (especially Communist) in theory was its ultimate inability to conceptualize the social nature of the movement itself, and particularly the system of power that had been institutionalized under the [significantly endless misnomers] such as 'socialist camp', 'communist regimes', 'Soviet-type societies', etc. (1991: 30)

Antisystemic movements have been rapidly losing their capability of intervention as main actors of social change since the late 1960s, not only in achieving their objectives but also in terms of their cohesion, mobilization, organization and strategies. In short, they have been declining, even disappearing.

This decline was common in slightly different degrees to political parties of Communist or social-democratic designation in or out of power; to labour organizations, whether or not linked to parties; and to former national liberation movements. If looked at since 1945, the trajectory of Communist organizations and political regimes in terms of their influence registered a steady increase (with an internal crisis of de-Stalinization in 1956, but then a recovery of the trend) up to the late 1960s when it started gradually to decline (1968 in Czechoslovakia and Poland, institutionalization of broadly defined 'dissident anti-politics'), falling precipitously after circa 1980 (the debt crisis; strong Western reaction in all zones newly 'associated' to the socialist bloc – Afghanistan, Nicaragua, Indochina, Angola, etc.; cruise missiles and the end of détente in Europe; irrepressible Solidarity in Poland and the beginning of generational transition in the Soviet leadership) – a trend of which the collapse of the USSR and the Eastern European regimes in 1989–91 can be seen as the ultimate confirmation. While socialist parties in some countries benefited from the relative decline of Communist parties at first, their growth reached its apex in the early 1980s; then, as the decade closed, they began to be affected as well by the decline in the credibility of welfare-state programmes.

In the 1960s all these issues were forcefully taken up and radically expanded and reformulated by the new social movements worldwide. In the 1980s the 'Green' movements came to be their first serious electoral expression. In the late 1980s, they began to appear as a contender to fill the niche of the old left parties. They registered a transient political success, first in the Federal Republic of Germany, then in other Western countries. They were then shaken by internal debate over where they would fit on the political checkerboard: on the far left, as a replacement for the old left, or as a new centrist force. These debates weakened them. This fact hardly signified an unmitigated defeat of the Green movement. The same is even more true in the case of human-rights activism. To be sure, environmentalist, anti-war, women's, minorities', or generic human-rights concerns were not exactly new, dating back in fact to the nineteenth century. Yet, until the 1960s they remained dependent discourses of liberalism, with Marxists and revolutionary nationalists usually being at best ambiguous about these issues, which were considered subordinate to the main cause of struggle. Elitist groups and personalities (Alfred Nobel, Bertrand Russell, Anatole France, H.G. Wells, Fritjof Nansen, and so on), or liberal Western governments and intergovernmental organizations (League of Nations, the UN and its subsidiaries), had been the major promoters and normsetters of pacifism, antidiscrimination, nature preservation, and general 'humane conduct', especially in times of war (Luard, 1967: 7–22).

The entry of the new social movements into the political arena seemed at first a radical innovation. But one could argue that they were almost instantly incorporated into the hegemonic liberal discourse and organizational frameworks of the core states, as reflected by the number of Nobel prizes won by the activists, invitations to address the UN and various prestigious conferences, or, in the case of the Soviet bloc dissidents, the extensive use that they made of the Cold War propaganda machine in the West. Nonetheless, by recognizing and promoting people like Martin Luther King, Havel, Mandela, Sakharov, and various civic resisters of the military regimes in Latin America and Asia, the core states had to accept and take into consideration their agendas, at least publicly. The fact that self-established watchdog NGOs, such as Greenpeace and Amnesty International, have been able to transform themselves into influential global agencies is certainly of major importance. Successive democratization waves that swept away or critically eroded dozens of dictatorial regimes of all sorts worldwide since the late 1970s were triggered by the Kondratieff-B squeeze. The concrete historical forms that the subsequent popular movements, reforms and revolutions took, however, were quite clearly far more part of the legacy of the politics of the 1960s than outgrowths of the post-1945 liberal discourse of US hegemony.

As to the former national liberation movements of the peripheries, a trajectory of decline, degeneration and collapse was equally pronounced since the mid-1970s, albeit with far more terrible cruelty, as always in the wretched zones of the world. Generically speaking, these movements found the difficulties of national development vastly aggravated by the worldwide economic stagnation, and the structural adjustment programmes imposed by the West. Joining the allegedly alternative socialist world-system seemed less and less attractive, as it became ever clearer that it was at most a geopolitical bloc within the world-system, and precisely lacked the economic foundations to become a system on its own. The Bandung era of Nasser, Tito and Castro was over. After the great offensive, the battlefield was littered with human and institutional wreckages and belonged to the marauders, such as Saddam Hussein, Yugoslavia's ex-Communist warlords, or Africa's lumpen-militariats, as Ali Mazrui wryly branded them (1973).

The last fortresses of states whose regimes derived from national liberation movements of one variety or another were besieged by anti-secular militants of despair (India, Egypt, Algeria, Sri Lanka, Tunisia, Peru, Tadjikistan). After 1979 an increasing number of antisecular movements were successful in storming the states (Iran, Sudan, Afghanistan) or, failing that, in being invited into the ruling coalitions (Israel, India, Pakistan, Turkey, but also the United States). Mainstream religious organizations worldwide have also been targets of religious militants, paying the price for their cohabitation with the secular authorities and accommodation to lay ideas. Religious fundamentalists represented genuine protest but hardly emancipatory movements, at least in contemporary terms. On closer look, it also becomes obvious that they have not been trying to reverse history, as is usually asserted about them, but rather to take over the discredited national developmentalist project and reformulate its values and social base (see Abrahamian, 1992, for the paradigmatic case of Iran; Sivan, 1992, for the Arab countries; and Hewitt, 1990, for the *Comunidades eclesiásticas de base* in Brazil). Essentially, the peripheral fundamentalists have tried to take over the cause of development just as the nationalists and the socialists of the previous period were in fact dropping it. Hence the stress on both the grassroots community of marginalized anomic Third World dwellers and the mythologized notions of religious meta-communities – Islamic Umma, Sikh Halsa, the caste order in Hinduism, the Christian brotherhood in liberation theology.

In the core, probably the first signs of the drift from secularism came in the bizarre form of the rapidly proliferating 'new religious movements' based on an avid interest in non-Abrahamic practices and doctrines. These movements recruited mostly among the younger generations in Europe and North America. In contrast to the theosophic elitism such movements exhibited at the turn of the twentieth century, the new mysticist groups actively proselytized and attracted quite a size-able mass base (tens of thousands of 'full-time' adepts with arguably hundreds of thousands of short-term followers). This phenomenon received an enormous amount of attention. Robbins has compared the impact of the 'new religious movements' on the sociologists of religion to 'the discovery of some 300 new species of lizard, including a few dangerous man-eaters, on a scholarly association of herpetologists' (1988: 13). The attention was, however, more than academic. At least in the core countries, most people still expected secularization and the Enlightenment to be irreversible. The explosive growth of the militant fundamentalist movements in the 1970s and 1980s came to shatter this belief and instil gloomy expectations of the return of the Dark Ages (incidentally, very similar to the now half-forgotten fears of a 'new obscurantism' in the interwar period, the previous Kondratieff B-phase). Fundamentalists certainly reflected an antisystemic strategy that challenged the West and its capitalist modernity, and saw the modern-izing state as the most oppressive aspect of it. Yet it is hard to conceive of these movements as a full-weight replacement to the national libera-tion movements. As with the Greens in relation to the 'old left', or the East European democrats to the Communists, the new stage resembles thus far more a life-after-death of the old movements and ideas than the dawn of truly new ones.

Considering the antisystemic movements in relation to the states, it seems ironically that the states have been losing their direct adversaries precisely since, and in large part because of, the revolutionary upheavals of 1967–73. Aside from the terrorists, who may be judged as still defiant but non-durable, other antisystemic movements no longer devote a central place to the state in their *Weltanschauung*. To use one of Lenin's typical phrases, this may 'reveal to *all* countries something – and something highly significant – of their near and inevitable future' (Lenin, 1975: 291–2).

Even the terrorist organizations differ from the older guerrilla movements in one very important sense. If the guerrilla movement of the pre-1967 epoch had essentially an 'old left'/national-liberation programme – that is, had as the most important middle-term aim the seizure of state power– most of the post-1967 terrorist organizations in both North and South did not envisage such goals. They were trying instead (somewhat like the underground movements of 1815–48 in Western Europe) to create conditions for a dramatic change in, or the total demise of, the state and social order as such. If the terrorism of the 1970s and 1980s represented an aftershock of 1968, then the distance between the latter and the earlier twentieth-century guerrillas may be compared to the distance between the new antisystemic movements and the old ones.

In addition, the murky world of espionage seems to have shared the difficulties of this time of troubles. The CIA and MI5 underwent major public scandals. The Soviet KGB and the Israeli Mossad and Shin Bet lost much of their mystique and myth of omnipotence due to numerous embarrassing defections and domestic power struggles. The competition offered by the newcomer special services of the Third World, terrorists, and international criminals enormously complicated the spy universe. The net result was that these espionage services began to lose some of the unquestioned aura and national legitimacy they had previously enjoyed, a further reduction of the real power of the states.

The arms race appears to have accelerated in the 1970s and early 1980s. Obviously, more and more states, after reacting to the new instability of the early 1970s by expanding their apparatuses of coercion and eventually embarking on internal and external war – Chad and Chad/Libya, Nigeria, Uganda/Tanzania, Somalia/Ethiopia, Sudan, Western Sahara/Morocco/Mauritania in Africa; 'internal wars' in Argentina, Uruguay, Chile, Colombia, Venezuela, Peru, Bolivia, Guatemala, Nicaragua in Latin America, plus the 'externalized' Falkland/

Malvinas South–North clash of prophetic significance; the entire Middle East with the special case of Lebanon; Afghanistan, Indo-Pakistani conflicts, Cambodia/Vietnam in South and Southeast Asia. Military takeovers also grew, although there is no clear pattern in the simple number of such events. By 1987, according to the above-cited UN report, there were fifty-nine military governments worldwide.

Yet very soon this trend towards military-bureaucratic regulation would be reversed in spectacular waves of worldwide 'democratization'. By 1990 there were hardly any military regimes in Latin America, while elsewhere a growing number of both weak states (Togo, Mozambique, Tanzania) and stronger states (South Africa, Turkey, Thailand, South Korea, Taiwan) began to democratize – that is, rely more on negotiation within the political and economic elites rather than outright military and police repression. This shift was not without certain reversals (Algeria being perhaps the most notable, but there was also the imposition of nationalist dictatorships in many former Communist states where national uprisings of the late 1980s helped to destroy the previous monopolies of state power). The effects of democratization on state cohesion seem mixed at best. While in some states situated in the zones of exonomic expansion (Chile, South Korea and Taiwan) democratization obviously made the states more legitimate in the eyes of their subjects, in many more places the trend appeared more like a desperate attempt of the local elites to prop up their positions in the changing world-system by explicitly subscribing to the dominant ideologies and thus getting external recognition. Many peripheral and semiperipheral states have been increasingly unable to control their territories, or have collapsed altogether. Between 1978 and 1990, Lebanon did not exist as a state. Lebanon was restored under Syrian 'proconsulship', but this kind of stabilization may be viewed rather as an instance of a conquest impossible to legitimate and thus as a sign of destabilization of the interstate system. As of 1990, there was no Liberian, Afghan, or Somali state, with few viable prospects for their restoration. The wars in former Yugoslavia and the conflicts in the former Soviet republics became the most 'northern' of the 'southern' state collapses, directly endangering a significant part of the core (Western Europe).

If one takes as an indicator one of the most respected compendia of indicators, the *UN Report on the World Social Situation*, we note that between 1952, when it began to appear, and 1982 it mainly consisted of chapters on demography, health, education and urbanization. In 1982 the structure of the report underwent a significant change. Chapters on civil and political rights and disarmament were introduced for the first time, and in the Preface a very interesting new tonality made its appearance:

Recent economic setbacks have not only dampened expectations but also exposed the limits of the role of the nation-state as a manager of socio-economic change.... Various forms of political instability occurred, especially where Governments were still faced with the formidable task of building simultaneously a nation and a viable economy. Often, more authoritarian types of government emerged as a response to this instability. It also took the form of decline in public and private behaviour. The weakening of various forms of authority and of accepted values which bound individuals together has gradually generated both a greater individual freedom and a more fragile society.... Attitudes towards public authorities were often marked with defiance. Laws, regulations, taxes were increasingly questioned and evaded. Alcoholism, drug addiction, criminality, irresponsibility vis-à-vis fellow men and the community were seemingly more frequent in many societies with different cultures and different levels of development (UN, 1982a: 1–2).

With the expectable lag in terminology and style proper to this international body, called upon to express nothing less than the aggregated opinion of global humankind, the report succinctly sums up the trend we have been trying to detect in its multiple and numerous manifestations. In 1985 the *UN Report* included yet another new chapter, 'Violence to Groups and Individuals'. Two more interesting statements were made:

Religious revival, however, appears to be a strong factor in several current civil wars and conflicts.... Also, the long-term trend of secularization, or laicization of the social order, has been increasingly questioned and, in some instances, reversed....

The welfare state was looked at critically.... In many developing countries financial resources became so scarce that ... these states had to face a struggle for survival (UN, 1985: 25–6, 89).

One of the expressions of this mounting instability and weakness of the state is undoubtedly the much lauded and hoped-for global democratization of the late 1980s and 1990s. Another indicator would certainly be the pressures for human rights and the new centrality of so-called 'minority issues', which came into the limelight in the 1970s, and now proliferate not only in the core but elsewhere in the world-system. In the case of the former Communist countries of Eastern Europe, it is most apparent that democratization is primarily a result of collapse of the states, and of social disorder.

The resistance of the core states to absorb ideologically the minorities of 'colour' (from the South) has led to calls for 'multiculturalism', which are in turn resisted. As a result, the states find themselves caught between two fires – the 'multiculturalist' pressures from the increasingly more effectively organized 'Southern' minorities on the one hand, and xenophobic Christian or even pre-Christian fundamentalist right-wing populists on the other.

Liberalism as the dominant ideology of the world-system is thus caught in numerous ideological and political complications that previously it could largely gloss over or ignore altogether. Minority rights undermine the 'one man, one vote' principle; affirmative action contradicts meritocracy; the state is viewed by the right-wingers as 'unduly meddling', and by the minorities as inadequate, untrustworthy and hypocritical.

What is at stake is the whole Jacobin project of political modernity – that is, nationalism as the primary mechanism of uniformization and articulation of populations into modern state apparatuses. Indeed, communities have to be imagined to become real, and when they are imagined as nations (Anderson, 1991) the principle of nationalism demands that ethnic units become congruent to political units – every Ruritanian upon becoming conscious of being Ruritanian must fight for all Ruritanians – usually regardless of the price (see Gellner, 1983). Meanwhile, the modern world-system appears to allow for far fewer states than there may be contenders. Thus, the very proliferation of nation-state-seeking undermines the state-imposed order.

More than sixty states – that is, more than one-third of the total, according to UN estimates – face grave and immediate separatist dangers. Very few separatist movements in the period since 1945 have succeeded in creating full-fledged states of their own (the most notable example being Bangladesh, which had the unusual advantage of great physical separation from the other part of Pakistan). However, the collapses of Yugoslavia and the USSR in 1991 brought into existence a sizeable number of new internationally recognized independent states, and brought in its wake the dissolution of Czechoslovakia.

Warlordism seemed once again to be rampant throughout the more and the not so distant zones of the world-system. Many guerrilla movements degenerated into this form of organization of power in the conditions of state collapse. Parts of the Philippines, Cambodia, Burma, Thailand, Sri Lanka, India, Afghanistan, Lebanon, Chad, Uganda, Mozambique, Angola, Somalia, Liberia, Sudan, Ethiopia, and now considerable stretches of the former Yugoslavia and USSR were being ruled by armed groups with or without nominal political agendas.

State decentralization has been another side of the same process. This phenomenon is much more general than the students of Western public administration have usually believed, since the re-emergence of 'traditional' or fundamentalist structures of public power in the South for them has been generally classified as anthropology, and hence divorced from the trend in the core zones towards localization of governance. The tendency, already present for the reasons described previously, has been much reinforced by the 'new openness' imposed through the IMF structural adjustment policies, which reversed most of the statist-nationalist policies of the previous A-phase. In the periphery and semiperiphery, the dismantling of the state, in favour of lower 'sub-state' and higher 'supra-state' levels was painfully obvious. The post-colonial putative nation-state was becoming merely a legitimizing mask for both levels. In this light, Baker poses the tantalizing question: 'The economic weaknesses and vulnerability of the colonial state at independence ... have persisted. Will the [post-colonial] state now become the *midwife of the new colonialism?*' (1991, 362: emphasis in original). The attempted intervention in Somalia, which was certainly meant to become a pattern of such neo-colonial humanitarian interventions, has shown that even this warning might be far-fetched. Imperialism requires far more political will and resources than were available in the end of the US hegemonic cycle, especially after the complicit USSR was no. longer a player in the peripheries.

At the same time, the planetary ecosphere and everything related to it ascended during the 1967–90 period to the position of being both the biggest scare and the biggest hope of humankind. By the beginning of the 1990s, environmentalism as a social phenomenon appeared to be deeply divided into several competing and disjointed currents. Some appeared quite antisystemic, but others clearly belonged to the core's Establishment. Furthermore, environmentalism operated at all levels, but it conspicuously tended to gravitate towards putting its aims above and below the nation-state, either in cosmopolitan global environmental agencies, private and international, or at the local levels of grassroots pressure groups within local communities or provinces. Though there were important examples of statist environmentalism, it was rather exceptional, typical only of countries with a traditionally strong state separated from the civil society, such as France (de Montbrial, 1990: 363).

The prevailing currents of environmentalism since the late 1980s were global environmental management and global ecology. In one or another form they were supported by the immense resources of Northern capitalist groups, state governments, and interstate agencies. This type of environmentalism clearly represented the latest version of liberal ideology in its two variants: conservative neo-liberalism and social-democratic reformism. It was apparently hoped that this brand of technocratic environmentalism in tandem with the slightly reformulated developmentalism of 'sustainable development' might represent a viable alternative to the crisis in the 'ideological cement' of late-twentieth-century capitalism.

This indicates one direction of possible future development in the capitalist world-system. The closely knit web of international and major nation-state bureaucracies, both scientific and managerial, public and private, may seek to legitimize themselves by assuming the functions of global management and security. Environmentalism, with its live human passion and exceptionally wide public acceptance and support, with its extremely successful propaganda campaigns and universally appealing slogans (nothing less than 'Save the Earth!'), its heroes and martyrs (Chico Mendes, Joy Adamson, Vladimir Chernousenko), may provide an exceptional opportunity for possible political restabilization in the 'post-modern' fragmentation and morass.

Indeed, 77 per cent of Americans polled in 1989 responded that their purchase decisions would be affected by a company's reputation with regard to the environmental issues (Miller, 1991: 216). DuPont is currently leading the way in advertising its 'eco-image'. In a spectacular move, US tuna producers adopted expensive dolphin-safe policies before they were mandated. In another example, sales of beneficent insects in the USA have tripled between 1985 and 1990, while the medical waste disposal industry was expected to further increase by $5 billion by 1995 (Miller, 1991: 216). Even more impressively, a 1989 *New York Times* poll showed that 80 per cent of regular US voters agreed with the statement: 'the standards for protecting the environment cannot be too high, and continuing improvement must be made regardless of costs'; in 1981, only 45 per cent agreed with this (Miller, 1991: 206).

It should be added that eco-safe technologies have been rapidly becoming another production advantage providing for monopolistic rent, while the enormous costs of an eventual global clean-up might offer taxpayer-sustained markets (managed through states or international agencies) capable of serving as a substitute for the increasingly discredited military-industrial Keynesianism of the twentieth century.

Curiously, modern-day ecological campaigns in many ways resemble Abolitionism, another great humanistic issue that had moved in the late eighteenth century into the centre of public debates to become a major tool of imposing British hegemony, and provided the Northern elites of the United States with an appropriate discourse in their struggle to become a world power. As in the case of slavery, the defence of an anti-environmental stance has today become an arduous task, the sign of an eccentric conservatism.

As compared to Abolitionism, the biggest problem with global environmental management is not even that the whole agenda may be too easily transformed into an antisystemic tool, or messed up by an effort of the ruling groups of the South, which might possibly unite on a platform of sustainable development and forcefully demand their share of the 'post-industrial' eco-safe technologies instead of the outdated smokestacks. After all, successful ideologies of historical capitalism have invariably been revolutionary in style, thus balancing close to the edge of antisystemic consequences.

The problem is that environmental management does not seem revolutionary enough; hence it may be an immanent failure from the outset. The crusade to save the Earth doesn't seem feasible given the present lack of coordinated political will and available resources among the possible contenders for an eventual future global hegemony, which leaves us with another very big question mark in the interrogation about the future.

Table 6.1 World heroin and cocaine seizures, 1947–82 (kg)

	Heroin	Cocaine
1947–66 (annual average)	187	41
1967–74 (annual average)	953	625
1975	1,708	2,406
1976	2,583	2,419
1977	2,377	3,977
1978	2,441	5,391
1979	2,070	8,365
1980	2,510	11,820
1981	5,613	9,541
1982	6,153	12,092

Source: UN Division of Narcotic Drugs MNAR/1/1984, Review of Trends in Drug Abuse and Illicit Traffic. Cited in Arlacchi, 1986.

Figure 6.1 Stability of the share of the vote among the generic political currents of twentieth-century Europe

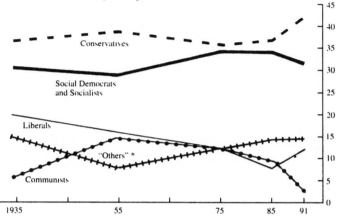

* "Others" are agrarian, nationalist, extreme-right and left, or Green parties.
For the 1980 s the major part of the "others" are fascists.

Source: The Economist, 23 November 1991: 79.

Figure 6.2a Italy, annual rate of murders and attempted murders per 100,000 population (1881–1990)

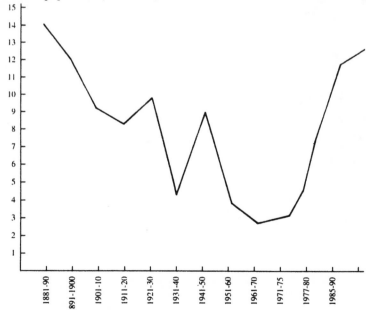

Source: Arlacchi 1986: 86; New York Times, 10 October 1990: A4.

Figure 6.2b   Homicide trend in the United States, per 100,000 population (1900–1985)

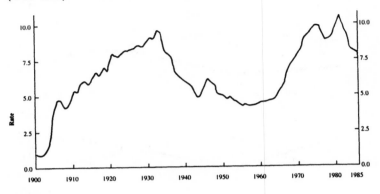

Source: Harries, 1990: 11.

Figure 6.2c   The common trend in crimes of theft and violence in Western societies (1830–1970)

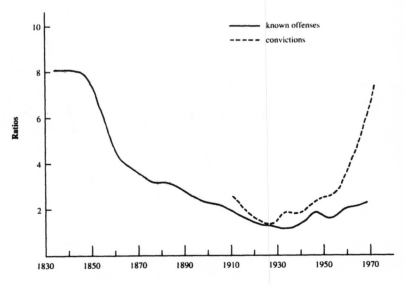

Source: Gurr, 1989: II, 22.

Figure 6.3 Total French taxes, 1597–1966, stated as worker hours of wages and worker hours per capita

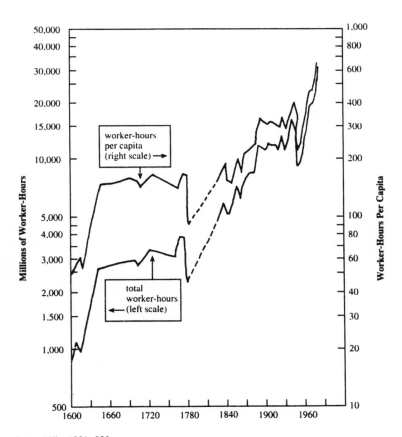

Source: Tilly, 1981: 230.

7

Structures of Knowledge

Richard Lee

A principal characteristic of the modern world-system has been that science has become the summit and the model in the hierarchy of its intellectual disciplines. This 'structure of knowledge' attained definitive ascendancy over religious, spiritual, transcendental 'belief systems' as the dominant mode of human understanding only in the nineteenth century, in complex articulation with the social and political struggles of the time and their institutional/intellectual manifestations. The old belief systems did not disappear. They have taken their place within the framework of a binary opposition, science/humanities, which has constantly deepened through internal, although not uncontested, transformation.

In 1959, C.P. Snow gave voice to a widespread perception of the contemporary situation: 'Literary intellectuals at one pole – at the other scientists, and as the most representative, the physical scientists' in which 'the feelings of one pole become the anti-feelings of the other' (1965, 4: 11). Others, however, have argued that between the two poles there has emerged a 'third culture': the human or the social sciences.[1]

The crisis of the long-term process reproducing this structure is at present manifest in its inability to contain internal contradictions. What we shall spotlight is the unfolding of the socio-cultural legitimation of conflicting modes of knowledge formation intimately related to (and not merely correlated with) economic and political life. Thus we hope to illuminate some of the shadowy premises grounding the seeming 'naturalness', or inevitability, of the structures of power and accumulation

---

1. See Lepenies, 1988, for the establishment of that 'third culture', the social sciences (especially sociology), between science and literature; see Williams, 1983: 87–93, for the concept of 'culture' itself.

which have been dominant during the last half century. We shall thus examine the intellectual terrain of the post-1945 conjuncture, then consider the complex articulation of countertendencies, and finally survey the contemporary scene of crisis and opportunity.

From 1945 to 1967/73: The Construction of Consensus

The period 1945–1967/73, the conjuncture of US hegemony and Kondratieff expansion, coincided with, was marked by, a deepened ideological commitment to a universal science, empirical and positivistic, expressing the Enlightenment ideal of endless progress implemented in an ultimately law-like (Newtonian, mechanistic, and hence in principle, predictable) world.

In 1945, the power of 'the bomb' sealed US hegemony. 'Atoms for Peace' (or better, the Manhattan Project itself, the prototype of 'big science') soon became the metaphor of material progress through rational (Western) science. Vannevar Bush, in his report to the US President, *Science, The Endless Frontier* (1945), linked well-being at home and geopolitical dominance abroad to progress in science/technology through government-sponsored basic research in academia and, to a certain extent, industry. US government expenditures for basic science increased a hundredfold from the pre-1945 to the immediate post-1945 period (Greenberg, 1967). And the United States has since dominated world knowledge production. This can be gauged by considering Nobel prizes awarded in science – 1940s, 43 per cent; 1950s, 48 per cent; 1960s, 49 per cent; 1970s, 52 per cent; 1980s, 56 per cent (Broad, 1991); or by comparing 'major social science advances' – 1900–29: Europe, 33, North America (USA), 12, Other, 4; 1930–65: Europe, 11, North America (USA), 41, Other, 0 (Deutsch, Markovits and Platt, 1986: 407). Political leaders and institutional policy-makers in the core, and eventually throughout the world, presumed a close correlation between science, technological progress and economic/military security, undergirded by a vast intellectual Establishment which reinforced the consensus.

From at least the middle of the nineteenth century, the dominant epistemology of science had been increasingly positivistic – truth associated with observable facts and the laws governing their relations. Logical positivism, in the analytic tradition and heir to the empirical legacy, gained ascendancy during the 1920s and 1930s.[2] Its 'verification principle' – the meaning of a proposition is the method of its verification –

---

2. See Hanfling, 1981; Ayer, 1959; and Weitz, 1966.

admits as meaningful tautological statements (such as mathematics and logic) or statements verifiable through observation. All others (such as metaphysics and theology), being unverifiable, are considered meaningless, neither true nor false. The corollaries – that the only valid knowledge is scientific and that science is unitary – deepened the gulf between the (ordered/lawlike, factual/expository) sciences and the (chaotic/ anarchic, impressionistic/poetic) humanities, with the position of that archipelago of in-between disciplines, the social sciences, a matter of fierce debate.

Periodically pronounced dead in favour of more flexible epistemologies, the ghost of logical positivism reveals itself a very active revenant. Attacks on the status of the principle of verification, critical review of such precepts as the presumed independence of 'facts', and the realization of the importance of context and models in explanation have discredited it. Nevertheless, in addition to the ideological infrastructure it offers, this philosophical lineage continues to profit from an enduring association with the very real accomplishments of twentieth-century science and technology (associated with determinism and predictability) in understanding and controlling the material world.

Associated with positivism, the reigning theoretical/methodological perspective of US social science(s),[3] was functionalism. It putatively examined 'the contribution which social items make to the social and

---

3. In 1942, Hempel renewed the idiographic/nomothetic debate by 'repudiat[ing the] rejection of law in historiography' (Weitz, 1966: 254). In assimilating the social sciences to one unified science, behaviourism (see Watson, 1925; Skinner, 1971) was integral to the arguments of the logical positivists:

> [S]ociology is not a 'moral science' or 'the study of man's spiritual life' (Sombart's 'Geisteswissenschaft') standing in fundamental opposition to some other sciences, called 'natural sciences', no, *as social behaviorism, sociology is a part of unified science.... The fruitfulness of social behaviorism is demonstrated by the establishment of new correlations and by the successful predictions made on the basis of them* (Neurath, 1959: 296, 317).

Behaviourism was fundamentally linked to empirical studies (often in animal psychology) of actual responses – an experimental method based on the observation of independent cases – and thus could claim 'objectivity'. By the 1950s, when its moment had waned somewhat in psychology, it became widely influential in political science. The tendency was to favour empirical, quantitative techniques, and hypothesis testing (see Dahl, 1963; Meehan, 1971). In the voice of a sociologist, '[a]s a science, sociology has as its objective the funding of knowledge with the goal of all science of achieving predictability and explanation through research' (Hauser, 1981: 63).

Sociologists 'of different persuasions joined hands in attempting, unsuccessfully, to have sociology included in the original legislation establishing the National Science Foundation' (Volkart, 1981: 65–6). Significantly, in 1968 the social sciences were added to a list of fields the Foundation was directed to support; a separate directorate for social science was created in 1991.

cultural life of human collectivities.... Functional analysis ... consists in examining social and cultural items by locating them in a wider context' (Cohen, 1985: 322–3). It informed anthropology, sociology, psychology, architecture, and even the philosophy of mind. In sociology this perspective took the form of structural-functionalism and was allied with survey analysis based on quantification and a comparative method; in practice, it de-emphasized social change and conflict. Modernization theory[4] represented the effort of Western social science (in the light of the Cold War and the political drive for national liberation) to come to grips with a world which included the non-Western and non-rich. It both expressed a real concern for development and harboured a political component in the search to control the appeal of Communism in the Third World. A Soviet version mirrored its Western counterpart. Theorists posited contemporary Western/Soviet society as an end point towards which the Third World was 'developing'. In so doing, it would achieve both the same economic successes (industrialization) and similar political organization (democracy/socialism). The comparative perspective defined each politically bounded state as a 'society' and cast it as an independent 'case' for analysis.

Whether in the form of logical positivism or structural-functionalism and modernization, the dominant intellectual currents in Western science and social science carried the humanities along on the same tides and swells. As Eagleton has written of US New Criticism, 'the literary text was grasped in what might be called "functionalist" terms: just like US functionalist sociology, it developed a "conflict-free" model of society, in which every element "adapted" to every other' (1983: 47). The political implications were clear.[5] Anglo-American empiricism wedded to description, the reality of external relations, and the independence of material objects (subject/object distinction) here found an echo. The 'scientific' psychology and behaviourist principles of I.A. Richards' work in the 1920s linked English 'close reading' to the American New Criticism which would carry through an absolute objectification of the text. Text,

---

4. See Rostow, 1960; Eisenstadt, 1966; 1973; and Huntington, 1968. For critical reviews of Rostow, see Baran and Hobsbawm, who specifically situate the importance of this work in its value as a cold war document rather than in its intellectual content (1961: 242); and for Huntington, Leys (1982).

5. '[It was a] recipe for political inertia, and thus for submission to the political status quo.... The limits of New Criticism were essentially the limits of liberal democracy: the poem, John Crowe Ransom wrote, was "like a democratic state, so to speak, which realized the ends of a state without sacrificing the personal character of its citizens". It would be interesting to know what the Southern slaves would have made of this assertion' (Eagleton, 1983: 50).

in fact, was largely equated with poetry by the New Critics. Its very opacity could be manipulated through an analysis of its internal 'tensions', 'paradoxes', 'irony' and 'ambivalences' to encapsulate it and place it outside history and floating above social context. The self-enclosure is evident in the title of Cleanth Brooks' 1949 classic, *The Well Wrought Urn*. These attributes put New Criticism in syntony with a garland of conservative undercurrents – that is, the aesthetic of the Old South of Ransom and the politics of T.S. Eliot. The New Critics presented themselves as anti-Establishment, while in fact buttressing it in the medium term.

Having flourished from the 1930s through the 1950s, the New Criticism finally succumbed to the onslaughts of structuralism and later poststructuralism. It was, nonetheless, a key element in the academic professionalization of criticism both for its 'objectivity' (which, in line with 'scientific' thinking, contributed to its legitimation as knowledge) and for its formalist characteristics (which made the instruction of large numbers of undergraduates considerably easier). However, much in the manner of logical positivism, it continued to be a practical formula, widely practised if not preached. Finally, 'traces of the New Criticism [we]re found in yet another way: in the repeated and often extremely subtle denial of history by a variety of contemporary theorists' (Lentricchia, 1980: xiii).

It was on this intellectual pegboard that the political struggles of the period were hung. Whenever opinion at the centre could not be homogenized, efforts were made to control the expression of dissent in the political domain.[6] In addition, a central arena of the campaign was the mass culture propagated from Hollywood. '[F]ar from being an industry representing traditional America, Hollywood was at the center of a contest to determine the future of politics and national identity in the postwar era' (May, 1990: 358). It soon became the major purveyor of film and television, and the cultural values that were their baggage, to the whole world, its products no less subject to the trends of the world-economy than any other commodities.

In the socialist East, dissent was managed through state censorship and individual repression (countered by underground organization and 'samizdat' literature) – unless it could be useful, as with the publication of Solzhenitsyn's *One Day in the Life of Ivan Denisovich* as part of Khrushchev's de-Stalinization programme. Protest, East and West, was regularly met with an array of force, from job pressures and individual intimidation, to proxy violence and covert operations, to incarceration.

---

6. For the literature on the USA, see Isserman, 1987: 221 n.2; 222 n.1.

Ideological battles were fought in the realm of 'high culture' as well. During the 1950s the stature of Russian/Soviet arts in the West was denigrated (socialist realism), or minimized (constructivism), or assimilated into a larger context, as the work of Berdyaev and Dostoevsky was to existentialism (see, for example, Friedman, 1991). US cultural imperialism was mobilized overtly through the United States Information Agency (USIA). and covertly through the CIA, but also through the Museum of Modern Art exporting abstract expressionism.[7] Asia and Latin America were specifically targeted along with Europe. The CIA 'recognized that dissenting intellectuals who believe themselves to be acting freely could be useful tools in the international propaganda war'. Rockefeller and others at MOMA 'consciously used Abstract Expressionism, "the symbol of political freedom," for political ends' (Cockcroft, 1992: 83, 90).

The European challenge to US hegemony in the cultural arena (as in the military and political arenas) came most notably from France. De Gaulle had shown his distrust of the USA as the tutor of European interests. In 1963 he withdrew French armed forces from NATO command and established an independent *force de frappe*. One response was 'cultural diplomacy'. The articulation of power, values and consensus came to a head in the events surrounding the 1964 Venice Biennale, which France had long dominated. The US presence, under financial strain as was the entire exhibition, found eventual funding through the USIA (the US government would 'save' modern art) and overflowed into an annex (unprecedented before or after) where pop art could be presented as a substantial movement. European critics dubbed this American expansionism.

> American critics explained Rauschenberg's victory in terms of aesthetic superiority.... Alan Solomon, the curator of the US exhibition, summed up ... sentiments in a public statement made just prior to the US victory: 'The whole world recognized that the world art center has moved from Paris to

---

7. Abstract expressionism (officially consecrated with the MOMA exhibit of 1951) – 'unequivocal expressions of terror, tragedy, and ultimate harmony in confrontations with Man and His actions, particularly with [the artists'] own inner selves and their activity as artists' (Reise, 1992: 262) – was explicitly contrasted with the 'superficial', 'state-controlled' Soviet socialist realism. This latter, 'the official vulgarity, the certified vulgarity' (Greenberg, 1948: 579), could be fused with Nazi and Fascist 'totalitarian' art, as Greenberg suggested (1948: 578; see also Golomstock, 1990). But establishing the superiority of Western (US) culture required dazzling *soubresauts*. Greenberg's rewriting of the history of the debates within the Soviet arts community – constructivism 'versus' socialist realism – was necessary for the eventual refusal to incorporate constructivism into the pantheon of the neo-avant-garde (Buchloh, 1990).

New York'. Yet Solomon admitted privately that 'we might have won it anyway (apart from the question of merit), but we really engineered it'. (Monahan, 1990: 369–70)

In the core, Great Britain discovered a 'new affluence'; the Federal Republic of Germany experienced an 'economic miracle'; and 'traditional American families' savoured the ideal (if not the reality for many) of an insular and achieved well-being – a status quo to be protected – in idyllic suburban Levittowns awash in Lawrence Welk and Norman Rockwell where everything on the 'other side of the tracks' could be ignored. Geoculturally, the hegemonic power exported the promise of development in the guise of images of progress. But always the 'new' was contrasted with 'old' forms (classical music, ballet, opera), which were the mainstays of Soviet cultural forays[8] and the French modernist presence (Roger Bissière) in Venice. The 'revolution' of Rauschenberg was presented as 'apolitical and affirmative' over against the abstract painters' traditionalism and formalism (Monahan, 1990: 387). Pop art could be billed as embodying the ideals of the new Kennedy administration, while the (advertised, constructed) essence of abstract expressionism had been perfectly suited to the conservatism of the Eisenhower years. Always, however, the 'new'. Certainly by 1964, as Monahan suggests, 'economic power ... had already won the battle. The force of the new issuing from American shores had already succeeded in dominating the world with its movies, its magazines, its culture' (1990: 407).

Cultural hegemony, then, in the post-1945 period consisted of a perspective derivative of positive science, universalizing and objectifying, and an experimental/comparative method leading to (disinterested, apolitical) progress associated with predictable results – a perspective that permeated not only the sciences but the social sciences as well and found strong echoes in the humanities in consistent, if shifting, articulation with US political hegemony and economic expansion. Even when challenged from within a discipline or through political activism,

---

8. It is not only what the Soviets exported – *classical* forms – but also when they did this. From the 1950s through the early 1960s New York saw the Bolshoi, yes, but also the English Royal Ballet and the French Madeleine Renaud and Jean-Louis Barrault Companies. Later, the opening to the People's Republic of China brought its national companies to the USA in similar bids for cultural legitimacy. The USA first seized the avant-garde but eventually US ballet companies toured Europe, the Far East, and even the USSR. Typical of hegemony, Wallerstein notes, is to 'encourage a culture of liberty, but to constrain it ... to garner the political and economic advantages for the prevailing dominant interests without reaping the whirlwind' (1982: 119).

ingrained ideas retained their commonsense quality: Pavlov's dog still wags its behaviourist tail in the popular consciousness and, as with the underclass in the core, the Third World is still shouldered with the guilt for its underdevelopment.

But all the while, this intellectual Establishment did not go un-challenged. It is, in fact, the more striking when placed in relation to its antisystemic, anomaly-projecting underside. The analytic tradition of positive (social) science, abutted phenomenology, existentialism and structuralism. Modernization theory was countered by the *dependentistas*. And the principles of the human sciences, and their institutional struc-tures, were challenged by Braudelian *Annales*. New criticism, abstract expressionism and pop art had to contend with structuralism, surrealism and the *nouveau roman*.

Countertrends, resistance and confrontation

On the Continent, phenomenology marked a reaction to positivism (as a clear alternative to the analytic tradition) and the perception of a disintegrating civilization in the wake of the First World War. Husserl, working in the tradition of the Cartesian project, sought a philosophy of certainty.[9] But the effect of his labour to place the human subject at the centre of a knowable world was not necessarily anti-Establishment:

> The subject was to be seen as the source and origin of all meaning: it was not really itself part of the world, since it brought that world to be in the first place. In this sense, phenomenology recovered and refurbished the old dream of classical bourgeois ideology ... pivot[ing] on the belief that 'man' was somehow prior to his history and social conditions. (Eagleton, 1983: 58)

The existentialists (Heidegger, Sartre and others) developed Husserl's ideas in directions he sometimes criticized. In breaking with Husserl, who was his teacher, Heidegger attempted to recapture the radically

---

9. Husserl's new beginning asserted that the heart of philosophical investigation was description, which should begin with deep introspection jettisoning any 'natural attitude' (of independently existing objects) in favour of the contents of consciousness alone. The aim was to return philosophy to the realm of the concrete, but a concrete which was internal and dependent on intuition for access. Schütz extended Husserl's method to the social world (an 'interpreted world') in a Weberian context in reaction to the prevalent positivism and behaviourism. Eventually arguing against the *a priori* individual, his work maintained an allegiance to description and common-sense knowl-edge (see Wagner, 1983). Phenomenology was the philosophical foundation for ethnomethodology and its study of everyday activities (Garfinkel, 1967; Sharrock and Anderson, 1986) and has also influenced literary criticism (Lentricchia, 1980: ch. 3).

historical dimension of meaning. Existence can never be completely objectified but remains problematic, a becoming and therefore constituted by history. Affirmation of knowledge through participation as against observation (the positive sciences) placed existentialism at a juncture with Dilthey's human studies. The historicism that followed entailed a relativism which repudiated eternal truths or all-encompassing systems of thought. The themes of repetition, destiny and the tragic comply with the vision of Being 'flattened' from the beginning to manifest an aversion to any easy doctrine of progress. Nonetheless, a re-evaluation of metaphysics in the descriptive sense (man's place in the world) instead of the speculative sense (the extension of reason beyond the observable to a transcendental reality) may also be attributed to the existentialist perspective: 'to raise the question of man is also to raise the questions of the world, of time, of history, and of man's relation to these' (Macquarrie, 1972: 241).

Since at least the time of the symbolists, artists and writers had organized resistance to Establishment models in just these terms. Dada, the immediate progenitor of surrealism, was the coming together of what was, in practice, already an international movement of resistance and rejection of a world at war which seemed to be at the end of its rope anyway. It 'aimed to destroy the reasonable deceptions of man and recover the natural and unreasonable order' (Arp, quoted in Ades, 1981: 114). Anarchic, against everything, it demolished itself (logically, as part of that world); but its anti-bourgeois, anti-art attitude survived in the surrealists' more constructive campaign against realism – 'the realist attitude, inspired by positivism ... has for me an air that is hostile to all intellectual and moral achievement' (Breton, 1972: 14)[10] – and the

---

10. Balzac had been Marx's favourite author and 'realism' had been the battle cry of 1848. On the eve of the Revolution, Jules Michelet contended that 'literature, emerging from the shadow of fantasy, will come alive and be real, will become a *form of action*; it will no longer be the entertainment of some individual, or of idlers, but the voice of the people to the people (cited in De Micheli, 1978: 11). Although the revolution 'failed', the artists who manned its barricades carried forward the movement in the spirit of De Sanctis ('art can be nothing other than the objective representation of reality, its undeformed expression'), or of Courbet, for whom art consisted 'in knowing how to discover the fullest expression of things that exist' (cited by De Micheli, 1978: 14–15, 17). However, realism soon became identified with the bourgeois liberal Establishment and finally exhausted its emancipatory appeal with the fall of the Paris Commune in 1871. The avant-garde movements of the late nineteenth century and twentieth century were oppositional too, but in a new way: they contested the premises of realism by figuring an internal rather than an external world and were anti-positivist and strongly influenced by non-Western cultural expressions.

recognition of the power of the unconscious and the imagination (Freud), for which 'automatic writing' (the manifestation of 'psychic automatism') provided a key technique.

Duchamp and Picabia led the movement in New York where it strongly influenced Jackson Pollock, the abstract expressionists, and pop art. To avoid diluting the home-grown superiority of his 'American-style painters', however, Clement Greenberg sought to expurgate the role of surrealism in their development. Thus the imposed consensus of the Establishment contained a suppressed resistance, a resistance which flowered as insurgent alternatives. Although heavy-handed, Dali's limp watches characterized well a disintegrating consensus about the nature of time, and Magritte's much more perplexing work 'questions one's assumptions about the world, about the relationship between a painted and a real object' (Ades, 1981: 133).

During the 1950s the *nouveau roman* confronted many of these same concerns – 'a rejection at last of any pre-existing order' (Robbe-Grillet, 1972c: 81). Robbe-Grillet's 'new realism' (1972f; 1972g: 15) or Butor's 'more highly developed realism' (1972a: 11) took up the baton espousing the creative and transformative potential of the imagination. 'The world is neither significant nor absurd; it simply *is*' (Robbe-Grillet, 1972e: 21). Any simplistic form of commitment was refused in favour of

> full consciousness of the current problems of one's own language, the conviction of their great importance, the determination to resolve them from within. That … is the only hope of remaining an artist, hence obscure and far-off, of someday being useful for something – perhaps even for the revolution. (Robbe-Grillet, 1972d: 46–7)

Although considering critiques from the surrealist camp as no different than the mainstream, Butor is generally positive in his assessment of surrealism, especially the (shared) postulate concerning the exploratory and transformative power of the imagination (over the 'real') (1972b: 182). To refuse character construction (associated with the high tide of the individual) and linear narrative (because it represented an order, and 'memory is never chronological') does not, however, assume the absence of human action. Writing for Robbe-Grillet is an intervention, 'less a matter of knowing than of conquering' (1972d: 33); the reader is invited to participate in the creation and thus learn to invent his own life (1972a: 168–9).

This is reminiscent of the existentialist vision. Sartre extolled existentialism as a humanism, as a 'style of philosophizing' beginning with man rather than nature. Stressing action and the themes of freedom, decision, responsibility and the emotions (within an environment of

factical possibility), existentialist discussion tended to centre on the individual, although as a unity, including both body and mind in a context:
being-in-the-world, being-with-others. This aspect was to be of primary
importance to the generation of young people who 'seized the moment'
in 1968. However, the individual component could come to predominate
over being-within-a-community. There was an easy slippage from an
anti-collectivism (as dehumanizing) to an anti-communal bias. And
authenticity, radical choice and self-affirmation unchecked could become
apologies for amoralism and totalitarianism,[11] or the simple excuse for
a 'me generation'.

But humanism, too, encountered challenges in both the social sciences
and humanities. Althusser's structuralist Marxism[12] rebuked economism
and empiricism, and the humanism and the historicism he found in
Sartre (and practically everywhere else). Here, it was a question of the
political *conjoncture*; writing in the early 1960s, Althusser (1969) situated
his rejection of humanism in the wake of the 'cult of the personality'
and the revelations of the Twentieth Congress of the CPSU. In his
condemnation of humanism, Robbe-Grillet pointed to the double-edged
and paralysing nature of the existentialist project which placed man at
the centre of meaning. For Robbe-Grillet the question was the very
hegemony of 'man', a fundamental ideological pillar of modern (world-
system) thought. His condemnation of 'habitual' humanism (in which
'man' is everywhere) and tragedy (as the sublimation of the difference
between man and things) rested on a profound sense of the way in
which being is separated from the world by the construction of an
anthropomorphic 'nature' (through adjectival metaphor – for example,
'majestic mountain'). Braudel (1958) found the humanistic framework
the great impediment to the 'convergence' of the social sciences.[13]

---

11. The case of Heidegger is exemplary, if discouraging.

12. The structuralist position was taken to task by E.P. Thompson (1978) in the
context of the history/theory and culture/ideology debates within English Marxism,
which date back to the 1950s (see Thompson, 1965; Anderson, 1964; 1966). Questions
of determinism and agency were central. Thompson and other 'culturalists' espoused
a socialist humanism (see Soper, 1990), which was attacked by Althusser along with
historicism (1969; also Althusser and Balibar, 1970). However, the culturalists' positions
were not always internally consistent (see Thompson, 1961). Thompson derided
'theory', and, in the extreme, structuralists could reject 'history' (see Hindess and
Hirst, 1975); however, both structuralists and culturalists repudiated any mechanical
economism.

13. Althusser emphasizes a slippage by which 'the relations of production, political and ideological social relations, have been reduced to historicized *"human relations"*,
i.e., to interhuman, intersubjective relations. This is the favourite terrain of historicist
humanism' (Althusser and Balibar, 1970: 139–40).

It was, nonetheless, the constitution by 'language', prior to the subject and in which we all participate, of the existentialist conception of a 'world' of being-in-the-world – a conception central to the *nouveau roman*: 'Language is not contained in consciousness; it contains it' (Robbe-Grillet, 1972g: 117, reproducing the phrase of Bousquet) – which meshed so felicitously with the structuralist programme. Structuralism, dormant for half a century, bloomed in European intellectual circles in the 1950s. Its time had come to be widely influential across the humanities and the social sciences.

Nothing satisfies Jameson's dictum that '[t]he history of thought is the history of its models' (1972: v) better than structuralism. Although its genealogy is long (Hawkes (1977) traces it back to Vico!), the work of de Saussure, the Swiss linguist, is fundamental. In his *Cours de Linguistique Générale* (1916), he insisted that language should be studied 'not only in terms of its individual parts, and not only diachronically, but also in terms of the relationship *between* those parts, and *synchronically*.... [This] involved recognition of language's current *structural* properties as well as its *historical* dimensions' (Hawkes, 1977: 20). Language is a total system, always and ever complete. Each unique utterance, *parole*, is referentially arbitrary and finds meaning only within a system of relationships, *langue*, which itself never appears. Individual sounds are assigned to particular ideas according to a system of oppositions, the differences between their sounds and those of other words. Languages are systems of signs which express meaning. But signs – and this is a key component in Saussure's theory – are inseparable wholes

---

Robbe-Grillet directly attacks the naturalistic error which persisted even in Saussurian linguistics (see Lentricchia, 1980: 119). He sees non-contingent, non-provisional nature as paralysing; he does not wish, however, to negate man.

A belief in nature can ... be seen to be the source of every kind of humanism, in the traditional meaning of the term.... To refuse our so-called 'nature' and the vocabulary that perpetuates the myth, to consider objects to be purely external and superficial [but not excluded], is not – as it is claimed – to deny man; but it is to refuse the idea of 'pananthropism'.... In the last analysis, it is nothing but the attempt to carry through to its logical conclusion the pursuit of liberty. (Robbe-Grillet, 1972c: 63–4)

Braudel suggests the themes of '*mathématisation, réduction à l'espace, longue durée*', for the orientation of collective research, and a 'convergence' among the social sciences which he esteemed had become a necessity due to the very progress of the *sciences de l'homme* ... 'at odds with a retrograde and insidious humanism which can no longer offer them a proper framework' (Braudel, 1958: 753, 725).

constituted by both the concept, the signified (*signifié*), and the sound-image or word, the signifier (*signifiant*).

This model was appropriated early on by anthropologists and applied to non-linguistic phenomena in the study of cultures/peoples without written histories. In his work on kinship, religion and myth, Lévi-Strauss (1963; 1964; 1966) looked for those contrastive relationships analogous to the structure of language which in a comparative perspective would yield insights into the fundamental form or essential nature of the mind, irrespective of the society in which it might appear. He characterized myth as the overcoming of contradictions. The modern engineer and the primitive *bricoleur* shared a universal activity: making things mean. His structuralist approach, anti-empiricist and challenging the one-to-one correspondence between reality or nature and constructions of meaning, contested former lines of research. The 'social' as substantive rather than adjectival was derived from Durkheim and Mauss; the ahistorical, synchronic, 'structuralist causality', as against historical determination, from the linguistic model. This approach (of internal arrangements) is positively present in Althusser and undergirded the new life he brought to the study of ideology. Particularly attractive to Marxists was the stress on determinate conditions.

An opening to the world was certainly a central part of the early programme of Barthes. He is unabashedly concerned with meaning, the construction of meaning – 'signification' – and its function. It is indicative that, during this period of anti-colonial struggle (Bandung Conference, Suez crisis, Algeria, Vietnam), Barthes, in a major theoretical exegesis of 1957, 'Myth Today', took as one of his primary examples the image (on the cover of *Paris-Match*) of 'a young Negro in a French uniform ... saluting':

> [W]hether naively or not, I see very well what it signifies to me: that France is a great Empire, that all her sons, without any colour discrimination, faith-fully serve under her flag, and that there is no better answer to the detractors of an alleged colonialism than the zeal shown by this Negro in serving his so-called oppressors. (1972: 116)

In 1970 Barthes wrote that the need for ideological criticism that had been evident in the 1950s was so again in May 1968 (1972: 9). This critique, carried out by a semiological analysis of the mechanics of language to 'account *in detail* for the mystification which transforms petit-bourgeois culture into a universal nature', was indebted, as he tells us, to his reading of Saussure (1972: 9).

Language *per se* can either formulate the concept by expressing it or expunge it by concealing it. Barthes' innovative reading of language as 'myth' accomplishes both.[14] This is how it transforms *history* into *nature* producing ideology: it is read as a factual system of expression (French imperiality is naturalized in the image of the saluting Black soldier), not a semiological system of values (the content – history, blood and struggle – of all the aspects of the image are drained away). This explicit concern for the construction of meaning and its relation to practice was, however, to remain temporally limited as a dominant programme.

Structuralism offered the promise of a new rigour and scientific status – non-reductionist and non-positivist – for the human sciences. This was clear in Lévi-Strauss, and in Althusser who was thinking about modes of production as structured like a language (Althusser and Balibar, 1970). However, just this possibility determined the closure of structuralism back in on itself: the realization of elegant formal analyses which privileged the internal relations of the text. The overly synchronic tendency[15] – the problem of accounting for historical change – along with the scarce significance accorded domains other than language, and the historical conditions of the emergence of structuralism itself, have been abiding difficulties in structural analysis. But 'emphasis on the "constructedness" of human meaning represented a major advance' (Eagleton, 1983: 107–8). It spelled the demise of European humanism and positivism alike, and the Romanticism of vital essences – material, human or poetic.

The primacy accorded to the analysis of relationships rather than of entities is also apparent in the positive resistance to the export of modernization theory. Third World scholars, especially from Latin

---

14. Barthes takes Saussure's first-order system one step further, and through a lateral shift employs the linguistic sign in an extended role as signifier in a second-order system, 'myth', which produces 'signification'. In the process, the original sign or collection of signs is drained of content, reduced to pure form, rendered arbitrary to serve as signifier in the new system. This innovation involves the particular qualities of the construction of meaning in the move from language to myth. At the level of myth, the image of the black soldier hails French imperiality as it establishes it, but with the loss of some knowledge, for the image is emptied of the history it had at the level of linguistic sign. In his words:

> *Myth hides nothing*: its function is to distort, not to make disappear.... the ubiquity of the signifier in myth exactly reproduces the physique of the *alibi*.... Myth is a *value*, truth is no guarantee for it; nothing prevents it from being a perpetual alibi: it is enough that its signifier has two sides for it always to have an 'elsewhere' at its disposal. (Barthes, 1972: 121, 123)

15. Although Lévi-Strauss did his utmost to do justice to both the synchronic and the diachronic, Braudel characterized the anthropologist's conception of time as 'very long' and 'too long', indeed as eternal; if it existed, said Braudel, it would be 'the time of the sages' (1958: 748).

America, led the way. Reservations about this Establishment perspective were advanced early in the 1950s by Prebisch and the UN Economic Commission for Latin America (ECLA). They observed anti-Ricardian deteriorating terms of trade between 'core' and 'periphery' (see Baer, 1962). The construction of this relation over the long term, 'the development of underdevelopment' (Frank, 1967; 1969) became the theme of dependency theorists (see Cardoso, 1977; Palma, 1978). Anomalies suggested that increased contact with the core (metropole, centre) impeded development in the periphery (satellite); the logic of modernization was inverted. Such was the strength of modernization as an official doctrine, however, that these critiques were largely ignored initially.

The nineteenth-century logic of the disciplines, 'universalizing, empiricist, sectioning off politics from economics and both from culture, profoundly ethnocentric, arrogant, and oppressive – Gramsci's hegemonic culture at the world level' (Wallerstein, 1978: 5), and the institutions through which that logic was realized, the universities, were met head-on by Braudel and the *Annales* school. Study of the economic and the social (rather than just the political) and the emphasis on the *longue durée* and *conjonctures* (instead of a chronological narrative of 'events' or individual biographies) were direct attacks on universalizing nomothetic thought and, even more so, on idiographic history, which had been dominant in France. During the Cold War period, *Annales* profited as a non-Anglo-Saxon and non-Soviet pole to which dissidents of any persuasion or nationality, including Marxists, could gravitate (Wallerstein, 1991b: 187–201). In this respect it represented another aspect of French, third-force, nationalism evident from world politics to the fine arts.

In May of 1968 the simmering world revolution exploded.[16] The 'old left' had succumbed to external pressures of Cold War McCarthyism and internal angst in the wake of Soviet de-Stalinization. A 'New Left' in the USA coalesced around themes including race relations (not to be

---

16. On 1968, including the international dimensions, see Caute, 1988; and Fraser, 1988. As a revolution in the world-system, see Arrighi, Hopkins and Wallerstein, 1989; and Wallerstein, 1991a: 65–83. On the Old and New Left, see Isserman, 1987; and Widgery, 1976. Throughout the 1960s the USA fought to hold on to hegemony in the face of mounting challenges on all fronts. In 1961 the Kennedy administration had established the Peace Corps and the Alliance for Progress. In 1962, Students for a Democratic Society issued the Port Huron Statement, still relatively mild and favouring 'party realignment' (Isserman, 1987: 202–19). Anti-insurgency warfare and winning 'the hearts and minds of the people' escalated to the debacle of full-fledged engagement in Vietnam, and the home-front revolt eventually culminated with the 'Weathermen' in 1969. Student movements were everywhere important, but nowhere more so perhaps than in France, which had lived through both a Vietnamese war and, even more traumatically, an Algerian war.

disassociated from a global dimension of Cold War decolonization), the anti-Vietnam War movement, and university reform. In Great Britain, 'positive neutralism', 'socialist humanism', and 'nuclear disarmament' had been the themes of the first flowering of protest in the late 1950s (Widgery, 1976). However, the lasting impact of 1968 corresponded to the underlying themes of *Annales*:

> The real impact of 1968 was ... on the *intellectual* life of the universities. It represented a challenge not only to the immediate consensus of the 1945–67 period, but to the deeper consensus that had governed world intellectual life since at least the mid-nineteenth century ... without however destroying its institutional base (Wallerstein, 1991b: 222).

Of course, movements are not at all times, or do not appear in all time frames, equally subversive. For example, existentialism had differing impacts according to the era, and the homophobic and phallocentric tendencies of the surrealists fit long-term trends in Western thought. The new women's movement is not alone in bleaching the credentials of these currents as radical alternatives. Poststructuralist strategies, presented and roundly criticized as profoundly radical, in fact produced new formalisms. Similarly, *Annales*, which aspired to a more 'scientific' history, lost its edge, failing to transcend the disciplines – with only a fig leaf of multidisciplinarity – and moving in both nomothetic and idiographic directions (the so-called *émiettement*) (Wallerstein, 1991b: 224).

From 1967/73 to 1990: Contradiction and Transformation

Turning to the recent, post-1968, period, we see that overt challenges to what the Establishment considers legitimate knowledge have intensified in attacks against three beliefs: (1) that instrumental science as public knowledge implemented through technology and applied to the real world engenders progress; (2) that there exist universal propositions reflecting timeless truths; (3) that there are substantial differences constituting a hierarchy of knowledge among the academic disciplines themselves.

Each refers to a material crisis; both universalizing and sectorializing processes are implicated. The first is associated with a crisis of linear chronosophy (see Pomian, 1979) – grave, in undermining the presumed (veiled) relation between progress and endless, capitalist, accumulation; the second is concerned with the crisis of the *longue durée* structure of knowledge dominated by universal science which underlay the very idea of progress; and the third addresses the crisis of the nineteenth-century *conjoncturel*, sectorializing, restructuring of the academic disciplines which has sustained the universal/particular (science/humanities) antinomy for over a century.

The ambiguity of progress

In the late 1960s, the ideology of a 'technological society', based on a value-neutral science providing unlimited growth and progress, reached a turning point. In April of 1968, barely two months after the Tet offensive in Vietnam, the Club of Rome met for the first time. They proposed to examine major trends, mutually interrelated, from a long-term, global, systems perspective. The study they commissioned reported that growth, far from a blanket panacea, if unchecked, would eventually result in 'sudden and uncontrollable decline in both population and industrial capacity' (Meadows et al., 1974: 29).

The development of new technologies based on discoveries in theoretical science, seconded by the managerial/organizational techniques for their large-scale deployment, had accompanied and in part made possible the massive destruction of the Second World War: atomic research (the Manhattan Project) and electronics (for example, radar). In the immediate postwar era it was presumed that this technology would undergo metamorphosis into 'too cheap to meter' atomic power. But during the next forty years the production of swords far outweighed that of ploughshares. Despite a relatively vocal anti-nuclear-weapons movement (associated with an antiwar movement that reached its apogee during the world revolution of 1968) only minor victories were attained, and these in the post-1968 period concerned deployment, as in the case of New Zealand, where ports were closed in the mid-1980s to ships carrying nuclear weapons. Proliferation continued and few credited science with making the world a safer place, although the assertion remained a staple of the political rhetoric of the strong and the legislative pitch of the military-industrial complex.

Nuclear power was not so obviously unprogressive as nuclear weapons; hence the movement contesting it got off to a slower start, only to become a real force in the post-1968 period, gaining support with each well-publicized incidence of radiation release or catastrophic 'meltdown' (Three Mile Island, 1979; Chernobyl, 1986), and most recently with concern over radioactive waste. As objection was based heavily on technical concerns – accidents, waste disposal, and damage compensation – the drawbacks of fossil fuels (the greenhouse effect) and growth of demand for electricity could well reverse the anti-nuclear consensus.

Nonetheless the Establishment did not envision as of the late 1980s the development of new, cleaner technologies; it perceived the problem as one of public relations (Nuclear Energy Agency, 1989: 9, 10). For, public outcry notwithstanding, the long-term commitment to nuclear power, buttressed by official public-relations campaigns, was massive in the core and increasing in the periphery. All the same, progress through technology represented by nuclear power has seemed a chimera.[17]

Vastly expanded chemical industries, many producing the pesticides and fertilizers necessary for the new high-yield strains of food grains of the 'Green revolution', were also typical of the postwar period. Rachel Carson in *Silent Spring*, published in 1962, exposed pesticide pollution. This marked the opening salvo of the contemporary concern for ecology, as distinct from the long-established (and Establishment) reformist conservation movement, and effectively launched it as a popular crusade in the core.[18] Even such mainstream, relatively conservative, conservation organizations as the Sierra Club and the National Audubon Society, although shunning any hint of radicalism, became more activist (for example, Mitchell with Stallings, 1970). The movement has exploded to include diverse philosophies, methods and goals: radical, confrontational direct action – Greenpeace and Earth First!; revolutionary rejection of any human-centred attitude toward nature – the Deep Ecology movement (Devall and Sessions, 1985; Wexler, 1990); grave concerns for the economics of growth (Brown, 1978; Meadows et al., 1974; Schumacher, 1973); and electoral politics (Ryle, 1988; Gorz, 1980).[19]

In the core zones of Europe and North America, some trade-offs have been negotiated between capital and the environment. However,

---

17. New construction is virtually at a standstill in Europe and the USA (although in Sweden nuclear power is favoured by legal limits on 'greenhouse' emissions) (Price, 1990). But for the moment there appears to be no substitute for the energy produced by the outdated reactors in Eastern Europe. New reactors are not the only ventures in trouble. Very large-scale hydroelectric projects (for example, Brazil, Canada, the Danube) have also faced reappraisal.

18. Carson's work resulted in the cancellation of the registration of DDT in the USA in 1971. In the USA the popular optimism launched with the first 'Earth Day' in 1970 gave way to official negligence during the Reagan administration. Alarm has been growing around the world, however, and during the 'Earth Summit' of 1992 (see Johnson, 1993), the US position was a minority one. The view from the periphery is drastically different to that from the core (Pearce, 1992; Ramphal, 1990; Durning, 1990).

19. Some of the more important organizations were founded around the turning point 1967/73: Friends of the Earth, 1969, as a lobbying group; the National Resources Defense Council, 1970, to draft bills and undertake educational programmes; Greenpeace, 1971, for nonviolent direct action. In both Eastern and Western Europe, 'Green' parties abound, but face the same structural dilemma with regard to state power that the old movements did.

in the former Comecon countries of Eastern Europe, the hazards of unbridled development through rapid industrialization may now be readily observed in the calamitous pollution of land, water and air. By the early 1970s the unexpected consequences of the Green revolution, one of the standard bearers of modernization – and Western science – had become painfully clear in the periphery.[20] Not surprisingly, many of the same concerns – long-term degradation of the life-support capacity of the biosphere (Sahel, tropical rain forests, ozone layer) and near-term catastrophe (Bhopal, 1984) – are shared, within the more restricted ambit of their activity, by the anti-nuclear-power movement.

In fact, support for social change remains broad but covert. According to Dellinger, 'the antinuclear movement has a hidden agenda: that is, fighting for a society based on equality and democracy rather than dependence on energy monopolies and the nuclear industry' (1982: 233). But is this so, and if so to what extent? Milbrath, in a study focusing on the core (the United States, Great Britain and the Federal Republic of Germany), documented quantitatively (both in terms of belief and behaviour) the efforts and relative success of a 'newly developing environmentally-oriented ethic' at odds with the 'dominant social paradigm' which posits humans as set apart from other creatures and masters of their destiny living in an unlimited world of ceaseless progress (1984: 7–8). What unites these tendencies with movements in the periphery, including those with other interests (for example, fundamentalism[21]), is their disenchantment with the old forms expressing the Enlightenment project (see Borgmann, 1992).

Few contemporary voices, in either core or periphery, have questioned more stridently the progressive nature of modern society by denouncing its scientific/technological fundaments than elements of the women's movement. In fact, women have been in the vanguard of the anti-nuclear movement and highly visible in calling for strong regulation of pollution and toxic waste (Milbrath, 1984: 75). They have singled out the female body itself as an exemplary locus of scientific confrontation (Gallagher and Laqueur, 1987). Despite the 'unprecedented cultural authority, and massive material investments guarantee[ing] its truths',

---

20. Glaeser (1987) profiles the Green revolution's negative spiral of the smallholder to the benefit of the rich in the periphery. Lappé and Collins' discussion of world hunger includes but transcends the issues of the Green revolution, finding that freedom as 'the right to unlimited accumulation of wealth-producing property, and the right to use that property however one sees fit … *is* in fundamental conflict with ending hunger' (1986: 131).

21. Seeking legitimacy, Christian fundamentalism, strong in the USA and unlike religious fundamentalisms in non-core zones, has cloaked itself in the language of ('creation') science (see Kitcher, 1982).

the demystification of 'the scientific discourse focused on the female body' proceeds apace. By the late 1960s, with roots in the reproductive issues of contraception, abortion and child care, feminist thinking began to take on a new aspect, challenging the previously unquestioned premisses of liberal society as well as the 'patriarchal privilege' they perceive to have been justified in the guise of 'scientific' principles, 'rejecting the linearity, the mechanistic thinking of technological society, replacing it with a sense of organic wholeness, roundness, inter-connectedness' (Rothman, 1989: 252–3).

For our Europe-centred system since 1500, progress has meant expansion. However, in the late twentieth century this movement seems to have reached its global limit of incorporating land (resources) and people (labour-power). Prior 'sceptical reassessments' of the idea of progress have been primarily core phenomena occurring in the wake of Kondratieff B-phases, but the structural reversal of expansion and geo-political change of the present conjuncture make 'doubts about progress ... stronger today than previously' (Wallerstein, 1991a: 232). The realiza-tion that living standards, if measured on a world scale, have exhibited a long-term polarization (Wallerstein, 1983: 98–105) has sowed doubts about the ideology of constructing a better world through universal science and technology (associated with endless capitalist accumulation and spatio-temporal universalism).

A questionable science

The premisses of classical science have come under attack from many of today's scientists. The unity offered by classical science has reached its limit, undermined by the internal development of science itself. Built on the model of celestial mechanics, it started to show cracks during the last quarter of the nineteenth century when mathematicians began to investigate continuous but non-differentiable functions and transfinite arithmetic, and proved the three-body problem insoluble (see Lee, 1992). Since the late 1960s, dynamical-systems research has led to a re-conceptualization of the world as one of complexity, determinate but unpredictable: order within chaos (strange attractors); order out of chaos (dissipative structures); visual representation of pathological functions and natural forms exhibiting non-integer dimensions (fractal geometry). An examination of publication data shows a veritable explosion of the relevant literature.[22]

---

22. The total number of entries in the Permuterm Index of the *Science Citation Index* has shown flat, linear growth since the 1960s, while entries under the rubric 'chaos' and its cognates have multiplied exponentially.

Davies (1989) characterizes contemporary scientific research as falling into three categories: at the frontiers of the very large; the very small; and the very complex. The new appreciation of complexity (Aida et al., 1985; Atlan et al., 1985) was foreseen by Weaver (1948).[23] Nicolis and Prigogine (1989) concentrate on natural complexity seen as part of everyday experience; limitations in predictability and self-organization of real systems are presented as intimately related to the inseparable notions of time and irreversibility. Peliti and Vulpiani (1988) cite the tendency to recognize the emergence of a science of complexity, dealing with the universal features of complex systems, irrespective of the peculiar aspects of the different systems.

This rethinking – a synthetic approach as opposed to a reductionist one, strong cross-disciplinarity, and the inclusion of 'intractable' problems (Pagels, 1988; Stein, 1989) – marks a transition away from the Newtonian world-view. Farmer and Packard (Farmer, et al., 1986: viii) speak of questions which 'cry out for *synthesis* rather than reduction' in this 'new wave science', where research on systems involving at least two time scales is based on simulation and cuts across disciplinary lines.

Evidence of an order underlying the seemingly chaotic evolution of certain dynamical systems had become apparent with the discovery of the 'strange attractors' associated with these systems, beginning with the weather models of Lorenz (1963a; 1963b; 1964) in the mid-1960s. With Feigenbaum's (1983) discovery of universal behaviour in cascading bifurcations of nonlinear systems, the meso-scale of humanly perceivable phenomena gained its universal constant.[24] Shaw argued that chaotic behaviour is '*completely* ubiquitous in the physical world' (1981: 107). Borrowing from information theory, he characterized the onset of turbulence as the passage of the system from an information sink to an information source. Strange attractors transmit perturbations from the microscale to the macroscale. The implications, according to Shaw, are that the nineteenth-century view of the world as a machine is wrong not only in the small but also in the large. 'The constant injection of new information into the macroscales may place severe limits on our

---

23. He distinguished three zones of science according to the number of variables: the *simple problems* of classical physics with few variables; *disorganized complexity* with very many variables amenable to description by statistical methods; and a middle region of *organized complexity* in which problem-solving must depend on analysing systems as organic wholes. He predicted that during the late twentieth century this latter activity – to be based on computers and interdisciplinary, 'mixed team' research – would comprise the third great advance of science.

24. Feigenbaum's 'δ' is the fixed value to which the rate of onset of complex behaviour converges as a limit.

predictive ability, but it as well insures the constant variety and richness of our experience' (1981: 108).

Markus, Müller, and Nicolis (1988) present the emergence of non-linearity as a unifying principle in which universalities in a variety of open self-organizing systems offer a common language to chemists, biologists, ecologists, physicists, mathematicians, and medical doctors. Prigogine and Stengers (1984) deal explicitly with the conceptual transformation of science challenging Newtonian mechanics as related to contemporary research in thermodynamics focusing on nonlinearity (instability, fluctuations, order out of chaos). The irreversibility of the evolution of far-from-equilibrium systems, characterized by self-organizing processes and dissipative structures, determines an arrow of time. The authors discuss the interconnectedness of chance and necessity and the reconciliation of being and becoming. Chaos is presented not as the opposite of order but as its source and confederate. Prigogine finds science and mankind to be in an age of transition. That the universe has a history including complexity supposes a new dialogue of man with man, and of man with nature. Nature is to be treated as active rather than passive, and science must go 'beyond a purely conservative approach to global problems, as is usually the case in the "ecological" point of view' (1986: 506).

Compared to the ordered mathematical world of Newton and Descartes, the world of Cantor's sets and Peano's space-filling curves seemed esoteric indeed. However, Mandelbrot (1982) has shown how the structures these (and other) late-nineteenth-century mathematicians conceptualized are ubiquitous in the everyday world around us. His fractal geometry of shapes which do not fit easily into the Euclidean categories of points, lines, planes and solids – but somewhere in between – describes such naturally occurring phenomena as coastlines and snow-flakes; branching systems such as trees, vascular and pulmonary systems; and oscillating systems such as sleep cycles and heart fibrillations.

All of these studies, contrasted with time-reversible classical science, call for a reconceptualization of time itself. Either time, as irreversibility, is an illusion, or it precedes existence (Géhéniau and Prigogine, 1986; Prigogine and Géhéniau, 1986). Gould (1989) denounces the idea of evolution as either the march of progress or a cone of increasing diversity, substituting an image of diversification and decimation – history as unrepeatable and therefore unpredictable – in an exciting exposition of the theme of contingency in the historical sciences. He also proposes another reconceptualization of the arrow of time: life's arrow, based on a statistical property, bottom-heavy asymmetry, of groups of clades (phylogenetic segments) to replace 'vague, untestable, and culturally laden notions of "progress"' (Gould; Gilinsky and German, 1987: 1437).

Bohm's (1980) concern for the relationship between reality and consciousness leads him to advance a new non-fragmented world-view with an emphasis on verbs rather than nouns. He argues that developments in science are away from the analysis of independent, divided, disconnected things, and advances a holographic theory of information storage, suggesting that memory is distributed throughout the brain, and a concept of implicate or enfolded order, in which everything is enfolded into everything else. This contrasts with the predominant explicate or unfolded order in which each thing lies outside the regions of other things.

A world in crisis is portrayed by Capra (1982): a crisis that parallels the challenge to the mechanistic conception of the universe of Descartes and Newton by developments in twentieth-century physics centring on descriptions of the material world as composed of relationships rather than of separate objects. He argues that the value system associated with this latter world-view seriously affects individual and social health, and that a 'turning point' for the planet as a whole is being reached – that is, a transformation based on a holistic or ecological perspective. In the case of human evolution, Laszlo (1987) contends that it is no longer genetic but sociocultural and that our age is not only the age of uncertainty but also the age of opportunity. The emerging 'transdisciplinary view of reality emphasizes creativity over adaptation and survival, openness over determinism, and self-transcendence over security' (Jantsch, 1981: v). Echoes and parallels to these arguments are to be found throughout the disciplines. It is to these that we now turn.

Collapsing disciplinary boundaries

That new developments in the sciences are serving as active models for some in the humanities[25] continues the strong direct opposition long expressed, and indeed growing, in the humanities to a hierarchy of academic disciplines presumed to reflect a hierarchy in the domains of knowledge. In the 1960s, various new forms – the 'new journalism'

---

25. Hayles (1990), originally trained as a chemist, draws parallels and traces analogies between contemporary developments in the sciences and in literature and critical theory. She argues that both have roots in a common cultural matrix: they share an interest in the relation between the local and the global; they are aware of the interpenetration of order and disorder; and they accept that complex systems may be determined but are nonetheless unpredictable (and acutely responsive in their development to initial conditions). Sobchack similarly catalogues some of the 'primary themes and aesthetic features that many cultural critics see as characteristic of post-modern representation and that apply equally aptly to models of chaos theory' (1990: 153).

(Wolfe, 1973); creative nonfiction – fiction in form, factual in content; the 'nonfiction novel' (Capote's term); Mailer's 'history "in the form of a novel" (Hollowell, 1977: x) – questioned the possibility of discriminating fact from fiction. When journalists such as Tom Wolfe, Gay Talese and Jimmy Breslin wanted to

> convey the immediacy of experience and give it coherence and significance, [they] turned to the *novelist*.... Novelists ... set out to gather the facts, not as an end in themselves, but as raw material for their art. The name for writers who set out to gather facts about people and events is *journalist*. (Agar, 1990: 76)

These are not the only indications of breaches in disciplinary ramparts. In 1968, Danto staked out a relationship between narrative and the *human* sciences:

> narratives ... re used to explain changes, and, most characteristically, large-scale changes taking place, sometimes, over periods of time vast in relationship to single human lives. It is the job of history to reveal to us these changes, to organize the past into temporal wholes, and to explain these changes at the same time as they tell what happened. (1968: 255)

And now, Rouse is linking scientific research as social practice to a similar idea of narrative:

> In contrast to earlier accounts of the epistemic significance of narrative ... narrative is important in natural scientific knowledge.... [W]e must understand narrative not as a literary form in which knowledge is written, but as the temporal organization of the understanding of practical activity. (1990: 179)

This view of the relationship of science and narrative may seem at odds with the science/humanities opposition depicted in recent work of Hayden White (1973; 1978; 1987), but his imagery resembles more a juxtaposition of a pristine positive science unaffected by the observer and the historical disciplines.[26] In this context,

> metahistory is a science and history is a text. Metahistory is the science which guarantees the stability of history. It is the vantage point from which the historical object can be stabilized and eventually understood. (Anderson, 1983: 268)

However, by redefining a 'scientific fact as a discursive event ... one eliminates the hierarchy science–literature that isolates the observer from

---

26. See his discussion of the *Annales* school: 'Getting the "story" out of "history" was ... a first step in the transformation of historical studies into a science' (White, 1987: 169).

what he is observing' (Anderson, 1983: 276–7). For White's conception
of history couldn't be further from Ranke's 'wie es eigentlich gewesen
ist': more poesis than mimesis, a history that can change the world
(Ermarth, 1975: 962–3); 'a new form of narrative, which would effect
the undisciplining of the discipline of history, … an exit from history,
as we understand it, and a sublimation of politics' (De Bolla, 1986: 50).
History, like science, is being transformed from within (Gearhart, 1987;
cf. Veeser, 1989).

And the message from contemporary science is that, between the
cold and rigidly deterministic on the one side and the impenetrable and
inaccessible on the other, there lies a world in which chaos is ordered.
The future is determined by present agency from materials of the past,
but its structure remains unpredictable. The world-systems perspective
radically reinstates history into the study of social change on a world
scale, without however reinventing 'total history'. Radical, because as
scientists open up the middle ground, world-systems analysis repudiates
the premisses of nineteenth-century social science. Change of *conjonctures*
is embedded in *longue durée* structures (cycles within trends). By positing
a unique, temporally bounded, and spatially delimited (but expanding)
social system defined by an axial division of labour as the coherent unit
of analysis, it rejects both idiographic particularism and nomothetic
universalism and comes to terms with the sectorializing resolution of
the nineteenth-century structural crisis. Process is the watchword; being
is always becoming.

As for the future of the 'in-between disciplines', Rosenau maintains
that if there is to be a postmodern social science it 'would be broad-
gauged and descriptive rather than predictive and policy-oriented …
encouraging interpretation' by an active reader (1991: 169–70). Those
who consider themselves postmodernists may question 'any possibility
of rigid … boundaries … in nearly every field of human endeavor'
(Rosenau, 1991: 6). Postmodern concepts like double-coding (Jencks,
1989), (ahistorical) fragmentation and scepticism (Lyotard, 1984), de-
centring leading to free play, the lapse of the signified, '*différance*' (Derrida,
1976; 1978; 1982), 'archeologies' and 'genealogies' of knowledge/power
(Foucault, 1970; 1972; 1980), may of course lead one to an infinite
deconstructive regress, and to a subjective, irrational, self-contradictory
void. Indeed, this is what happened to the structuralists as they began
to concentrate solely on the sign. '[F]ormal deconstruction of the most
elegant, mannered kind' was the result, divorced from any politically
active referent. '[T]heir contribution to the resolution of the cultural
crisis [was] nonexistent' (Hall, 1990: 22). This does not necessarily have
to happen to the postmodernists themselves. However, in the late 1980s,

amidst the wailings of conservative intellectuals, poststructuralist/ deconstructionist views were entering the academic mainstream (even constituting it in some areas), and an expectable degree of political devitalization has followed.

The postmodern makes sense only in relation to the modern – that is, to those processes guaranteeing the primacy of endless capitalist accumulation; and to the modernist consciousness in the form of the concepts of progress, chronological historical time, and representational realism (where a turning point was reached with the invention of perspective in the fifteenth century at the very beginning of the history of the modern world-system). What Foucault and Derrida have sought to do is to 'rule out a historical consciousness that is "neutral, devoid of passions, and committed solely to the truth".... [Rather, they have sought to] uncover ... presiding logocentric urges, rules, and oppositions' (Lentricchia, 1980: 208). This would have the effect of opening up the possibility for postmodern narrative to redefine time as rhythmic time,

> as a function of position, as a dimension of particular events.... Postmodern time belongs to a figure, an arrangement in which 'the other world surrounds us always and is not at all the end of some pilgrimage' (Ermarth, 1992: 10– 11, 16).

This is only a small step away from Braudel's plurality of social times, a concept that requires imaginative (but explanatory) constructs rather than icy essentialism.

The '[p]ost-modern view ... will support relative absolutism, or fragmented holism ... the developing and jumping nature of scientific growth, and the fact that all propositions of truth are time- and context-sensitive' (Jencks, 1989: 59). All the same, language (like time) does not necessarily lose its symbolic, syntactical, representational dimension with the restoration of the digressive, rhythmic, semiotic disposition. Post-modernism does not rule out reuniting the two: meaning, which is 'the power to sustain linear arguments, transfer information, communicate conclusions', and play, which may be 'discredited ... [but belongs to a] realm of qualitative values like proportion, complexity, flexibility, pleasure, and eroticism taken in its most expanded sense' (Ermarth, 1992: 146, 143).[27] Thus, although the postmodern problematizes any nine-

---

27. We are reminded of a material parallel: 'hypertext', an information technology which redefines the classical document (generally of a maximum of four or so pre-conceived layers – text proper, notes, illustrations, over a bibliographic foundation). With hypertext, the reader assembles his own document (infinitely re/de-centerable) in the process of reading through electronic search-and-retrieval mechanisms, upsetting hierarchies and transcending reader/owner/author relations (see Landow, 1992).

teenth-century idea of the 'social', we have not thereby reached the end of responsibility and social agendas.

A World in Transition

In sum, the symptoms of the ideological crisis of the current conjuncture are apparent. It is no longer possible unabashedly and uncritically to associate science with progress. As the humanities become more open to analytic constructs, the internal development of science itself is tending to undermine its own position of authority. And the disciplinary boundaries reflecting a hierarchy of knowledge, with the sciences at the privileged pole, are already effectively blurred; indeed, the trend is one toward increasing 'fuzziness'.

Thus our argument, at the level of dynamics, is situated at one remove from most discussions of ideology. Yes, the modern world-system has produced three great political ideologies: conservatism, liberalism and socialism.[28] And, undoubtedly, both conservatism and socialism have had important functions legitimating struggle against dominant groups. But, over time, the differences among the three paled such that liberalism became the reigning ideology of the modern world-system. Socialism and conservatism have converged to a left and right liberalism (Wallerstein, 1992a; 1992b). This is understandably so, for liberalism, unlike its siblings, legitimates a politics of the *conjoncture*. Medium-term increments of reformist change adding up to endless (long-term), linear, progress suggest a golden, extrapolatable 'now' with no allusion to either a future transformation (socialism) or an idyllic past (conservatism).

The parallel to Newtonian dynamics is clear, and self-fulfilling. The very success of the system has taken the process to its limit. Science itself offered the linear-development model, based empirically and epistemologically on the ontological reality of independent units. It now provides us with alternative models of physical reality: relationally constituted self-organizing systems and fractal geometry; models of change, complexity theory; and models of transition, chaos theory – all in defiance of the law of the excluded middle so fundamental to classical science, classical logic, and current common sense (or 'bottom line' thinking).

No longer can phenomena in the natural world be perceived as falling into exhaustive, mutually exclusive categories. Likewise, with the realization that all knowledge is social and fundamentally interrelated, the

---

28.. See Eagleton, 1991; Gray, 1986; McLellan, 1986; Nisbet, 1986.

historical boundaries distinguishing disciplines are becoming increasingly blurred by the inquiry scholars practise. Since universities, departments, professional associations, and individual professors have institutional interests in preserving their domains, only limited observable movement, beyond so-called interdisciplinary studies programmes and the phenomenon of the 'electronic university' (important as a network model), is as yet evident. Multiculturalism may signal an advance, but the easy cooption of the 1970s 'Marxism' by departments and professional associations is not organizationally encouraging. The institutionalization of 'cultural studies' with programmes explicitly aimed at 'bridging the gap between the social sciences and the humanities' may or may not succeed in avoiding this fate.

Rearrangement of subjects and fresh organizational strategies are also being experimented with outside of established organizations and institutions. The 'think tank' model has become common, particularly in policy areas. For example, the Santa Fe Institute (founded 1984), devoted to the study of complex systems, does both experimental and theoretical work through networks of overlapping, multi(non)disciplinary groups (Pines, 1988).

Science is forging beyond the world of independent, hard-bodied units for one of open systems and relationships just as, congruently, the humanities tilt with humanism. That social construct, the rugged, independent, self-interested but responsible individual of liberalism, the 'subject', has lost his/her ideological underpinnings and now declares overlapping allegiances. The unique object – and the individual creator, the hero of modernism – has also been toppled (see, for example, Barthes, 1972: 109–59; 1977: 142–8; Krauss, 1981). The erosion of the law of the excluded middle may be observed symptomatically in the efforts in some places to reinstitutionalize limited, overlapping sovereignties, to find a legal interspace that will meet the demands of various groups for autonomy while retaining the wholeness of some larger structure. The activities of non-governmental organizations like Amnesty International, which confines itself to operations across borders, may also offer a glimpse of the future.

---

29. Michael Apple argues that 'neutral' scientific/technological processes underwrite as legitimate knowledge the clinical, psychological and therapeutic perspectives and evaluations which serve 'as mechanisms by which schools engage in anonymizing and sorting out abstract individuals into preordained social, economic, and educational slots' and justify 'already existing technical, cultural, and economic control systems that accept the distribution of power in American society as given' (1990: 126, 129).

Even as the relationship between science and ideology is being unveiled in such practical fields as curriculum studies,[29] scientists themselves are dissolving Poulantzas's 'mask of *science* dissembling power' (Eagleton, 1991: 154). And the cultural surrogate of this science, modernity, appears more and more to be a source of subjugation, oppression and repression than of liberation (Rosenau, 1991: 6). So 'crisis', yes, but one whose pulse is one of opportunity offered by success and demise: transition, where the *bricoleur* meets the engineer.

Part II
Overview

8

The Global Picture, 1945–90

Immanuel Wallerstein

There are three conclusions that one can draw from a review of the series of vectors that we have analysed. The first is that there is clear evidence that the period 1945–90 shows all the usual characteristics of a Kondratieff cycle (although the B-phase had not yet ended in 1990). The second is that the cycle of US hegemony in the world-system seems to have reached its peak somewhere in the middle of this period, and that the 1970s and the 1980s were the beginning of a downward phase in the cycle, even though as of 1990 the USA still remained in many (even most) ways the most powerful state in the world-system.

The third conclusion is more complicated and its meaning less clear. Aside from phenomena that can be associated with or explained by a Kondratieff B-phase and the B-phase of a hegemonic cycle, there seem to be the beginnings in the 1970s and 1980s of reversions in a series of several multisecular trends in the history of the world-system, as well as the levelling off of other trends as they seem to be reaching structural asymptotes.

We have chosen 1967/73 as the turning-point in this period, although of course the exact dates are open to much empirical debate. We chose these dates on the grounds that they are bounded by two major economic shocks – the first serious troubles for the US currency at the one end and the OPEC oil shock at the other – and that a series of political events occur during this period that together seem to add up to a significant break in the patterns of the earlier period: the worldwide revolution of 1968 (which in fact went on to 1970), the Tet offensive, the proclamation of US–Soviet détente, the US–Chinese resumption of more normal relations, and the undermining of the US imperial presidency with Watergate.

210   *The Age of Transition*

Let us summarize the data we have accumulated concerning the two cycles (the Kondratieff and the hegemonic), as well as such data as points to a possible systemic turning point.

I

The year 1945 can be taken to mark the beginning of a classical Kondratieff A-period. Kondratieff waves are notoriously controversial to date, given the lags in alternative measures of economic expansion (for example, prices, production, investment, profit rates), which are variously given priority in different models.[1] Some would start the upturn in 1940. There had been, of course, a significant worldwide expansion of both production and employment during the Second World War, but there had at the same time been worldwide destruction of fixed capital and people, as well as considerable interference with production and trade. It seems more reasonable to begin in 1945 (or even a few years later) if we wish to denote an overall expansion of the world-economy.

In fact, as of 1945, the destruction on the Eurasian land mass was quite extensive; and production, trade and transport had been sufficiently hindered such that there were widespread insufficiencies in basic food, clothing and shelter, not to speak of the enormous displacement of people. Yet we know that these difficulties were in fact overcome within a few years. The significant fact is that the world-economy thereupon entered into a period of rapid, steady, and indeed unprecedented expansion. A sharp upward boost came with the onset of the Korean War in 1950; its economic effects were felt not only in North America, Western Europe and East Asia, but in much of the Third World as well.

The USA played a central role as generator and promoter of the worldwide economic expansion – directly, in its economic activities at home; and indirectly through state assistance, primarily to Western Europe and East Asia, but to a lesser degree to much of the Third World (especially Latin America and the Middle East). US transnational corporations in this period accounted for the overwhelming majority of foreign direct investment. As noted, this was initially in Latin America but very soon throughout Western Europe. The US dollar served as the base currency of the world financial system, backed by a substantial gold

---

1. For a review of alternative models and their consequences for dating, see Goldstein, 1988. For a discussion of the problems of dating the current Kondratieff, see Wallerstein, 1979.

reserve. Hence, it was US Treasury and Federal Reserve Board decisions that in effect governed the world money supply.

The 1950s and 1960s saw ever greater production in the world-system as a whole, and especially of all those products which were highly profitable, the so-called leading industries. Western Europe, under the impetus of the Marshall Plan and the early European institutions, and East Asia (particularly but not only Japan), under the impetus of Cold War-related economic expenditures by the USA, not only recovered fully from wartime destruction but set out on the path of becoming highly competitive on the world market in the major industrial sectors. They recovered dominance in their home markets quite rapidly and by the 1960s were competing actively within the USA in non-home markets.

The so-called socialist bloc, whose trade external to the bloc was kept minimal in the 1950s and 1960s by deliberate policy of both the USSR and the USA, set out on its own simultaneous economic expansion. Its agenda emphasized multiple and more or less parallel national programmes of intensive industrialization, which had the effect of expanding overall world production in the leading industries still more. Finally, in Third World countries outside the socialist bloc, the objective of industrialization was similarly pursued, if somewhat less intensively on the whole.

The massive expansion of world industrial production required, of course, a massive expansion of so-called primary products. This translated into economic prosperity in agricultural and mining zones, particularly important in expanding the state income base in peripheral areas of the world-system. This meant that many, perhaps most, of the states that independence movements were seeking to wrest from colonial powers were, or seemed to be, economically prospering concerns. This in turn permitted expansion of the wage-earning sector (before and especially after political independence), particularly but not only in the state bureaucracies and state-managed enterprises. It also permitted the massive world-wide expansion of resources devoted to the educational and health-institution sectors. All in all, this added up on a world scale to what one French analyst called 'the thirty glorious years' (which, in his view, ran to 1973).

Our data clearly show that, in terms of generalized prosperity, upward climb in the standard of living, and relatively full employment, these glorious years came to an end perhaps as early as 1967, certainly by 1973, when the downward turn was dramatized (but surely not caused) by the so-called OPEC oil shock. The key element, no doubt, was that worldwide profit levels had begun to fall. The explanation seems straightforward. Whereas in the 1950s the leading sectors had been relatively monopolized by a small group of enterprises on the world level, the number of competitors had grown considerably in the 1960s; the field had become crowded.

The 1970s and 1980s were marked overall by a considerable slow-down of growth in production, and, given the continued demographic expansion, probably a decline in world per-capita production. This was accompanied, as would be expected, by a rise in the rates of active unemployment. Of course, this was not evenly distributed spatially in its effect. Furthermore, the negative effects were constantly shifting geographically, as various countries did what they could to suffer least, 'exporting unemployment' (or trying to do so) to the others. But, overall, the trend was one of stagnation, as compared to the previous Kondratieff A-phase. In particular, the spectacular expansion of transnational corporations, as measured by total production, by total real value, or by rate of profit, slowed down, at times considerably.

To be sure, efforts were constantly being made to counteract the insufficiency of total worldwide effective demand. The oil price rises of the 1970s served this purpose very well in two important ways. The dramatic rise in the costs of fuel energy had the obvious consequence of increasing the costs of production everywhere, and hence served as a pressure to reduce world production, which thus brought it more into line with world effective demand. The oil price rises also served as a vacuum of surplus-value throughout the world (but, of course, as a percentage of GDP, this affected the Third World most dramatically). In the end, this money was distributed in part as rent consumed by oil producers (most of whom were state enterprises in a limited set of countries), in part as rent (or exceptionally high profits) consumed by the transnational oil corporations, and in part as deposits invested in banks in core countries. These deposits were then 'recycled' in the 1970s as loans to peripheral and semiperipheral states (including those in the socialist bloc).

The recycled money enabled a large number of governments in the periphery and semiperiphery to solve balance-of-payments difficulties during the 1970s, difficulties that had been caused in part by the oil price rise, but caused as well by the falling terms of trade for peripheral products in the Kondratieff B-phase. The borrowed funds were used to import goods, primarily of course from states in the core zone, thereby restoring momentarily some of the lost demand for their exports. However, the artificial stimulus of exaggerated loans could not last. The ever-growing cost of servicing the debt led ineluctably to the so-called debt crisis of the 1980s.

The decline in the rates of profit in the production sector had three structural consequences of note. In the first place, it led to an urgent search for ways to reduce the costs of production. One classic method in times of economic downturn is the shift of loci of production from core to semiperipheral and peripheral zones in the expectation of reducing significantly the cost of labour. This shift began on a substantial basis in the 1970s and accelerated further in the 1980s.[2]

The second structural consequence was a considerable shift of investment from productive activities to the financial sphere in the search for profit. This led to the well-documented series of financial takeovers of major corporations and the flourishing of junk bonds, made all the more possible by the weakened profit position of major corporations. Of course, these financial manipulations also had the consequence of precipitating additional difficulties in the now heavily debt-laden private sector, with collapses that were quite costly in the long term, as in the case of the US savings-and-loan bankruptcies.

The third structural consequence was the turn to increased military expenditures as the counter-cyclical Keynesian measure most likely to be politically acceptable when seeking to increase governmental expenditure in times of economic squeeze. This occurred in two ways. The first was increased arms purchases by Third World countries from the great powers, especially from the USA, but also from some semiperipheral states, absorbing a significant part of the profits generated by the oil price rise. This, of course, had the consequence of increasing the amount of intra-state violence in the Third World, as well as exacerbating civil war situations.

The second form of military Keynesianism was increased expenditure on arms in the 1980s by the USA itself (as well as, to a lesser extent, by the USSR). While this major increase in expenditure by the USA had the effect of reducing the level of unemployment, at least in the USA, it did so at the very high price of increasing drastically the US debt level. The world-economy thus acquired in this B-period three major loci of debt: the Third World (and socialist) governments, large corporate enterprises, and the US government.

The consequences of these transformations on the workforce were seen in falling real wages for all those located in the former leading sectors, and increased unemployment (or irregularity of employment). Since these were precisely the sectors in which the trade unions were strongest, this weakened the labour movement considerably. This went along with a shift throughout the world to forms of work that were

---

2. The shift was already visible and documented by 1977, and explained theoretically in Fröbel et al., 1980.

under less legal control (home-working, the informal economy) and a major expansion of subcontracting. This shift constituted, in fact, an expansion of the numbers of wage-workers worldwide while at the same time reducing the average wage-level and also reducing the average percentage of total work time in wage work.

The downturn in the world-economy was accompanied by an acute downturn in food production in peripheral zones, for two reasons. In the A-period, core countries considerably expanded food exports, in part through food aid programmes. They thereby displaced economically local food production. This new food dependency of the peripheral zones was then accentuated in the B-period when these states turned with ever greater eagerness to export-led production as the solution to their balance-of-payments difficulties, thereby further transforming food-production areas into zones producing industrial or non-staple exportable crops.

The resulting hunger and homelessness accentuated the migration from rural to urban areas, but with an important difference from the previous A-period. Previously that part of the migration which was intra-Third World had been primarily to primate and/or capital cities, in search of wage employment, given the expansion of the state sector. Now such migration was emphasizing lesser cities nearer to the rural zones of emigration because of the new emphasis on seasonal, informal and temporary work. One consequence was the flattening of the urban–rural distinction, a point to which we shall return.

The decline of the state sector resulting from the decline of the income potentials of states not only led to a reconstruction of the workforce but to a significant decline in the ability of the state sector to maintain the level and expansion of educational and health facilities. This was true worldwide and came to be perceived as a general problem of decline in urban environments due to the cumulative effect of popular violence and the decrease in state services.

The world interzonal migration pattern began to shift as well. In the A-period the South–North migration was largely planned and encouraged by the state structures of the North. The economic stagnation led to a job squeeze in core countries, with the expectable political consequence of a reduced welcome for legal migrants. But the now increased need of employers in the core for low-paid workers led to a *de facto* collusion with those operating machinery for evading border controls, which greatly increased the flux of illegal (or undocumented) workers, a phenomenon further encouraged by the deteriorating political-economic (and hence security) conditions in peripheral zones.

Women workers in the B-period found more jobs, but this was far from indicating more equality at the workplace. On the one hand, they were more sought after precisely because of their socially constructed lower wage levels. Since their increased employment was often deliberately at the direct expense of male workers, this seemed to reduce somewhat the statistical gap in pay between male and female workers, but primarily by reducing the male level. On the other hand, to the degree that these male and female workers were located in income-pooling households, the total average income of the households in cash went down, thereby accentuating the reduction in real wages. Furthermore, the amount of part-time wage work went up worldwide as a percentage of all wage work, and employers of part-time workers tended to prefer to recruit women. Thus, although more women were in the world workforce, their subordinate role was in fact reinforced by the fact that the percentage of work done by women that was full time became less.

Finally, it should be noted that there were ecological consequences. The 1950s and 1960s led to a considerable increase in the exhaustion of primary resources precisely because of the enormous expansion of world production. The 1970s and 1980s saw no similar expansion. Instead they saw a shift in locus of the major ecological costs from core to peripheral and semiperipheral areas.

II

The role of the USA in the world-system had been steadily growing stronger since at least the 1870s. As British hegemony entered into its B-phase, the USA became increasingly important as a competitor on the world market, its principal rival being Germany. This rivalry culminated in the two world wars, actually to be thought of as one long 'thirty years' war' from 1914–45, which ended as we know in the unconditional military triumph of the USA and its allies.

In 1945, the USA was the only major industrial power of the time to have emerged from the military conflicts not merely unscathed in terms of any physical destruction of its fixed capital but, on the contrary, enormously strengthened in terms of its productive capacity and efficiency. It was able quickly to transform this economic advantage into a political, military and even cultural advantage that continued and grew in the immediate postwar period. Thus, 1945 marks the beginning of the heyday of unquestioned US dominance or hegemony in the world-system. US strength grew greater and greater in the twenty-five years or so thereafter.

The only other country with significant geopolitical and military strength in 1945 was the USSR, a country whose official ideology seemed to set it at direct odds with the USA in terms of long-term objectives for the structure of the world-system. The USSR, however, did not have anything near the productive strength of the USA (not to speak of commercial or financial strength). Its presumed great military strength would never be tested directly, for both the USA and the USSR were at pains to avoid a military collision. However, the USA had an initial nuclear edge in potential full-scale warfare, which was at most neutralized by the Soviet acquisition of nuclear bombs and the subsequent arms developments on both sides. The Soviet political appeal in the world arena, although considerable, turned out to be less than anticipated in 1945. And US claims to moral leadership, while constantly contested very strongly, always found a wide audience, especially in Western Europe and Japan.

The evaluation of the US–USSR relationship during the post-1945 years is bounded by limits contained in two slogans: the Cold War and Yalta. The Cold War symbolized total antagonism, albeit in a (relatively) cold form. Yalta, to the contrary, symbolized mutual accommodation (or for some a 'sell-out' by the USA to the USSR). In reality, looking back on the years 1945–1967/73, the actual story seems to be neither total antagonism nor mutual accommodation/'sell-out'.

Rather, the relationship, while noisy in rhetoric and full of tactical manoeuvring, was one primarily of mutual self-restraint. In the successive major military-political confrontations (the Greek Civil War, the Berlin blockade, the Korean War, the Quemoy-Matsou dispute, the Cuban missile crisis), the ultimately decisive operative slogan seems to have been prudence and the restoration of the status quo. The *de facto* consequence in terms of the world-system as a whole was the ghettoization of a Soviet 'bloc' within which Soviet authority was unchecked, which was minimally involved in worldwide commodity chains, and which in Europe respected perfectly the military frontiers established in 1945. Furthermore, the Cold War rhetoric enabled both the USA and the USSR to exercise a strong hand in their respective spheres, often without any significant challenge from the other (the German Democratic Republic 1953, Poland and Hungary 1956, Czechoslovakia 1968, Iran 1953, Guatemala 1954, Lebanon 1958, Dominican Republic 1965).

The USA worked to create politico-military alliances with all the major industrial countries – Western Europe, Japan, the White Commonwealth countries. This required initially significant assistance in physical reconstruction and renewed investment, a project which resulted in political advantage (a 'free world' bloc in the interstate system), military security (NATO, US–Japan Defence Pact, ANZUS), and economic opportunity (foreign direct investment by US transnationals). This habit of automatic US leadership and unilateral decision-making in the world arena had its cultural counterpart: the rise to centrality of US intellectual structures in all the fields of knowledge; New York as the world's art capital; and the so-called 'coca-colonization' of the popular culture of the world (but, first of all, of its allies in the industrialized core zone).

In peripheral zones, the period was marked by relative prosperity and the expansion of investment in infrastructure, educational and health facilities. In that large part of this zone which was still under formal colonial rule, nationalist movements gained strength steadily. The colonial powers launched, for the most part reluctantly, programmes of 'decolonization', first throughout Asia, and then in Africa, the Caribbean and Oceania. In general, this process was relatively smooth, particularly in British colonies, meaning that it was relatively peaceful (with some notable and well-noted exceptions). The USA encouraged this kind of peaceful, minimally disruptive transfer of power to 'responsible' movements, although the USA refrained from placing excessive pressure on the European colonial powers. Wherever colonial powers dragged their feet, for whatever reason, nationalist movements demonstrated a will and a capacity to force the pace (Dutch East Indies, French Indochina, Algeria, Kenya, the Portuguese colonies in Africa), and their energetic mobilization bore fruit not only for themselves but for their neighbours and fellow-colonized as well.

Finally in this period of great expansion of the world-economy under US hegemony, the USA in particular did extremely well, in terms of both the economy and social cohesion. It virtually eliminated the labour–capital conflicts at home that had been so acute in the 1930s. There was a significant rise in the standard of living of skilled workers and lower-middle-class strata, which began now to enjoy home and car ownership, durable goods, leisure-time activities, and higher education for children as normal expectations. The acute oppression of Blacks was alleviated by a higher rate of better-paying employment, accompanied by urbanization plus the ending of legal segregation (first of all in the military forces). These measures, in tandem with a ferocious anti-Communist ideological crusade plus the clear benefits deriving from US hegemony, seemed to fashion an exceptionally high degree of national unity.

And yet, by 1967/73, the skein of US hegemony began to unravel, something that seemed to be caused by the very successes of the USA in the establishment of its hegemonic authority. The most acute difficulty was posed by the growth in economic strength of other states in the core zone, in particular Western Europe (especially the Federal

Republic of Germany) and Japan. This showed up quite clearly in the patterns of foreign direct investment by transnational corporations. Whereas at first such investment was almost entirely a phenomenon of US-based TNCs, first European and then Japanese corporations began to represent a larger and larger percentage of the total. This began to pose a particularly acute problem for US corporations, given the overall slowing down of the rate of growth.

The same pattern was repeated in terms of financial structures. The first sign of difficulty was the emergence of a new phenomenon at the beginning of the 1960s: the so-called Eurodollars – US dollars that were physically located in Europe and therefore not subject to direct US financial controls. By the end of the 1960s, this weakening of the US government's financial leverage was compounded by the shrivelling of the US gold stock, accentuated (but not solely explained) by the heavy outflows occasioned by Vietnam War-related expenditures.

The ending of the fixed rate of gold in US dollars would relieve the pressure on the US gold supply, but only at the price of creating a world currency variability outside the unilateral control of the USA. Over the subsequent twenty-five years, the US dollar fell considerably (with, of course, ups and downs) vis-à-vis the currencies of other major states. By 1990, even the post-1945 practice whereby virtually all world economic transactions were denominated in dollars was coming into question.

One major consequence was the loss of effective authority over the world financial markets by the US government (Treasury Department and Federal Reserve Board) and the rise of rival centres of decision-making – other national institutions (for example, the Bundesbank), the 'gnomes of Zurich', and the trio of interstate world financial/economic structures (the IMF, the World Bank and GATT). The annual meetings of the G7 economic summit, launched in 1977, and itself one of the major consequences of US economic decline, became a locus of negotiated decisions among the major powers in the core zone. The world-system found itself in the 'obligatory adventure' of financial globalization.[3]

Of course, the other great powers in the core zone drew the appropriate geopolitical conclusions. De Gaulle's distancing of France from the USA (including the withdrawal from the NATO command structure) was the harbinger. It was followed by Willy Brandt's *Ostpolitik* and the European pipeline. European unification began to shed its anti-Soviet, Atlanticist flavour in favour of a more autonomous patina.

---

3. This is the title of the 1990 book by Aglietta, Brender and Coudert.

The unwillingness of the Third World to await the largesse of modulated decolonization had already been strongly demonstrated, first by the Chinese Communists and later, but with even more enervating effect, by the national liberation movements in Vietnam, Algeria, Cuba, and southern Africa. Even, however, with these experiences under the belt, the world-system (and the USA in particular) was caught off guard by the Iranian Revolution, and in particular by the total unwillingness of Khomeini and his supporters to respect the 500-year-old conventions of interstate diplomacy. The nose of the Great Satan was sharply tweaked, Mr Carter lost his helicopters in the desert, and Mr Reagan found he had to purchase the freedom of the US hostages.

When President Nixon proclaimed 'Let Asians fight Asians', he was already thereby admitting the limits of direct US military intervention in the world-system. Yet, the creation of subimperialist regional guardians was shown to be a substitute of limited effectiveness with the relatively easy destitution of the Shah of Iran. Nonetheless, this did not slow down the increasing militarization of the Third World, in which US interest was now becoming more immediately commercial and less a matter of middle-range strategy. Indeed the commercial need became very strong. The USA, to be sure, wanted to retain control of, or at least limit the availability of, the most advanced weapons. In fact, of course, the proliferation of weapons of mass destruction, despite the active opposition of the USA, constantly expanded in the 1980s, to the point that nuclear, chemical and biological weapons came to be a part of the arsenal of many semiperipheral states (even if the latter still felt pressure to deny publicly their possession, or felt obliged to keep their nuclear potential in an almost-but-not-quite-ready state).

Meanwhile, the world revolution of 1968 served as a protest everywhere against US hegemony in the world-system, but a protest simultaneously against the USSR, accused of *de facto* collusion with US hegemony. The revolutionaries pushed their analyses further, making a fundamental critique of all the major historic antisystemic movements without exception: social democrats (Labourites, New Deal Democrats), Communist parties, and national liberation movements. They launched a demand for an entirely new strategy, one far less cooptable by the hegemonic liberalism of the USA. This call effectively undermined the old antisystemic movements, but it also marked the beginning of the end of the US cooption strategy.

The disintegration at the end of the 1980s of the Soviet bloc and then of the USSR itself can be deemed a US victory only if one takes seriously the assertion that the destruction of this bloc had represented the (or even a) primary objective of US world policy since 1945. In

terms of US hegemony in the world-system, the disintegration of the
Cold War scaffolding of interstate relations can more pertinently be
seen as a vital blow to US pre-eminence, and therefore as something
that occurred despite (and not because of) US political will.

The decline of US relative power in the 1970s had permitted the
Brezhnev regime to seek to stretch the terms of Yalta, most notably in
Afghanistan. The USA was thereupon able effectively to use this new
Soviet assertiveness as an argument to slow down during the 1980s the
growing aspirations of Western Europe and Japan for political autonomy
from US world leadership.

The world economic stagnation, accentuated by the debt crisis, was
to have in the 1980s a destabilizing effect on the governments in
peripheral and semiperipheral states. The crisis of legitimacy, especially
but only in states which had claimed to be antisystemic in inspiration,
first drew world attention in Poland in 1980, followed by a long series
of instances such as the fall of the military regimes in Brazil and
Argentina, the crisis of the FLN in Algeria, and the agonizing collapse
of the Congress Party in India. Throughout Asia, Africa and Latin
America, the fiscal crises of the states led to the internal clamour for
'democracy' but simultaneously to the 'restructurings' imposed by the
IMF. The collapse of the east-central European Communisms was merely
the culminating event of this series.

The Gulf War crisis of 1990–91, in the very drama of US military
triumph, illustrated well the declining strength of the USA in the world-
system in two fundamental ways. The first was in the fact that this crisis
was deliberately and knowingly provoked by Iraq, whose government
resisted every attempt to avoid the actual outbreak of warfare. In the
period since 1945, this was the first such provocation of the USA. In
other cases where US strength had been tested, the provocation was
surreptitious and tacit (Berlin blockade, Cuban missile crisis) and never
was allowed to culminate in warfare. US hegemony had been tested, not
challenged. Now it had been defiantly challenged, and the inability of
the Iraqis to win the battle militarily was less important than the
precedent they were setting.

Second, it was clear that the USA could win this battle only on two
conditions: that it mounted a collaborative effort under UN aegis, and
that the battle was financed externally. The first condition demonstrated
the new political constraints on the USA, and the second the new
financial dependence of the USA on its former client states. These two
realities have been subsequently confirmed in the inability of the USA
to depose Saddam Hussein despite the military victory.

III

There are some observations about the 1970s and 1980s which are not easily accounted for merely by viewing this period as that of a Kondratieff B-phase or as the beginning of the period of decline of a hegemonic power. One of the most striking of these other occurrences is the widespread and rather profound attack on state power. The power of states – their centralization vis-à-vis regional forces, their authority over subjects/citizens, their clear definition vis-à-vis other states in the interstate system – has been on a steady rise since the creation of the modern world-system; that is, for some 500 years now. Of course, there have always been localized challenges to this growing authority, but the momentum of 'statism' has seemed not only to be unrelenting but to have had a remarkable thrust forward, thus reaching a new and exceptional peak precisely in the period 1945–1967/73. In this period, even conservative forces in core zones were openly lauding the virtues of *dirigisme*.

The hegemonic power had in a sense demonstrated the successful model of the New Deal, a model whose true blossoming was in the post-1945 period. The Western European states and Japan followed the same path. The Communist bloc shouted that they did it better. And the Third World frantically sought to use the state machinery to 'catch up' under one ideological guise or another. So large a proportion of enterprises had become state-run that a special term, the parastatals, was invented to designate them. Above all, the states were committed to serving the function of providing a wide range of basic services, as well as a so-called safety-net – social security, education, health, income for those out of the work network, finding employment for those who became unemployed, and in general countering cyclical downturns. The atmosphere was clearly expressed in the extraordinary statement in 1971 of a conservative US president, Richard Nixon: 'We are all Keynesians now.'

Suddenly, this secular trend began to reverse itself sharply in a series of ways. The unity of the state machineries began to come unglued in one crucial way in the core zones. The central banks began to assume a degree of real autonomy in decision-making vis-à-vis the central executive authorities that powerfully subverted the ability of these authorities to control their economic parameters. Whereas state authorities always had to take into account a gamut of political forces, central banks were responsive almost exclusively to a small segment of transnationals. Similarly the growing power of interstate structures like the IMF, seen in peripheral zones as agents of the core, could be viewed by authorities in the core zone as agents perhaps of core forces but subversive of the state machineries of the core zone.

The revolutions of 1968 put a serious crimp in the intellectual hold of centrist, reformist liberalism on intellectual and political norms. As a result, conservative forces were liberated to return to their original anti-statist, anti-reformist bias. This was alternately called neo-liberalism or neo-conservatism, and was exemplified ideologically by the Thatcher and Reagan regimes. The revolutions of 1968 also detached the commitment of the world left to statist reformism. The rise of various kinds of movements promoting the coherence and solidarity of groups whose boundaries were not congruent with those of the states combined with the convulsions of 1989 to put a serious damper on the remaining efforts of the historic antisystemic movements (the 'old left') to strengthen state structures. Slogans such as 'think globally, act locally' pointedly omitted the state level. While the new antisystemic movements turned anti-statist as a mode of radicalizing their action, the old antisystemic movements thereupon began to renege on their commitment to welfare-statism as a mode of staunching the loss of electoral support to more openly conservative movements. Swept up in the language of the 'free market', they were acknowledging the (at least momentary) appeal of the Friedmanite counter-Keynesian offensive of the 1980s.

All of this rhetorical turmoil seemed to reflect the exhaustion of the two-century-long ideological model of reformist liberalism, arriving at human progress through incrementalist state enactment and encouragement of rational change, as devised by technological experts. But the shift from reformist liberalism to the free market as political ideology was not a simple operation. For the old ideological model had one major trump card: it had acquired popular legitimacy over its history, by persuading popular forces that political activity paid off eventually. This belief served consequently to constrain 'revolutionary adventurism' and hence was profoundly stabilizing. The new ideological substitute had no historic popular base. It will therefore have to prove itself rapidly, or risk losing adherents as fast as it gained them.

Thus the disintegration of state structures, which we begin to see in the 1970s and 1980s, took on a new, more menacing, flavour. Whether it was the *de facto* replacement of state authority and state functions in local zones by integrist religious movements, or drug mafioso operations, or militarized sub-ethnicities, or urban gangs, or movements like Sendero Luminoso, the phenomenon was spreading. But the most important aspect of this phenomenon was not that it was spreading, but that the major world powers seemed unable or unwilling to do much about it. The disorder seemed to be slowly spreading, limited primarily by the degree of local exhaustion from the acute insecurity and economic suffering such disintegration of state authority involved.

This seeming reversal of the upward trend of statism appears to have been matched by the seeming reversal of the upward trend of secularism. This is not surprising, since statism and secularism were both historically and theoretically linked. Secularism was an essential concomitant of statism because it removed a very major obstacle to the necessary definition of citizenship as pertaining at least to all those born within certain arbitrary boundaries and having thereby both duties and obligations. The state was a secular institution *par excellence* and had needed to liberate itself from all non-secular claims in so far as it intended to centralize authority.

Secularism succeeded as long as the vision of progress, under the aegis of reformist liberalism, reigned supreme. Religion was kept out of politics so long as people felt that they could attain their political ends by political means in the only political arena that seemed to matter, the state. In so far as statism came under attack, however, secularism began to lose its major political justification. The re-emergence in new strength of fundamentalist/integrist/neo-traditionalist religious movements in every corner of the globe should thus be seen not as a reversion to some patterns predating the modern world-system, but rather as a revised, anti-statist mode of seeking to achieve the unfulfilled goal of modernity, equality in the realization of a decent quality of life.

The question, of course, is whether the new anti-secularism is a merely momentary reaction to a passing B-phase or is more fundamental. To the extent that it is linked with the cultural 'revolution' expressed in both 1968 and the collapse of reformist liberalism, it is likely to feed the creation of a new politics, of which the 1980s has heard much: identity politics, or the new faith in a crosscutting multiplicity of 'groups' and hence of group claims and group rights.

The third new trend of the 1970s and 1980s was the assault on the claims of scientistic science – both by the 'new sciences' and by the proponents of 'culture'. Of course, one might argue that a shift in paradigm is a cyclical phenomenon in the history of thought. But there is a difference here. The old paradigm – Newtonian, positivist, determinist science – was not merely a mode of defining normal science for a small group of specialists. It had become in the last two centuries one of the reigning faiths of the modern world-system, perhaps *the* reigning faith.

As such, the faith in science was more than an epistemological issue. It was a political phenomenon. Liberal reformism justified its self-confidence on the certainty of technological advance guaranteed by science. It was no accident that even the leading anti-liberal ideologist of the nineteenth century, Karl Marx, argued the merits of his programme as constituting 'scientific socialism'. Hence, as in the case of secularism, scientism was a necessary ideological prop of statism. Removing this prop has serious political and general cultural consequences.

Finally, in looking at developments in the 1970s and 1980s, we see three long-term curves reaching asymptotes, which may lead to further profound shocks to the system. The first is the transformation of the workforce. Analysts have long perceived proletarianization as a secular trend of the modern world-system. Actually we have underestimated how slow it has been in reality. And we have neglected how crucial to the modern world-system its non-universalization as a work form has been.[4]

In fact, the data seem to indicate that we are not reaching a fully proletarianized workforce (as defined classically), but rather a workforce in which there is a flattening of the variation of the degree of prole-tarianization across core–periphery and urban–rural differences. Indeed, we are seeing an evening out of population distribution such that it is increasingly difficult to delineate clear urban–rural dichotomies (at least within states). The political impact of such flattening is as yet uncertain. But it seems to remove one of the major mechanisms by which historic returns to economic expansion were engineered – that is, via the prole-tarianization of some 'reserve' labour force, which quite often meant the urbanization of persons previously resident in rural areas.

A second asymptote can be seen in the field of education. As late as 1945, there was a very sharp hierarchy, worldwide and within each state, of educational levels within the adult population. But the post-1945 economic expansion, accompanied by the triumph of statism and in-creased urbanization, led to an incredible expansion of primary educa-tion, a major expansion of secondary education, and even a remarkably large expansion of tertiary education. The rate of expansion slowed down in the 1970s and 1980s but continued nonetheless. In any case, the curves inch up to limits.

The problem with the universalization of education is that its success has undermined its political virtues. Education had been seen as a primary guarantor of liberal reformism, offering both opportunity and upward mobility on the one hand and social integration on the other. But the education of everyone has not meant that hierarchy is dis-

---

4. See the discussion in Smith and Wallerstein, 1992.

appearing; it has rather meant that the absolute level of education could no longer serve as the primary criterion of hierarchization. The political consequence became rapidly visible. Education came under attack because of its presumed lack of 'quality'. This has been a cover for creating a hierarchy of levels of quality of education within levels of quantity, and the quality has been identified with the particular schools which individuals have attended. Of course, this qualitative measure has always existed, but it has been revived and amplified to counter the effects of democratization of access. The consequence is that the faith in the redemptive virtues of education in the dissolution of inequalities has been undermined, and thereby one further systemic stabilizer has been vitiated.

Finally, the third asymptote we seem to be reaching is ecological degradation. Over 500 years, the accumulation of capital has been predicated on the vast externalization of costs by enterprises. This necessarily meant socially undesirable waste and pollution. As long as there were large reserves of raw materials to be wasted, and areas to be polluted, the problem could be ignored, or more exactly considered not to be an urgent one. The dramatic economic expansion after 1945, aided by further scientific advances, has led more and more people to believe that the world has crossed the threshold of danger – that is, to believe that the problem is now an urgent one.

Hence, in the 1970s and 1980s, ecology became a major political issue. The traditional political forces have tried the patchwork solution of verbal cooptation of the issue. But the problem is too dramatic to be affected by minor adjustments, and too expensive to be paid for easily. The real costs involved in ending waste, undoing pollution, and then not re-creating the problem are extraordinarily high. Paying for these costs threatens to overwhelm the possibilities for continued accumulation of capital. In any case, the issue directly opens up the question of the legitimacy of the current polarization of wealth and resources.

None of the problems discussed here is totally new. All seem to have posed, however, acute dilemmas as of the 1970s and 1980s. None seems soluble simply by entering a new Kondratieff A-phase or a new hegemonic A-phase. Indeed, all three problems would probably be exacerbated by an upturn.

9

The Global Possibilities, 1990–2025

Immanuel Wallerstein

In the light of the patterns of the world-system that we have analysed for the years 1945–90, what can we plausibly expect of our present/ future, 1990–2025? Formally, there are only two real possibilities. One is that the world-system will continue to function more or less in the ways that it has been functioning for five centuries now, throughout its life, as a capitalist world-economy, with to be sure the constant necessary adjustments to the machinery of the system. This would mean, in terms of the cycles that we have been analysing in this work, that the Kondratieff cycle would turn upwards again, and that the longer hegemonic cycle would begin again its path of reconstruction. The world-system might be different in many ways, but essentially it would remain a capitalist world-economy, based on an axial division of labour, unequal exchange, and an interstate system.

The second possibility is that those new phenomena which began to be noticeable in the 1970s, but which we argued could not be analysed as being simply the reflections either of a normal Kondratieff B-cycle or of the beginning of a hegemonic decline, prove sufficiently important and massive that it becomes no longer reasonable to expect that the system will continue more or less in the same manner, with merely some adjustments. In this case, we would rather expect the burgeoning of a systemic crisis or bifurcation, which would manifest itself as a period of systemic chaos, the outcome of which would be uncertain. The basic methodology we shall use is very simple. We shall assemble the arguments that might be made for the second hypothesis, that of systemic crisis. If the arguments we put forward do not seem plausible or convincing, then the first alternative, the normal continuance of the system, would be upheld, and it therefore will not be necessary to argue it separately.

It may be useful to distinguish in this analysis the 1990s from the period 2000–2025. We are already living in the 1990s. It seems clear that this is the final subperiod of the Kondratieff B-phase in which the world-economy has been since 1967/73. It is now widely asserted in the media and in political discourse that the 1990s are a period of 'recession'. This is, of course, *no more* true than it has been for two decades now. But since the final years of a B-phase are often the worst in terms of unemployment and general belt-tightening, it is harder for commentators to deny the reality of the worldwide 'recession', a denial in which the powers that be indulged themselves during the 1970s and the 1980s.

We may possibly, but not certainly, have a dramatic 'crash' of prices soon. This is simply one way (but not the only way) to clear the decks of the weakest economic performers in a period of stagnation, to prepare the way for a fresh expansion of the world-economy. We may also witness an acute increase in social unrest. It is normal that, in the early years of a Kondratieff B-phase, the working classes tend to be conciliatory in the hopes of retaining their jobs in a threatened job market. But in the later years, the advantages of further conciliation pale by comparison with the threat to their already lowered standard of living, and greater militancy is a normal response. While more intense class struggle is a rational response (rational in that it speaks directly to the problem at hand), such moments also see the intensification of less 'rational' inter-ethnic struggle, in response to the sense many people have of being threatened by the economic squeeze ever more immediately. It is no different this time: in the 1990s we are seeing an increase (by comparison with earlier moments in the post–1945 period) of both class struggles and inter-ethnic struggles around the world.

The coincidence of a Kondratieff B-phase with the beginning of hegemonic decline poses special problems for great powers, especially for those that are located in the core zone. Their internal equilibrium is much more shaky than usual, and fear of social unrest at home becomes the compelling priority. They also know that the possibility of doing well in the expansion of the prospective A-phase depends on their ability to be competitive in one particular subfield of world production, that of the new leading products. This, too, leads these states to turn inward, in search of formulas that will reward the workforce in these new product areas while remaining very prudent about concessions to the working classes in what are considered outdated arenas of production. If such a period coincides with the culminating phase of a long struggle for hegemonic supremacy, it can lead to world war. But if it is at only the beginning of such a struggle for hegemony, as we are now, the combination of the two internal concerns leads these powers instead to be quite cautious in the international arena. The utilization of threats of force, implying sending troops outside the national frontiers, risks social explosion at home, given a situation of pre-existing social unrest. Geopolitically, such a situation can be rather paralysing, and this is precisely what we are seeing in the 1990s – in Bosnia, in Somalia, in Haiti, in Korea, and elsewhere.

To be sure, the situation of the 1990s would normally be quite transitory. At some point, probably ±2000, there should be an economic upturn. There will have been enough 'cleaning-out' of unprofitable productive enterprises worldwide, enough elimination of accumulated rent situations, and enough innovations in the prospective new leading industries, plus enough restoration worldwide of global demand through a combination of new proletarianizations and the increase in social benefits acquired as a result of the renewed class struggles, such that there will once again be an adequate basis for an expansionary momentum in the world-economy. Not only is this a normal expectation, but there is little reason to think that it will not occur this time too.

Thus, at one level we may expect the normal continuance of the patterns of the world-system. The question is how this ongoing pattern will be affected by, interact with, the new elements of which we have been speaking. We shall analyse the mixture in terms of the same six vectors we used to analyse the period 1945–90: the interstate system, world production, the world labour force, world human welfare, the social cohesion of the states, and the structures of knowledge.

It is now a commonplace observation that, given the relative decline of US economic strength, the world-system has become triadic, by which is meant that there are now three loci, or central nodes, around which economic activity is organized, and that the three are sufficiently competitive with each other – that is, near enough in the prices at which they can supply major products on the world market – that none of the three, now or in the immediate future, will be able easily to outdistance the others. This triadic distribution has been discussed primarily as an economic phenomenon, and of course this is the heart of its existing reality. But such a triadic distribution of economic strength cannot fail to have geopolitical implications.

The end of the Cold War has made archaic all institutions that had their origins in the Cold War. This is the basic problem of NATO. It is the object of lavish rhetorical support while at the same time it has been given in fact a relatively minor role to play in the post-1989 geopolitical arena. In short, it is being treated by the great powers in the way we have observed them acting for almost fifty years towards the United Nations, as a secondary adjunct.

The USA remains in the 1990s by far the strongest military power in the world, *a fortiori* given the collapse of the USSR. But it is a power whose force is on the wane, given the decline in its internal financial base and its internal legitimacy. On the contrary, it is most probable that each of the other potentially major military powers in the world – the European Community, Japan, Russia and China – will, in the twenty-five years to come, become stronger than they are in the 1990s. Furthermore, it is quite clear that nuclear weapons are no longer technically out of the reach of the so-called middle powers. Who among them already has such weapons, who will have them soon, who will only have them twenty-five years from now is a matter of considerable debate, but nuclear proliferation is already occurring. How fast things move is a function of how much the USA can and will still invest in rearguard manoeuvres against this proliferation. It is hard to believe that by 2025 there will not be at least several dozen states who will have nuclear weapons at their disposal. There is in addition the present reality and prospective spread of chemical and bacteriological weapons, which are inherently more difficult to monitor than nuclear weapons.

Thus, it is scarcely adventurous to put forward the picture of a world-system in which there will be widespread diffusion of significant military power without the comforting concentration of this power in two efficacious (and mutually restraining) command posts such as existed in the world-system during the Cold War. The absence of such command-posts opens up three major possibilities, all of which may occur: a proliferation of 'minor' wars that will be relatively unchecked; the possibility that multiple forces in the South, coincidentally or conjointly, will deliberately engage in military challenges to the North; and a difficult search in the North for new alliance patterns in the hope of stabilizing the interstate system.

The ability of the North to contain a military disintegration of the world-system would depend on the degree to which the so-called major powers could in fact re-create stabilizing alliances. This is, of course, what is being discussed under the heading of 'finding a new role for NATO'. The likelihood of this depends, however, on the current struggle over the creation of new quasi-monopolies in world production. It is this struggle that will determine the ability of each of the three triadic nodes to retain and augment their overall economic strength and consequently their ability to accumulate capital and to sustain and improve their national standards of living.

During the Kondratieff A-phase, the competition between the three nodes will be acute, each trying to secure a sufficient economic edge such that it can 'lock in' some technological advantage, and thus achieve the rents deriving *de facto* from middle-term monopolies. It is in part a battle over concentrating the key patents which will bring in their wake high profit margins. If the three nodes are not too far apart as of the 1990s, it is not likely that they will remain in this relative equilibrium in the period 2000–2025. One of them will probably pull ahead, as has happened so regularly in past competitions of this sort.

The economic competition poses two sorts of problem. The TNCs which are located primarily in the one node or the other are individually, and also in collusion with fellow-national TNCs, seeking optimal arrangements to pursue their ability to accumulate capital. This requires the making of inter-enterprise alliances and it requires as well support from their state machineries. The fact that there are three nodes and not two means that the structure is unstable. As the competitive battle goes on, it will be tempting to try to reduce the triad to a dyad, since in this case the two of the three that link up will have a clear advantage over the third. On the other hand, any struggle to reduce the triad to a dyad will exacerbate the latent tensions among them, and make it more difficult for the governments to reach accord on a common front of the North vis-à-vis the incipient military challenges from the South.

The manoeuvring by TNCs is already going on, and no clear pattern has yet emerged. In the effort to secure control of the new leading products – microcomputers, biotechnology, metals that permit super-conductivity, multimedia informatics, waste management, and so on – the USA has the advantage of the largest existing markets but the disadvantage of structures of production that are less than maximally efficient with an overextended, indeed bloated, network of middle-management cadres. Japan is in virtually the opposite situation: relatively efficient overall structures of production (including, of course, the whole system of subcontracting) with insufficient internal markets to absorb the production. Western Europe seems to fall in between on both criteria. Of course, governments and the TNCs are aware of these differences, and have been moving to reduce the negatives. But this is more easily said than done.

Like teams preparing for the big contest, the three nodes have been assembling their forces. This has taken the form of constructing regional networks which are potentially, but not yet actually, protectionist redoubts. The European Community is an entity of approximately the same weight as the USA and Japan, or perhaps the USA plus Canada and Japan plus the so-called four dragons. Each of the three has been moving to expand its node by including some countries that are lower-cost production zones in a privileged relationship: Mexico for the USA (NAFTA), parts of Southeast Asia for Japan, possibly east-central Europe for Western Europe.

In this situation, the result of any struggle to reduce the triad to a dyad is more likely to see Japan and the United States coming together than either of them with Europe. The reasons are not primarily economic, since economically any of the three combinations could probably work about equally well. The reasons are more broadly political and cultural.

First of all, there is what may be called the special positions of China and Russia. These two countries combine present and potential military and political weight with large populations who are very eager and ready to serve both as an import market and as a source of cheaper labour for world production. There are, of course, other countries that have the second characteristic, but it is the combination of the two features that gives them their special position, and considerable bargaining power. Including China or Russia in one or another of the nodes will constitute a major prize in the struggle for primacy. Japan clearly wishes to include China in its node, but for historical reasons will find it difficult to do this; it would be easier for both Japan and China if the USA were to join them in a three-legged alliance. Europe has little to offer China but much to offer Russia, and will work hard to bring Russia within its node. Russia might be interested in a link with the USA, but it is unclear that the USA would have the political and economic energy to develop such relations with both China and Russia; and, for geopolitical as well as historical reasons, the USA is more interested in China.

Aside from how the triad relate to Russia and China, there is a second consideration that brings the USA and Japan closer together, and forces Europe and the USA further apart: the politics of military power. Japan will be politically unable fully to develop its military potential for at least another twenty-five years. It therefore needs a military ally, and the USA is the obvious candidate. Europe, on the other hand, wants very much to develop *now* a fuller military presence on the world scene, and it can only really do this to the extent that it loosens its links with the USA.

The military issue is linked to a third factor, what might be called the general cultural issue. Japan and China are both interested in re-asserting an East Asia centrality on the world cultural scene, a reassertion which goes against the grain of the Eurocentrist assumptions of the geoculture of the world-system. Clearly, they cannot do this if they ally with Europe. The USA is, of course, culturally derivative of Europe, but given its hybrid cultural structure is probably more flexible in the long run in this regard than Europe. Europe, on the other hand, wishes to reassert itself as the heartland of European culture, a role that the USA usurped from Europe in the post-1945 period. Europe can more easily achieve this by distinguishing itself from the USA rather than by drawing closer.

These, then, are the reasons why we may expect the emerging dyad, if there is one, to be Japan/USA/China versus Europe/Russia. In the 1990s we are still in a triadic situation, and there is much public quarrelling between the USA and East Asia. But does each side mean what they say? It may well be that the public quarrels are merely a smokescreen of rhetoric behind which the geopolitical alliances of the early twenty-first century are steadily being forged.

The real question is whether any dyadic outcome, whatever its shape, will allow the North to deal with any challenges from the South that are more than rhetorical. One question is how the South will react to an emerging dyadic situation in the North. Initially, many countries in the South may seek to become part of the nodes. They will, so to speak, offer themselves for closer integration into the production networks under construction; indeed many are already doing so. But it is not enough to offer oneself for exploitation; one has to be accepted. The economic energy of the North in terms of monetary and human investment is not unlimited. The famous FDI coming from the strong states tends therefore to be directed where it will pay off the most. Most of it goes, as we have seen, from one part of the core zone to another, or to those semiperipheral zones which have privileged political ties. Another large amount goes normally to those countries which, for political and/or economic reasons, are newly given priority, and we have already suggested the reasons why China and Russia will be such priority areas. Finally, some of it must go to appease restive understrata in the major states of the core zone. After all this investment is distributed, how much will be left over in the coming A-phase for the other half of the globe? Probably not very much at all. There will, of course, be selective investment in enclaves all over, but, as we know from past A-phases, this may not add up to very much – almost certainly not enough at the level of larger states in the South to satisfy increasingly restive, increasingly large, populations.

What seems very possible is that we shall enter into a vicious circle of low investment, leading to an increased sense of exclusion, leading to social unrest, leading to these countries becoming increasingly unsafe as loci of investment and therefore to still further exclusion. And all this would be occurring at a time when the new expansionary A-phase will seem to offer a more glittering standard of living than ever to populations in the North, or at least to its large middle strata. The gap between zones which has always existed, and whose increasing width the world was already discussing loudly during the 1945–90 period, may become magnified both in reality and above all in perception.

The consequence for the structure of the world labour force of dyadic competition in the North combined with an increased North–South gap in the coming world-economic expansion will be reinforcement of the patterns already described for the 1945–90 period. The continuing deruralization of the world labour force will push ever larger numbers into sprawling urban centres, where they will be employed, to the extent that they are, in widening networks of part-time, informal, subcontracting structures. These will be located worldwide, North and South, but in a hierarchical pattern that will constantly encourage the stronger individuals to seek upward mobility by upward migration.

Upward migration on an ever more massive scale may prove to be enormously politically disruptive for states in the North. Once there is a new A-phase, there will be a very strong lobby of employers to permit more legal migration, or failing that to collude in widening mechanisms of illegal immigration, which in turn will meet constant resistance from groups who see their wage levels and even their jobs threatened by this influx.

Economically this may seem to be a development that would be moving in a direction opposite from polarization, since it would involve some flattening of wage disparities between North and South to the degree that the influx of migrants effectively lowered average wage levels in the North. Actually, the modern world-system will be coming full circle in the structuring of the world labour force. Originally, low wages were the norm throughout the world-system, with only pockets of high-wage activities. The early patterns of industrialization led to a geographical concentration of higher-wage pockets, such that states in which core activities were located had larger and larger percentages of persons for whom the 'iron law of wages' was a meaningless referent. With the increasing deruralization of the world labour force, and the depreciation of the profitability of those kinds of industrial production which employ large labour forces, we are once again returning to a situation where the distribution of lower and higher level wage jobs is becoming somewhat more even worldwide. With, however, one major difference: the income gap between those whose wages are at survival level and those whose wages are more than that is now considerable, unlike in the fifteenth to eighteenth centuries. Thus an increasing core–periphery gap will become less and less seen or defined as a clearly geographical phenomenon, and more and more as a class phenomenon in all countries.

This is the worst of all situations for those interested in the political stability of the existing world-system. On the one hand, the populations in the South, who will still be the worst off and the most desperate, may be ready to contemplate more serious antisystemic disruption. On the other hand, the bottom strata in the countries of the North will no longer enjoy some of the amenities which they had been invited to share in the post-1945 period, and even more importantly will no longer believe that it is certain that their children will enjoy a higher standard of living than they.

In the states of the North, this could lead not merely to disorder, but quite extensively to the end of Jacobinism, the ideal of the integrative nation-state, whose ultimate rationale was the disparity it could guarantee between the working strata of the North and those of the South. The cultural-political expression of the breakdown of Jacobinism is the rise of 'multiculturalism' in its many guises. Even if only partially successful, the assertion of 'group rights' will interfere with the ability of states of the North to mobilize politically (and militarily) against states of the South. But this will be happening at a point in the historical development of the world-system where, as we have seen above, it will be all the more necessary for states in the North to mobilize mass support at home because of the increased destructiveness of weapons available to the South at the raised minimum threshold level. That is to say, even though the states of the North will no doubt continue to maintain a considerable technological edge in their military capacities, the power of the weak states will for the first time be sufficiently destructive as to be truly threatening. If, on top of this, national identity breaks down in northern states, it is not clear how they can effectively oppose military defiance from southern states.

It is here that the vector of world welfare raises its head as a crucial political variable. The seemingly steady increase over time of formal education, health services, and availability of nutritious food has served as a pillar of the world-system, however unevenly this welfare has been distributed. The exigencies of dyadic competition and vast migratory transfers of population will put enormous pressure upon – have already been putting enormous pressure upon – the abilities of governments, both South and North, to maintain their current levels of services. At the same time, the flattening of urban distribution, both within and among countries, combined with the long-term effects of the rhetorical commitments of the world-system to human welfare, have led to a much increased demand for democratization, a concept whose reality has long been *de facto* measured in very large part by the distribution of welfare services.

What this means is very simple. For the first time in at least 200 years, governments are seeking to cut back everywhere on previous levels of expenditures on social services of all kinds. But this is the very moment where populations are pressing for a significant increase in government expenditures on social services of all kinds. Furthermore, the movements of the ethnic understrata and of women are insisting precisely on a further and special increase of these services to them as previously neglected groups. Quite obviously, this is a scissors effect of the sharpest sort, and expresses itself as the 'fiscal crises of the states'.

To the extent that states do not resolve their fiscal crises, they undermine the contextual stability that capitalist enterprises need in order to permit relatively rational risk-taking. On the other hand, to the extent that they seek to resolve their fiscal crises by some kinds of cutbacks, the cutbacks they will be able to make that would be most financially significant – the so-called entitlements – form a good part of the income of the middle strata in the states of the North. These are the same middle strata whose bloated numbers are the target of those enterprises which are seeking greater leanness in the competitions of the world market. The combination of reduction of middle-strata jobs (by enterprises, and by governments who will support fewer such jobs in research-related activities) and the reduction of direct benefits to these middle strata in terms of entitlements would constitute an attack on precisely those elements who have been the political stalwarts of the liberal states of the North, and their major soldiers in the effort to contain the discontents of the lower strata.

In addition, it is not only the middle strata of the North who are thus in peril, but also (albeit in somewhat different ways) the smaller yet equally politically crucial middle strata in the South. In the post-1945 period, the improvement of the political and economic situation of middle strata in the South was even more spectacular than that in the North, although this group constitutes a much smaller percentage of its national population. They were the primary beneficiaries of the national projects of the national liberation movements, and they have taken as the measure of what they ought to expect the standard of living of their equivalents in the states of the North. Their sustenance has been costly to state budgets, in part through the legal dispensing of perquisites, in part through illegal acquisitions. They have begun now to be squeezed, in part by the structural adjustment programmes imposed by the IMF and other world structures and in part by popular rebellion against precisely their privileges. In addition, they have lost the sense of mission that the national liberation project had offered them, and which had given them legitimacy in the eyes of the popular strata and in their own eyes. From revolution to corruption is not a very exhilarating collective trajectory. Of course, this has been a trajectory not only of strata in the South but in most of the North, as the political upheaval of the 1990s in Italy amply demonstrated. This, of course, further weakens the political framework of the world-system.

The decline in world welfare, and above all the decline of the confidence that world welfare is rising, constitutes a major blow to the social cohesion of the states. Nor is it the only such blow. Indeed, it is in large part a consequence of the far more important decline of the faith in the traditional antisystemic movements, and thereby the rupture of the belief in the efficacy of rational reformism. This is not a mere cyclical up and down, or at least it is more than that. We have argued that the world revolution of 1968, completed in 1989, involved a process of irreversible shift in collective social psychology. It marked the end of the dream of modernity – not the end of the search for its goals of human liberation and equality, but the end of the faith that the state within the capitalist world-economy could serve as the facilitator and guarantor of steady progress towards achieving these goals.

The great stabilizer of the system, which made possible the social cohesion of the states, has been an underlying optimism of the long term. It is no longer there. It is not that long-term pessimism has replaced it, but rather acute uncertainty and lingering fear. Fear is not new, but it has been fear of certain people or groups or institutions; such fear could be countered by struggle to overcome them. The fear that now pervades is much less tangible; it is the fear that the situation is crumbling and that nothing is being or can be done to stop the crumbling. This kind of fear leads to much more erratic behaviour, much more uncontrollable behaviour.

Individual states have, of course, frequently been weak, or under attack from within. But normally they were under attack from alternative organizing structures which had clear long-term projects. There were not only the structures and projects of the old left. There were also the structures and projects of the dissenting Churches (broadly defined), and even those of the mafias. All of these structures with projects carried within them an internal optimism which made members impatiently militant in the short run but patiently confident in their long-term prospects. To the extent that such movements had been able by their militancy to achieve interim gains for their members (that is, an increase in human welfare), their anti-state rhetoric has in fact resulted historically in an increase, not a decrease, in the social cohesion of the states.

Today, there are some substitute movements that have been putting themselves forward, with similar anti-state rhetoric. Some have taken the guise of religious integrisms, some a renewed claim for ethnic separatisms. The question is not whether such movements can mobilize populations in the short run, but whether they can achieve interim goals for their members in the middle run. At some point, these movements will be called upon to assume some responsibility for governance, as has always been the case. And at this point their ability to meet expectations is less a function of their programmes or wisdom than of the structural possibilities the world-system offers them. It is this latter that has changed. In this case, we are in another vicious circle: disillusionment with the old antisystemic movements and the prospects for liberal reformism leads to the weakening both of such movements and of the social cohesion of the states; this opens space for other movements, which may gain local successes, followed by an inability to perform better in the provision of human welfare; and this leads to a further weakening of the social cohesion of the states. We seem to be in precisely that circle now.

There is one final problem, which affects simultaneously the stability of the interstate system, the profitability of world production, and the social cohesion of the states. It is addressed in the social issue that became for the first time a major concern in the last twenty-five years: ecology, or the health of our ecosystem. Ecology had long been a local concern; but it is only recently that it became a global concern. The reason is very clear: the steady expansion of both world production and world population had begun to use up remaining margins of waste within the world ecosystem. The objective constraints became blatantly evident, and in many cases frightening. The point is not to rehearse this story, but simply to outline the dilemmas involved in responding to the problem. There are two collective tasks involved: repair to damage already done; minimizing future damage. Each is costly, but the mode of payment is different. Essentially, repair to damage already done is a task that can only be undertaken in a significant way by governments, and financing the work requires taxation. Minimizing future damage can most effectively be done by forcing enterprises to internalize the costs.

The basic question is who will bear the costs, and what priority such costs will have vis-à-vis alternative expenditures. Within each state, the costs for repair can be seen as part of the overall bill for welfare, since the main issue is public health. Within a context in which the current level of expenditures on welfare is diminishing and under constant attack, how plausible is it that a bill for significant repair of damage will in fact be incorporated into state budgets? To what extent, that is, will the taxation be progressive, or 'user-related'? Clearly, we have added a very divisive element to an already explosive debate about the role of governments in reducing or sustaining internal inequalities.

In terms of the system of world production, forced internalization of the (not small) costs of waste management will seriously constrain the profitability of enterprises in a situation where secular global rises of wage levels are already putting serious pressures on profit levels. To be sure, if all enterprises were under exactly parallel pressures (a dubious proposition), this would not affect their competitive position, but it could still affect the overall profit level, on the assumption that the elasticity of demand was less than one. To be sure, waste management has itself become a profitable enterprise, but it is profitable to firms specializing in it; it remains a cost for all the other firms.

One solution that will appeal to many in the North is to export the costs to the South, by exporting waste and by exporting industries that do not wish to internalize the costs of waste management and seek therefore to avoid bureaucratic controls. In terms of the interstate system, this will involve a significant further increase in the North–South polarization, and this at a time when, as we have seen, the military stability of the interstate system will be much weakened, especially in relation to the North–South axis.

The final difficulty is located in the structures of knowledge. The modern world-system has been built on the faith in science – science as unlimited technological advance, and hence as the foundation of the world production system; science as progress, and hence as the foundation of world human welfare; science as rationality, and hence as the guarantor of social stability and the inspirer of rational reformism. We have explored the degree to which this faith in science has been called into question in the last twenty-five years in ways that are more fundamental and more corrosive of collective faith than any critiques with which science has been confronted for at least 200 years.

The intellectual and moral challenges to the simple trust in a science that could and would perform its social task of making possible collective improvement comes at precisely the moment when, with the end of the Cold War, organized science is losing the extraordinary financial base it had obtained in the post-1945 era. Everywhere, big science is being subjected to budget cuts, and has to face the challenge of alternative uses of collective resources, without the advantage of hiding such expenditures as military costs. We must not forget that science as an enterprise is as much a social organization as it is an intellectual activity, and bureaucratic attack affects recruitment, confidence and optimism.

Organized science finds itself in a position similar to that of the antisystemic movements. Disillusionment is creeping in, albeit not yet to the degree that has affected the antisystemic movements. The new science represents an attempt to respond to the intellectual culs de sac. It may also have implications for the social organization of science. The very attempts to regain antisystemic energy by inventing new social movements, less linked to the search for state power, has served as an additional obstacle, both intellectual and organizational, for organized science to overcome in the struggle to maintain and/or restore its privileged position. The question is whether the new science may not be caught in a squeeze between a still strong group unflinching in their commitment to positivism and those advocating a rejection of science *per se*. This is in part an organizational question, but it is also in great part an intellectual one. By insisting on the inherent indeterminacy of the future, on the impossibility of quantitative accuracy, on the transitory nature of theories, the new science may have solved many of the intellectual conundrums posed by Newtonian science. But its practitioners may equally find themselves in the position of reform movements: wanting to save the house of science, they may have undermined its social legitimacy, at least within the framework of the existing system.

Does this series of dilemmas for the major institutional vectors of the world-system add up to a situation of systemic chaos? We shall, of course, know the answer to this only in the observation of the social reality as it develops. We shall be able to monitor this reality in five major arenas, for each of which we can observe the degree to which there will be great oscillation in behaviour which the system might be unable to contain. Each of these arenas constitutes a sensitive zone, in which too great an oscillation may, if one may be permitted the metaphor, force the vehicle permanently to leave its groove.

The first is the arena of 'groups', or, to be more precise, of *Gemeinschaften*. A *Gemeinschaft* is the kind of group defined in terms of a (fictive) commonality and which lays claim to loyalty over and above egoistic interests. The story of the modern world-system has been *not* the elimination of *Gemeinschaften* but their subordination to the primacy of one particular one, that of 'citizenship'. Citizenship has, of course, been identified totally with states. In principle, in the modern world-system, for at least two centuries now, everyone has been a citizen of some country and normally of only one country. There have been exceptions to this rule, but they were considered as anomalies. Of course, the rule still holds. The question for the immediate future is not whether citizenship continues to exist and even to command loyalty, but whether it will continue to exert primacy of loyalty.

As the ability of the states to respond to the currently expressed demands of its citizens lessens (for the reasons explained previously), and as, above all, the faith of the citizens that the state can and eventually will respond to its demands disappears, it is natural that the claims of priority of other groups, other *Gemeinschaften*, become more persuasive. Indeed, as we have argued, this process has already begun. It is fuelled by two quite different sources. One is fears concerning survival in a situation where states seem less capable of ensuring security and stability. The other is the demand for democratization, the sense that the states have systematically ignored the needs of certain groups, who have thus *de facto* been excluded from the benefits obtained by other citizens. Both concerns lead to the militant organization of such groups. But the second motivation leads groups to oppose them-selves to the states, whereas the first motivation leads groups to oppose themselves to other groups.

The problem is that, in real social organization, the line between the two motivations is not very clear, and the actual groups are often divided among themselves as to strategy, the argument being one about whether the primary objective is self-protection (and hence group-aggrandizement) or democratization (or equality). One can well imagine a scenario in which *three* forces are at work: those favouring group-aggrandizement, those favouring democratization, and those favouring the status quo ante of 'citizenship' (formal equality but *de facto* hierarchy). In a situation of economic polarization, the absence of a stable geopolitical equilibrium, and a collapse of some of the ideological fundamentals of the world-system, it is not implausible to see a confused zigzag of battles between these three forces, within and among states, which will feed upon itself.

The second arena is what we may call police order. The ability of any historical system to operate is predicated upon a certain minimum of police order – that is, of a certain degree of general confidence in daily security of person and property. The level of security is never perfect, but it is normally high. If it is not, the system of production cannot operate and very soon there are major problems of material distribution. In addition, it becomes very difficult to operate any kind of political or cultural institution.

In our modern world-system, police order is guaranteed by the states, who use force, reward and faith to enforce order. The degree of internal order has, of course, not been uniform across the states. States contain-ing a high quota of core-like processes have always had more resources (material and spiritual) with which to maintain internal order effectively. But the remarkable feature of the modern world-system has been its ability to promote ever higher degrees of internal order worldwide on the basis of secular states that are legitimated by popular sovereignty and participate in the singular division of labour of the world-economy.

We have reviewed some of the reasons why this secular growth of 'stateness' (which is another name for this police order) may have passed its apogee and be for the first time declining. The question is whether it will decline as gradually as it ascended historically. There is reason to doubt this. The increase of stateness can be gradual because it is sustained by the assumption that it will grow greater, which was the result of the belief in progress, the faith in science, and the credibility of rational reformism. But if these pillars fail, the effect may be dramatic. In a scenario of prospective decline of stateness, the rush for advantage (or rather the rush to avoid disadvantage) can be precipitous. Such precipitation would, of course, be reinforced by the kind of confused inter-group struggle previously adumbrated.

The third arena is that of military order, which is an aspect, of the interstate system. Wars have, of course, been as chronic within the modern world-system as previously in world history. It is, however, important to see that, over time, the wars have tended to be of two principal varieties. The first is that of the wars of conquest, which have been part and parcel of the establishment of a core–periphery axial division of labour. In our language of today, they have been wars launched by the North to subordinate the South. The second is that of the wars of hegemony, the struggle among states in the North with each other for primacy, culminating in the world wars. In the historic process, two other kinds of wars have not occurred, or have been eliminated. Wars among states in the South have been suppressed. Indeed, the 'restoration of order' in the South was one of the great imperialistic themes of the nineteenth century. And wars launched by the South against the North have not been possible. The wars of national liberation have, of course, been launched by the South but they were by definition and by objective territorially limited.

What has begun to happen in recent years is the re-emergence of wars among the states of the South as well as wars launched by the South against the North that go beyond national boundaries. It is the sign of a diminution of collective military strength of the North. Once again, we have already analysed the sources of this decline: technological, economic and, above all, those deriving from collective social psychology. Here again, as in the case of police order, the question is whether a decline in military order can be as gradual as its ascent. And here again, one may doubt that this is truly possible. The possibilities of warfare are as much conditioned by what is in the heads of the war-makers as by what is or can be in their hands. A 'failure of nerve' in the North can precipitate a disintegration of the protective dikes against the two kinds of wars that were suppressed in the modern world-system. Of course, any kind of breakdown in the military order will immediately affect the degree of police order that is possible, and intensify the intergroup struggles.

The fourth arena is that of welfare, and in particular that of public health and food distribution. The great achievement of the modern world-system has been the steady improvement of public health and food distribution for at least the privileged third of the world's population. We have examined some of the reasons why this has begun to be challenged: malfunctioning of the ecosystem, the intensification of migratory flows, the persistent demands of the non-privileged to be included in the benefits, the growth of world population.

In the last 200 years, the ideologues of the world-system have been congratulating themselves on the conquest of diseases and the elimination of famines. Here, too, one must ask whether we have not passed the apogee and now find ourselves on a descending curve. The general feeling still is, faced with new pandemics like AIDS and new signs of famine revival as in Africa, that this is a technological problem open to solution with enough investment of money and intellectual energy. And this may be the case, provided that the numbers of such problems do not grow and provided that we are not faced with breakdowns of police and military order. But, of course, we have just indicated why we may be faced with such breakdowns of order, in which case it may well be that the basic health problems expand very rapidly and overwhelm the capacities of the world health system to cope with them. In this arena as in the others, the oscillations can rapidly become quite wild.

The final arena is the stability of our religious institutions. In a sense, the legitimacy of religious institutions has long been thought to have been undermined by the emergence of the secular, scientific geoculture of the modern world-system. In fact, the reality has been that the religious institutions have survived, and even in a real sense, tamed the challenge of secularism. Not only have the passions of anticlericalism begun to be a faint memory of things past but we are said to be living a great religious revival across the world.

Such a reading of the present misses the fact that the world's religious institutions are today facing a much more fundamental challenge than that of Newtonian science or liberalism, which have proved to be paper tigers in this regard. The greater challenge is that of the demand for full equality of women. It is a historic fact that all the world's major religious structures have been built on assumptions about and attitudes towards women that are not in fact compatible with the demand for the full equality of women. This is no doubt because all the world's religious institutions have been centrally concerned with the control of sexuality.

We do not propose here to suggest how this conflict could in fact be resolved. We merely wish to point to the fact that the conflict is very acute and socially extremely disruptive. The rise of groups not giving priority to citizenship has allowed both new religious integrisms and new feminist movements to flourish. But each of the two is building its strength on the basis of arguments that lead it into direct conflict with the other. This is not merely one more intergroup conflict, because it has implications for the entire organization of social life. It will therefore not be something that can be 'handled' by the kind of social compromise that postpones resolution. Or rather, it might be so handled, if the world-system were otherwise stable. But given the multiple instabilities which we have been analysing, it is quite improbable that this conflict will be shelved. And since this conflict will interact with at least the arenas of group conflict, police order and world welfare, it will have a cumulative effect.

It may be possible to contain the conflicts in one or more of the five arenas. The question is, will this happen? And even if it does, will it be enough? Since the arenas interact, containing the conflicts in one arena may turn out to be provisional, as the conflicts erupt in another. In a tinderbox, which is the picture we have been drawing of the world-system, the fire can spread. This is precisely what is meant by systemic chaos.

To be sure, after systemic chaos will come some new order, or orders. But here we must stop. It is not possible to discern what such a new order would be. It is only possible to assert what we would like it to be, and to struggle to make it so.

Bibliography

Abel-Smith, Brian (1990). 'The Economics of Health Care', in T.A. Lambo and S.B. Day, eds, *Issues on Contemporary International Health*. New York: Plenum Medical Book, 55–71.

Abrahamian, Ervand (1992). 'Khomeini: A Fundamentalist?', in L. Kaplan, ed., *Fundamentalism in Comparative Perspective*. Amherst: University of Massachusetts Press, 109–26.

Acheson, Dean (1969). *Present at the Creation: My Years in the State Department*. New York: Norton.

Ades, Dawn (1981). 'Dada and Surrealism', in N. Stangos, ed., *Concepts of Modern Art*, rev. edn. London: Thames & Hudson, 110–37.

Agar, Michael (1990). 'Text and Fieldwork: Exploring the Excluded Middle', *Journal of Contemporary Ethnography*, vol. XIX, no. 1, April, 73–88.

Aglietta, Michel (1979). *A Theory of Capitalist Regulation: The U.S. Experience*. London: New Left Books.

Aglietta, Michel and Brender, Anton (1984). *Les métamorphoses de la société salariale: la France en projet*. Paris: Calmann-Levy.

Michel Aglietta, Anton Brender and Virginie Coudert (1990). *Globalisation financière: l'aventure obligée*. Paris: Economica.

Aharoni, Yair (1993). 'Globalization of Professional Business Services', in Y. Aharoni, ed., *Coalitions and Competition: The Globalization of Professional Business Service*. New York: Routledge, 1–19.

Aida, Shuho et al. (1985). *The Science and Praxis of Contributions to the Symposium Held at Montpelier, France, 9–11 May 1984*. Tokyo: UN University.

Alexandratos, Nikos (1988). *World Agriculture towards 2000*. New York: New York University Press.

Alperovitz, Gar (1985). *Atomic Diplomacy: Hiroshima and Potsdam: The Use of the Atomic Bomb and the American Confrontation with Soviet Power*. New York: Penguin.

Alperovitz, Gar and Bird, Kai (1994). 'The Centrality of the Bomb', *Foreign Policy*, no. 94, Spring, 3–20.

Althusser, Louis (1969). *For Marx*, trans. B. Brewster. London: Verso.

Althusser, Louis and Balibar, Etienne (1970). *Reading Capital*, trans. B. Brewster. London: New Left Books.

Ambrose, Stephen E. (1983). *Rise to Globalism: American Foreign Policy Since 1938*, 3rd rev. edn. New York: Penguin.

Ambrosius, Gerold and Hubbard, William (1989). *A Social and Economic History of Twentieth-Century Europe*. Cambridge, MA: Harvard University Press.

Amin, Ash (1993). 'The Globalization of the Economy: An Erosion of Regional Networks?', in G. Grabher, ed., *The Embedded Firm: On the Socioeconomics of Industrial Networks*. New York: Routledge, 278–95.

Anderson, Benedict R. O'Gorman (1991). *Imagined Communities: Reflections on the Origin and Spread of Nationalism*, 2nd edn, revised and expanded. London: Verso.

Anderson, Dennis and Leiserson, Mark W. (1980). 'Rural Nonfarm Employment in Developing Countries', *Economic Development and Cultural Change*, vol. XXVIII, no. 2, 227–48.

Anderson, Perry (1966). 'Socialism and Pseudo-Empiricism', *New Left Review*, no. 35, January–February, 2–42.

———— (1964). 'Origins of the Present Crisis', *New Left Review*, no. 23, January–February, 26–53.

Anderson, Wilda C. (1983). 'Dispensing with the Fixed Point: Scientific Law as Historical Event', *History and Theory*, vol. XXII, no. 3, 264–77.

Antle, John M. (1988). *World Agricultural Development and the Future of U.S. Agriculture*. Washington, DC: American Enterprise Institute for Public Policy Research.

Apple, Michael W. (1990). *Ideology and Curriculum*, 2nd edn. New York: Routledge.

Apter, David (1987). *Rethinking Development: Modernization, Development, and Post-Modern Politics*. Newbury Park, CA: Sage.

Arlacchi, Pino (1986). *Mafia Business: The Mafia Ethic and the Spirit of Capitalism*. London: Verso.

Armstrong, Philip; Glyn, Andrew and Harrison, John (1984). *Capitalism Since WWII: The Making and Breakup of the Great Boom*. London: Fontana.

Arnove, Robert F. (1980). 'Comparative Education and World-Systems Analysis', *Comparative Education Review*, vol. XXIV, no. 1, February, 48–62.

Arrighi, Giovanni (1991). 'World Income Inequalities and the Future of Socialism', *New Left Review*, no. 189, September–October, 39–66.

———— (1990a). 'Marxist Century, American Century: The Making and Remaking of the World Labour Movement', *New Left Review*, no. 179, January–February, 29–64.

———— (1990b). 'The Three Hegemonies of Historical Capitalism', *Review*, vol. XIII, no. 3, Summer, 365–408.

Arrighi, Giovanni and Drangel, Jessica (1986). 'The Stratification of the World-Economy: An Exploration of the Semiperipheral Zone', *Review*, vol. X, no. 1, Summer, 9–74.

Arrighi, Giovanni; Hopkins, Terence K. and Wallerstein, Immanuel (1989a). *Antisystemic Movements*. London: Verso.

———— (1989b). '1968: The Great Rehearsal', in G. Arrighi, T.K. Hopkins and I. Wallerstein eds, *Antisystemic Movements*. London: Verso, 97–115.

Arrighi, Giovanni; Ikeda, Satoshi and Irwan, Alex (1993). 'The Rise of East Asia: One Miracle or Many?', in R. A. Palat, ed., *Pacific-Asia and the Future of the World-System*. Westport, CT: Greenwood, 41–65.

Arrighi, Giovanni and Silver, Beverly (1984). 'Labor Movements and Capital Migration: The United States and Western Europe in World-Historical Perspective', in C. Bergquist, ed., *Labor in the Capitalist World-Economy*. Beverly Hills: Sage, 183–216.

Atlan, Henri et al. (1985). *La sfida della complessità*, a cura di Gianluca Bocchi e Mauro Ceruti. Milan: Feltrinelli.

Ayer, Alfred Jules, ed. (1959). *Logical Positivism*. Glencoe, IL: Free Press.

Baer, Werner (1962). 'The Economics of Prebisch and ECLA', *Economic Development and Cultural Change*, vol. X, no. 2, January, 169–82.

Bairoch, Paul (1988). *Cities and Economic Development: From the Dawn of History to the Present*. Chicago: University of Chicago Press.

Baker, R. (1991). 'The Role of the State and Bureaucracy in Developing Countries Since World War II', in A. Farazmand, ed., *Handbook of Comparative and Development Public Administration*. New York: Dekker, 353–63.

Balbo, Laura (1987). 'Family, Women and the State: Notes Toward a Typology of Family Roles and Public Intervention', in C. Maier, ed., *Changing Boundaries of the Political*. New York: Cambridge University Press, 201–20.

Baran, Paul A. and Hobsbawm, E.J. (1961). 'The Stages of Economic Growth', *Kyklos*, vol. XIV, no. 2, 234–42.

Barnet, Richard J. (1983). *The Alliance – America, Europe, Japan*. New York: Simon & Schuster.

Barnet, Richard J. and Cavanagh, John (1994). *Global Dreams: Imperial Corporations and the New World Order*. New York: Simon & Schuster.

Barraclough, Geoffrey (1990). *An Introduction to Contemporary History*. Harmondsworth: Pelican.

Barthes, Roland (1977). *Image/Music/Text*, trans. S. Heath. London: Fontana.
——— (1972). *Mythologies*, trans. A. Lavers. New York: Hill & Wang.

Beardsley, Edward H. (1987). *A History of Neglect: Health Care for Blacks and Mill Workers in the Twentieth-Century South*. Knoxville: University of Tennessee Press.

Beechey, Veronica and Perkins, Tessa (1987). *A Matter of Hours: Women, Part-time Work and the Labour Market*. Cambridge: Polity Press.

Bergquist, Charles; Penaranda, Ricardo and Sanchez, Gonzolo, eds. (1992). *Violence in Colombia: The Contemporary Crisis in Historical Perspective*. Wilmington, DE: SR Books.

Betts, Richard K. (1987). *Nuclear Blackmail and Nuclear Balance*. Washington, DC: Brookings Institute.

Bill, James A. (1988). *The Eagle and the Lion: The Tragedy of American–Iranian Relations*. New Haven, CT: Yale University Press.

Bird, Kai (1992). *The Chairman: John J. McCloy, The Making of the American Establishment*. New York: Simon & Schuster.

BIS (Bank for International Settlements) (1992). *Annual Report*.

Black, Jan Knippers (1977). *United States Penetration of Brazil*. Philadelphia: University of Pennsylvania Press.

Bleeke, Joel and Ernst, David, eds (1993). *Collaborating to Compete: Using Strategic Alliances and Acquisitions in the Global Marketplace*. New York: Wiley.

Block, Fred (1977). *The Origins of International Economic Disorder: A Study of United States International Monetary Policy from World War II to the Present*. Berkeley: University of California Press.

Bohm, David (1980). *Wholeness and the Implicate Order*. Boston, MA: Routledge & Kegan Paul.

Borden, William S. (1989). 'Defending Hegemony: American Foreign Economic Policy', in T.G. Paterson, ed., *Kennedy's Quest for Vic tory: American Foreign Policy, 1961–1963*. New York: Oxford University Press, 57–85.

—— (1984). *The Pacific Alliance: United States Foreign Economic Policy and Japanese Trade Recovery, 1947–1955*. Madison: University of Wisconsin Press.

Borgmann, Albert (1992). *Crossing the Postmodern Divide*. Chicago: University of Chicago Press.

Boserup, Ester (1990). *Economic and Demographic Relationships in Development*. Baltimore: Johns Hopkins University Press.

—— (1986). 'Shifts in the Determinants of Fertility in the Developing World: Environmental, Technical, Economic and Cultural Factors', in D. Coleman and R. Schofield, eds, *The State of Population Theory: Forward from Malthus*. London: Blackwell, 239–55.

—— (1970). *Woman's Role in Economic Development*. London: Allen & Unwin.

Bosworth, Barry P. (1993). *Saving and Investment in a Global Economy*. Washington, DC: Brookings Institute.

Bowles, Samuel and Gintis, Herbert (1976). *Schooling in Capitalist America: Reform and the Contradictions of Economic Life*. New York: Basic Books.

Brands, H.W. (1989). 'The Limits of Manipulation: How the United States Didn't Topple Sukarno', *Journal of American History*, vol;. LXXVI, no. 3, December 785–808.

Braudel, Fernand (1981). *Civilization and Capitalism, 15th–18th Century*, I: *The Structures of Everyday Life: The Limits of the Possible*. New York: Harper & Row.

—— (1958). 'Histoire et sciences sociales: La longue durée', *Annales: E.S.C.*, vol. XIII, no. 4, October–December, 725–53.

Breton, André (1972 [1924]). 'Manifeste du surréalisme', in *Manifestes du surréalisme*. Paris: Gallimard, 11–64.

Broad, Dave (1991). 'Global Economic Restructuring and the (Re)Casualisation of Work at the Center', *Review*, vol. XIV, no. 4, Fall, 555–94.

Broad, Robin (1988). *Unequal Alliance: The World Bank, the International Monetary Fund, and the Philippines*. Berkeley: University of California Press.

Broad, William J. (1991). 'For U.S., No Nobels May Mean a Fluke', *New York Times*, 29 October, C5.

Brodersohn, M. (1988). 'Developing Countries' Delicate Balance', in H. Stein, ed., *Tax Policy in the Twenty-first Century*. New York: Wiley, 118–24.

Bromley, Simon (1991). *American Hegemony and World Oil: The Industry, the State System and the World-Economy*. Cambridge: Polity Press.

Brown, Lester R. (1988). *The Changing World Food Prospect: The Nineties and Beyond*. World Watch Paper 85. Washington, DC: World Watch Institute.

—— (1978). *The Twenty-Ninth Day: Accommodating Human Needs and Numbers to the Earth's Resources*. New York: Norton.

Brown, Lester R. et al. (1989). *State of the World 1989*. New York: Norton.

—— (1987). *State of the World 1987*. New York: Norton.

Bryceson, Deborah F. (1989). 'Nutrition and the Commoditization of Food in Sub-Saharan Africa', *Social Science and Medicine*, vol. XXVIII, no. 5, 425–40.

Buchloh, Benjamin H.D. (1990). 'Cold War Constructivism', in S. Guilbaut, ed.

Reconstructing Modernism: Art in New York, Paris, and Montreal, 1945–1964.
Cambridge, MA: MIT Press, 85–112.

Bull, David (1982). *A Growing Problem: Pesticides and the Third World Poor.* Oxford:
OXFAM.

Bundy, McGeorge (1988). *Danger and Survival: Choices About the Bomb in the First
Fifty Years.* New York: Random House.

Bunker, Stephen and O'Hearn, Denis (1993). 'Strategies of Economic Ascend-
ants for Access to Raw Materials: A Comparison of the U.S. and Japan', in R.
A. Palat, ed., *Pacific Asia and the Future of the World-System.* Westport, CT: Greenwood, 83–102.

Burawoy, Michael (1979). *Manufacturing Consent: Changes in the Labor Process Under
Monopoly Capitalism.* Chicago: University of Chicago Press.

Burrows, William E. and Windrem, Robert (1994). *Critical Mass: The Dangerous
Race for Superweapons in a Fragmenting World.* New York: Simon & Schuster.

Bush, Vannevar (1945). *Science, The Endless Frontier: A Report to the President.* Washington, DC: US GPO.

Bushnell, P. Timothy et al., eds (1991). *State Organized Terror: The Case of Violent
Internal Repression.* Boulder, CO: Westview.

Butor, Michel (1972a [1960]). 'Le roman comme recherche', in *Essais sur le roman.*
Paris: Gallimard, 7–14.

——— (1972b [1964]). 'Réponses à "Tel Quel"', in *Essais sur le roman.* Paris:
Gallimard, 7–14.

Buttari, Juan J. (1979). *Employment and Labor Force in Latin America: A Review at
National and Regional Levels,* 2 vols. Washington, DC: OAS.

Camilleri, Joseph and Falk, Jim (1992). *The End of Sovereignty? The Politics of a
Shrinking and Fragmenting World.* Brookfield, VT: Elgar.

Capra, Fritjof (1982). *The Turning Point: Science, Society, and the Rising Culture.* New
York: Simon & Schuster.

Carnoy, Martin (1974). *Education as Cultural Imperialism.* New York: McKay.

Carnoy, Martin and Levin, Henry M. (1985). *Schooling and Work in the Democratic
State.* Stanford: Stanford University Press.

Cardoso, Fernando Henrique (1977). 'The Consumption of Dependency Theory
in the United States', *Latin American Research Review,* vol. XII, no. 3, 7–24.

Castles, Stephen; Booth, Heather and Wallace, Tina (1984). *Here For Good: Western
Europe's New Ethnic Minorities.* London: Pluto.

Catrina, Christian (1988). *Arms Transfers and Dependence.* New York: Taylor &
Francis.

Caute, David (1988). *The Year of the Barricades: A Journey Through 1968.* New York:
Harper & Row.

Chaliand, Gérard and Rageau, Jean-Pierre (1990). *Strategic Atlas: A Comparative
Geopolitics of the World's Powers,* 3rd edn. New York: Harper & Row.

Chetley, Andrew (1990). *A Healthy Business? World Health and the Pharmaceutical
Industry.* London: Zed.

Chomsky, Noam (1991). *Deterring Democracy.* London: Verso.

——— (1982). *Towards a New Cold War: Essays on the Current Crisis and How We
Got There.* New York: Pantheon.

Clark, Joseph (1964). 'Higher Education is a National Problem', in P. Woodring
and J. Scanlon, eds, *American Education Today.* New York: McGraw-Hill.

Cleaver, Harry M. (1979). 'The Contradictions of the Green Revolution', in C.K. Wilbur, ed., *The Political Economy of Development and Underdevelopment.* New York: Random House, 223–33.

Clegg, Jeremy (1987). *Multinational Enterprise and World Competition: A Comparative Study of the U.S.A., Japan, the U.K, Sweden and West Germany.* London: Macmillan.

Cleland, John and van Ginneken, Jerome (1989). 'Maternal Schooling and Child-hood Mortality', *Journal of Biosocial Science, Supplement,* no. 10, 13–34.

Cockcroft, Eva (1992 [1974]). 'Abstract Expressionism, Weapon of the Cold War', in F. Frascina and J. Harris, eds, *Art in Modern Culture: An Anthology of Critical Texts.* New York: Icon Editions, 82–90.

Cohen, Linda R. and Noll, Roger G. (1991). 'Government Support for Commercial R&D', in L. R. Cohen et al., *The Technology Pork Barrel.* Washington, DC: Brookings Institute, 17–36.

Cohen, Percy S. (1985). 'Functional Analysis', in A. Kuper and J. Kuper, eds, *The Social Science Encyclopedia.* Boston, MA: Routledge & Kegan Paul, 322–25.

Cohen, Stephen S. and Zysman, John (1987). *Manufacturing Matters: The Myth of the Post-Industrial Economy.* New York: Basic Books.

Collins, Randall (1988). *Theoretical Sociology.* San Diego, CA: Harcourt Brace Jovanovich.

Cooper Weil, Diana et al. (1990). *The Impact of Development Policies on Health: A Review of the Literature.* Geneva: WHO.

Costigliola, Frank (1989). 'The Pursuit of Atlantic Community: Nuclear Arms, Dollars, and Berlin', in T.G. Paterson, ed., *Kennedy's Quest for Victory: American Foreign Policy, 1961–1963.* New York: Oxford University Press, 24–56.

Cremin, Lawrence A. (1990). *Popular Education and Its Discontents.* New York: Harper & Row.

Crime and Social Justice (1987). Issue on 'Contragate and Counter-Terrorism: A Global Perspective', nos 27–8.

Crouch, Harold (1978). *The Army and Politics in Indonesia.* Ithaca, NY: Cornell University Press.

Cumings, Bruce (1994). 'Japan and Northeast Asia into the 21st Century', un-published paper delivered at workshop, 'Japan and Asia', Cornell University, May 19–20.

——— (1993). 'Japan's Position in the World System', in M. Miyoshi and H.D. Harootunian, eds, *Japan in the World.* Durham, NC: Duke University Press, 34–63.

——— (1990). *The Origins of the Korean War,* II: *The Roaring of the Cataract, 1947–1950.* Princeton, NJ: Princeton University Press.

——— (1987–88). 'Power and Plenty in Northeast Asia: The Evolution of U.S. Policy', *World Policy Journal,* vol. V, no. 1, Winter, 79–106.

——— (1987). 'The Origins of Northeast Asian Political Economy: Industrial Sectors, Product Cycles and Political Consequences', in F.C. Deyo, ed., *The Political Economy of New Asian Industrialism.* Ithaca, NY: Cornell University Press, 44–83.

——— (1984). 'The Origins and Development of the Northeast Asian Political Economy: Industrial Sectors, Product Cycles, and Political Consequences', *International Organization,* vol. XXXVIII, no. 1, Winter, 1–40.

———— (1981). *The Origins of the Korean War,* I: *Liberation and the Emergence of Separate Regimes, 1945–1947.* Princeton, NJ: Princeton University Press.

Dahl, Robert A. (1963). *Modern Political Analysis.* Englewood Cliffs, NJ: Prentice-Hall.

Dahlberg, Kenneth (1979). *Beyond the Green Revolution.* New York: Plenum.

D'Amico R. and Piccone P. (1991). 'Federalism. Introduction', *Telos,* no. 91, Spring, 2–15.

Danto, Arthur C. (1968). *Analytical Philosophy of History.* Cambridge: Cambridge University Press.

Darling, Martha (1975). *The Role of Women in the Economy: A Summary Based on Ten National Reports.* Paris: OECD.

Darknell, Frank A. (1980). 'The Carnegie Philanthropy and Private Corporate Influence on Higher Eduction', in R. Arnove, ed., *Philanthropy and Cultural Imperialism: The Foundations at Home and Abroad.* Boston, MA: G.K. Hall, 385–411.

Davies, Paul, ed. (1989). *The New Physics.* New York: Cambridge University Press.

Davies, Robert and Martin, William G. (1992). 'Regional Prospects and Projects: What Futures for Southern Africa', coordinated by S. Vieira; W.G. Martin and I. Wallerstein, *How Fast the Wind? Southern Africa, 1975–2000.* Trenton, NJ: Africa World Press, 329–64.

Davis, Lynn Etheridge (1974). *The Cold War Begins: Soviet–American Conflict Over Eastern Europe.* Princeton, NJK: Princeton University Press.

Davis, Mike (1986). *Prisoners of the American Dream: Politics and Economy in the History of the US Working Class.* London: Verso.

———— (1982). 'Nuclear Imperialism and Extended Deterrence', in *New Left Review,* ed., *Exterminism and Cold War,* London: Verso, 35–64.

Davis, Zachary S. (1994). 'Nuclear Proliferation and Nonproliferation Policy in the 1990s', in M.T. Klare and D.C. Thomas, eds, *World Security: Challenges for a New Century,* 2nd edn. New York: St Martin's Press, 106–33.

De Bolla, Peter (1986). 'Disfiguring History', *Diacritics,* vol. XVI, no. 4, Winter, 49–58.

Deger, Saadet (1990). 'World Military Expenditure', in *SIPRI Yearbook.* Oxford: Oxford University Press, 143–202.

Dehio, Ludwig (1962). *The Precarious Balance: Four Centuries of the European Power Struggle.* New York: Knopf.

Dehm, Alfred (1990). 'Investment Flows Between Korea and Europe', in J.L. Maurer and P. Regnier, eds, *Investment Flows Between Asia and Europe, What Strategies for the Future?* Geneva: Modern Asia Research Centre, 139–42.

de Janvry, Alain; Sadoulet, Elisabeth and Young, Linda Wilcox (1989). 'Land and Labour in Latin American Agriculture from the 1950s to the 1980s', *The Journal of Peasant Studies,* vol. XVI, no. 3, April, 396–424.

Deldycke, Tilo; Gelders, H. and Limbor, Jean-Marie (1968). *La population active et sa structure.* Brussels: Université Libre de Bruxelles.

Dellinger, David (1982). 'The Antinuclear Movement', in M. Kaku and J. Trainer, eds, *Nuclear Power, Both Sides: The Best Arguments For and Against the Most Controversial Technology.* New York: Norton, 233–7.

De Micheli, Mario (1978). *Le avanguardie artistiche del Novecento.* Milan: Feltrinelli.

de Montbrial, Thierry, dir. (1990). *RAMSES 91: Le monde et son évolution*. Paris: Dunod.

de Oteyza, Luis G. (1972). 'Restructuration des entreprises affectées par l'émigration: L'Espagne', in C.A.O. Van Nieuwenhuijze, ed., *Emigration et agriculture dans le bassin mediterranéen*. The Hague: Mouton, 50–81.

Derrida, Jacques (1982). *Margins of Philosophy*, trans, A. Bass. Chicago: University of Chicago Press.

—— (1978). *Writing and Difference*, trans, A. Bass. Chicago: University of Chicago Press.

—— (1976). *Of Grammatology*, trans, G. Spivak. Baltimore: Johns Hopkins University Press.

De Swaan, Abram (1988). *In Care of the State: Health Care, Education, and Welfare in Europe and the USA in the Modern Era*. New York: Oxford University Press.

Deutsch, Karl W.; Markovits, Andrei S. and Platt, John, eds (1986). *Advances in the Social Sciences, 1900–1980: What, Who, Where, How?* Lanham, MD: University Press of America.

Devall, Bill and Sessions, George (1985). *Deep Ecology: Living as if Nature Mattered*. Salt Lake City: G.M. Smith.

Dewey, Kathryn (1989). 'Nutrition and Commoditization of Food in Latin American and the Caribbean', *Social Science and Medicine*, vol. XXVIII, no. 5, 415–24.

Didericksen, Finn (1990). 'Health and Social Inequalities in Sweden', *Social Science and Medicine*, vol. XXXI, no. 3, 359–68.

Dixon, John A.; Talbot, Lee M. and LeMoigne, Guy J. M. (1989). *Dams and the Environment*. Washington, DC: WHO, World Bank Technical Paper No. 110.

Dobb, Maurice (1964 [1947]). *Studies in the Development of Capitalism*, rev. edn. New York: International.

Doctor, Kailis C. and Gallis, Hans (1966). 'Size and Characteristics of Wage Employment in Africa: Some Statistical Estimates', *International Labour Review*, vol. XCIII, no. 2, February, 149–73.

Douglass, Mike (1988). 'Transnational Capital and Urbanization on the Pacific Rim', *International Journal of Urban and Regional Research*, vol. XII, no. 3, 343–55.

Dower, John (1972). 'The Superdomino in Postwar Asia: Japan In and Out of the Pentagon Papers', in N. Chomsky and H. Zinn, eds, *The Pentagon Papers: Critical Essays*, Vol. V, Senator Gravel Edition. Boston, MA: Beacon, 101–42.

Duch, Danuta and Sokolowska, Magdalena (1990). 'Health Inequalities in Poland', *Social Science and Medicine*, vol. XXXI, no. 3, 343–50.

Dunning, John H. (1993). 'The Internationalization of the Production of Services: Some General and Specific Explanations', in Y. Aharoni, ed., *Coalitions and Competition: The Globalization of Professional Business Service*. New York: Routledge, 79–101.

Durand, John Dana (1975). *The Labor Force in Economic Development: A Comparison of International Census Data, 1946–1966*. Princeton, NJ: Princeton University Press.

Durning, Alan B. (1990). 'The Third World Fights Back: People Overcome Poverty and Pollution', *The Progressive*, vol. LIV, no. 7, July, 24–7.

—— (1989). *Poverty and the Environment: Reversing the Downward Spiral*. World

Watch Paper, No. 92, November, Washington, DC: Worldwatch Institute.

Eagleton, Terry (1991). *Ideology: An Introduction*. London and New York: Verso.

———— (1983). *Literary Theory: An Introduction*. Oxford: Blackwell.

Ehrenreich, Barbara and Ehrenreich, John (1978). 'Medicine and Social Control', in J. Ehrenreich, ed., *The Cultural Crisis of Modern Medicine*. New York: Monthly Review Press, 39–79.

Eisenberg, Carolyn (1983). 'Working-Class Politics and the Cold War: American Intervention in the German Labor Movement, 1945–49', *Diplomatic History*, vol. VII, no. 4, Fall, 283–306.

Eisenstadt, Shmuel N. (1973). *Tradition, Change, and Modernity*. New York: Wiley.

———— (1966). *Modernization: Protest and Change*. Englewood Cliffs, NJ: Prentice-Hall.

Elliot, William Y., ed. (1955). *The Political Economy of American Foreign Policy*, report of a study group sponsored by the Woodrow Wilson Foundation and the National Planning Association. New York: Holt.

Ellsberg, Daniel (1986a). 'The Construction of Instability: U.S. First-Use Threats and the Risks of Nuclear War', unpublished MS.

———— (1986b) 'Iran Arms', unpublished MS.

———— (1981) 'Introduction: Call to Mutiny', in E.P. Thompson and D. Smith, eds, *Protest and Survive*. New York: Monthly Review Press, i–xxxviii.

———— (1972). *Papers on the War*. New York: Simon & Schuster.

Enderwick, Peter (1989). 'Some Economics of Service-Sector Multinational Enterprises', in P. Enderwick, ed., *Multinational Service Firms*. New York: Routledge, 3–34.

Ermarth, Elizabeth Deeds (1992). *Sequel to History: Postmodernism and the Crises of Representational Time*. Princeton, NJ: Princeton University Press.

Ermarth, Michael (1975). 'Hayden White. *Metahistory*', *American Historical Review*, vol. LXXX, no. 4, October, 961–63.

Ethier, Wilfred (1983). *Modern International Economics*. New York: Norton.

Etzold, Thomas and Gaddis, John Lewis, eds (1978). *Containment: Documents on American Policy and Strategy, 1945–1950*. New York: Columbia University Press.

Evers, Hans-Dieter (1989). 'Urban Poverty and Labour Supply Strategies in Jakarta', in G. Rodgers, ed., *Urban Poverty and the Labour Market*. Geneva: ILO, 145–72.

Fanon, Frantz (1963). *The Wretched of the Earth*. New York: Grove Press.

FAO (Food and Agriculture Organization of the United Nations) (1958–75). *Production Yearbook*. Madrid: UN.

Farmer, Doyne et al., eds (1986). *Evolution, Games and Learning: Models for Adaptation in Machines and Nature*, Proceedings of the Fifth Annual International Conference of the Center for Nonlinear Studies, Los Alamos, NM, 20–24 May 1985. *Physica D: Nonlinear Phenomena*, 22D.

Feige, Edgar (1990). 'Defining and Estimating Underground and Informal Economies: The New Institutional Economic Approach', *World Development*, vol. XVIII, no. 7, 989–1002.

Feigenbaum, Mitchell J. (1983). 'Universal Behavior in Nonlinear Systems', *Physica D: Nonlinear Phenomena*, 7D, 16–39.

Feis, Herbert (1970). *From Trust to Terror: The Onset of the Cold War, 1945–1950*. New York: Norton.

Fibbi, Rosita and de Rham, Gérard (1988). 'Switzerland: The Position of Second-Generation Immigrants on the Labour Market', in C. Wilpert, ed., *Entering the Working World: Studies in European Migration*. Gower: Aldershot, 24–55.

Filias, Vassilios (1972). 'Restructuring of Agricultural Enterprises Affected by Emigration: Greece', in C.A.O. Van Nieuwenhuijze, ed., *Emigration et agriculture dans le bassin mediterranéen*. The Hague: Mouton, 122–43.

Filippelli, Ronald (1989). *American Labor and Postwar Italy, 1943–1953: A Study of Cold War Politics*. Stanford: Stanford University Press.

Forsberg, Randall (1994). 'Wasting Billions', *Boston Review*, vol. XIX, no. 2, April/May, 3–6.

Foucault, Michel (1980). *Power/Knowledge: Selected Interviews and Other Writings, 1972–1977*. Edited and translated by C. Gordon. Brighton: Harvester.

———— (1972). *The Archeology of Knowledge and The Discourse on Language*, trans. A.M. Sheridan Smith. New York: Pantheon.

———— (1970). *The Order of Things: An Archeology of the Human Sciences*. New York: Vintage.

Fox, Mary Frank (1984). *Women at Work*. Palo Alto, CA: Mayfield.

Frank, Andre Gunder (1981). *Crisis: In the Third World*. New York: Holmes & Meier.

———— (1980). *Crisis: In the World Economy*. New York: Holmes & Meier.

———— (1969). *Latin America: Underdevelopment or Revolution*. New York: Monthly Review Press.

———— (1967). 'The Sociology of Underdevelopment or the Underdevelopment of Sociology', *Catalyst*, no. 3, Summer, 20–73.

Fraser, Ronald (1988). *1968: A Student Generation in Revolt, An International Oral History*. London: Chatto & Windus.

Fraser, Steve (1989). 'The Labor Question', in S. Fraser and G. Gerstle, eds, *The Rise and Fall of the New Deal Order, 1930–1980*. Princeton, NJ: Princeton University Press, 55–84.

Friedman, David (1988). *The Misunderstood Miracle: Industrial Development and Political Change in Japan*. Ithaca, NY: Cornell University Press.

Friedman, Maurice, ed. (1991 [1964]). *The Worlds of Existentialism: A Critical Reader*. New York: Pantheon.

Fröbel, Folker (1982). 'The Current Development of the World-Economy: Reproduction of Labor and Accumulation of Capital on a World Scale', *Review*, vol. V, no. 4, Spring, 507–55.

Fröbel, Folker; Heinrichs, Jürgen and Kreye, Otto (1980). *The New International Division of Labour: Structural Unemployment in Industrialised Countries and Industrialism in Developing Countries*. New York: Cambridge University Press.

Fursov, A.I. (1991). 'Est li mesto dlia levykh v griadushchem mire?' [Is there a place for the left in the coming world?], *Mirovaia ekonomika i mezhdunarodnye otnoshenia (MEIMO)*, no. 7, July, 30–38.

Gaddis, John Lewis (1987). *The Long Peace: Inquiries into the History of the Cold War*. New York: Oxford University Press.

Gallagher, Catherine and Laqueur, Thomas (1987). *The Making of the Modern Body: Sexuality and Society in the Nineteenth Century*. Berkeley: University of California Press.

Galtung, Johan (1971). 'A Structural Theory of Imperialism', *Journal of Peace Research*, vol. VIII, no. 2, 81–117.

Gardner, Richard N. (1980). *Sterling–Dollar Diplomacy in Current Perspective: The Origins and the Prospects of Our International Economic Order*. New York: Columbia University Press.

Garfinkel, Harold (1967). *Studies in Ethnomethodology*. Englewood Cliffs, NJ: Prentice-Hall.

Garthoff, Raymond L. (1985). *Detente and Confrontation: American–Soviet Relations from Nixon to Reagan*. Washington, DC: Brookings Institute.

Gearhart, Suzanne (1987). 'History as Criticism: The Dialogue of History and Literature', *Diacritics*, vol. XVII, no. 3, Fall, 56–65.

Géhéniau, J. and Prigogine, I. (1986). 'The Birth of Time', *Foundations of Physics*, vol. XVI, no. 5, 437–43.

Gellner, Ernest (1983). *Nations and Nationalism*. Oxford: Blackwell.

George, Susan (1992). *The Debt Boomerang: How Third World Debt Harms Us All*. Boulder, CO: Westview.

——— (1977). *How the Other Half Dies: The Real Reasons for World Hunger*. Montclair, NJ: Allanheld, Osmun.

Ghilan, Maxim (1991). 'Thoughts on the After-Gulf War', *New Politics*, vol. III, no. 3, Summer, 25–36.

Gilpin, Robert (1987). *The Political Economy of International Relations*. Princeton, NJ: Princeton University Press.

——— (1975). *U.S. Power and the Multinational Corporation: The Political Economy of Foreign Direct Investment*. New York: Basic Books.

Gittell, Marion (1991). 'Education in a Democratic Society', in L. Wolfe, ed., *Women, Work and School: Occupation Segregation and the Role of Education*. Boulder, CO: Westview, 31–35.

Glaeser, Bernhard (1987). *The Green Revolution Revisited: Critique and Alternatives*, Boston, MA: Allen & Unwin.

Gleijeses, Piero (1994). "Flee! The White Giants Are Coming!": The United States, the Mercenaries, and the Congo, 1964–65', *Diplomatic History*, vol. XVIII, no. 2, Spring, 207–37.

Goldstein, Joshua (1988). *Long Cycles: Prosperity and War in the Modern Age*. New Haven, CT: Yale University Press.

Goldstein, Morris, et al. (1992). *International Capital Markets: Developments, Prospects, and Policy Issues*. Washington, DC: IMF.

Golini, Antonio and Bonifazi, Corrado (1987). 'Demographic Trends and International Migration', in *The Future of Migration*. Paris: OECD, 110–36.

Golomstock, Igor (1990). *Totalitarian Art: In the Soviet Union, the Third Reich, Fascist Italy, and the People's Republic of China*. New York: Icon Editions.

Gordon, David (1988). 'The Global Economy: New Edifice or Crumbling Foundations', *New Left Review*, no. 168, March–April, 24–64.

Gorz, André (1980). *Ecology as Politics*. Boston, MA: South End Press.

Gould, Stephen Jay (1989). *Wonderful Life: The Burgess Shale and the Nature of History*. New York: Norton.

Gould, Stephen J.; Gilinsky, Norman L. and German, Rebecca Z. (1987). 'Asymmetry of Lineages and the Direction of Evolutionary Time', *Science*, vol. CCXXXVI, no. 4807, 12 June, 1437–41.

Gover, James E. (1993). 'Review of the Competitive Status of the United States Electronics Industry', in W. Aspray, ed., *Technological Competitiveness: Contemporary and Historical Perspectives on the Electrical, Electronics, and Computer Industries.* New York: Institute of Electrical and Electronics Engineers, 57–74.

Gray, John (1986). *Liberalism.* Milton Keynes: Open University Press.

Greenberg, Clement (1948). 'Irrelevance versus Irresponsibility', *Partisan Review*, vol. XV, no. 5, May, 573–79.

Greenberg, Daniel S. (1967). *The Politics of Pure Science.* New York: New American Library.

Griffin, Keith B. (1987). 'World Hunger and the World-Economy', in W.L. Hollist and F.L. Tullis, eds, *Pursuing Food Security: Strategies and Obstacles in Africa, Asia, and Latin America, and the Middle East.* Boulder, CO: L. Rienner, 17–36.

Grigg, David (1983). 'Output and Population 1950–1980', *Geography*, vol. LXVIII, no. 4, October (No. 301), 301–6.

Grubel, Herbert G. (1989). 'Multinational Banking', in P. Enderwick, ed., *Multinational Service Firms.* New York: Routledge, 61–78.

Gurr, Ted R., ed. (1989). *Violence in America*, 2 vols. Newbury Park, CA: Sage.

Gwynne, Robert N. (1985). *Industrialization and Urbanization in Latin America.* London: Croom Helm.

Hagedoorn, John (1993). 'Strategic Technology Alliances and Modes of Cooperation in High-Technology Industries', in G. Grabher, ed., *The Embedded Firm: On the Socioeconomics of Industrial Networks.* New York: Routledge, 116–37.

Haggblade, Steven; Hazell, Peter and Brown, James (1989). 'Farm-Non Farm Linkages in Rural Sub-Saharan Africa', *World Development*, vol. XVII, no. 8, August, 1173–1201.

Halbach, Axel (1989). *Multinational Enterprises and Subcontracting in the Third World: A Study of Inter-Industrial Linkages.* Geneva: ILO.

Hall, Stuart (1990). 'The Emergence of Cultural Studies and the Crisis of the Humanities', *October*, vol. LIII, Summer, 11–23.

Halliday, Fred (1990). 'The Ends of Cold War', *New Left Review*, no. 180, March–April, 1–23.

Hanfling, Oswald (1981). *Logical Positivism.* Oxford: Blackwell.

Hanlon, Joseph (1986). *Beggar Your Neighbors: Apartheid Power in Southern Africa.* Bloomington: Indiana University Press.

Haraszti, Miklos (1977). *Worker in a Workers' State: Piece-Rates in Hungary.* Harmondsworth: Penguin.

Hargert, Michael and Morris, Deigan (1988). 'Trends in International Collaborative Agreements', in F. J. Contractor and P. Lorange, eds, *Cooperative Strategies in International Business.* Lexington, MA: D.H. Heath, 99–109.

Harries, Keith (1990). *Serious Violence: Patterns of Homicide and Assault in America.* Sprinfield, IL: Charles Thomas.

Hartmann, Betsy (1987). *Reproductive Rights and Wrongs: The Global Politics of Population Control and Contraceptive Choice.* New York: Harper & Row.

Harvey, David (1989). *The Condition of Postmodernity: An Enquiry into the Origins of Cultural Change.* New York: Blackwell.

Hauser, Philip M. (1981). 'Sociology's Progress Toward Science', *American Sociologist*, vol. XVI, no. 1, February, 62–64.

Havens, Thomas R.H. (1987). *Fire Across the Sea: The Vietnam War and Japan,*

1965–1975. Princeton, NJ: Princeton University Press.

Hawkes, Terence (1977). *Structuralism and Semiotics*. Berkeley: University of California Press.

Hayles, N. Katherine (1990). *Chaos Bound: Orderly Disorder in Contemporary Literature and Science*. Ithaca, NY: Cornell University Press.

Helgeson, Ann (1986). 'Geographical Mobility – Its Implications for Employment', in D. Lane, ed., *Labour and Employment in the USSR*. Brighton: Wheatsheaf, 145–75.

Henderson, Jeffrey (1989). *The Globalisation of High Technology Production: Society, Space, Semiconductors in the Restructuring of the Modern World*. New York: Routledge.

Hersh, Seymour (1994). 'The Wild East', *The Atlantic*, vol. CCLXXIII, no. 6, 61–86.

Hershberg, James G. (1993). *James B. Conant: Harvard to Hiroshima and the Making of the Nuclear Age*. New York: Knopf.

——— (1990). 'Before "The Missiles of October": Did Kennedy Plan a Military Strike Against Cuba?', *Diplomatic History*, vol. XIV, no. 2, Spring, 163–98.

Hewitt, Warren E. (1990). 'Catholicism, Social Justice, and the Brazilian Corporate State Since 1930', *Journal of Church and State*, vol. XXXII, no. 4, Autumn, 831–50.

Hicks, John (1969). *A Theory of Economic History*. New York: Oxford University Press.

Hindess, Barry and Hirst, Paul Q. (1975). *Pre-Capitalist Modes of Production*. Boston, MA: Routledge.

Hirschman, Albert O. (1986). 'Exit and Voice: An Expanding Sphere of Influence', in *Rival Views of Market Society and Other Recent Essays*. New York: Viking, 77–101.

Hogan, Michael (1987). *The Marshall Plan: America, Britain, and the Reconstruction of Western Europe, 1947–1952*. New York: Cambridge University Press.

Hollingsworth, J. Rogers; Hage, Jerald and Hanneman, Robert (1990). *State Intervention in Medical Care: Consequences for Britain, France, Sweden, and the United States, 1890–1970*. Ithaca, NY: Cornell University Press.

Hollowell, John (1977). *Fact and Fiction: The New Journalism and the Nonfiction Novel*. Chapel Hill: University of North Carolina Press.

Humes, Samuel (1993). *Managing the Multinational: Confronting the Global-Local Dilemma*. New York: Prentice Hall.

Hunter, John M; Rey, L. and Scott, David (1982). 'Man-made Lakes and Man-made Diseases', *Social Science and Medicine*, vol. XVI, no. 11, 1127–45.

Huntington, Samuel P. (1968). *Political Order in Changing Societies*. New Haven, CT: Yale University Press.

Ibbotson, Roger G. and Brinson, Gary P. (1993). *Global Investing: The Professional's Guide to the World Capital Markets*. New York: McGraw-Hill.

ILO (International Labour Organization) (1986). *Economically Active Population: Estimates and Projections, 1950–2025*, 6 vols. Geneva: ILO.

——— (1984). *World Labour Report*, 3 vols. Geneva: ILO.

IMF (International Monetary Fund). *Balance of Payments Yearbook*, various issues. Washington, DC: IMF.

Isaacson, Walter and Thomas, Evan (1986). *The Wise Men: Six Friends and the World They Made: Acheson, Bohlen, Harriman, Kennan, Lovett, McCloy*. New York: Simon & Schuster.

Isserman, Maurice (1987). *If I Had a Hammer … The Death of the Old Left and the Birth of the New Left*. New York: Basic.

Itoh, Makato (1990). *The World Economic Crisis and Japanese Capitalism*. London: Macmillan.

Ives, Jane (1985). 'The Health Effects of the Transfer of Technology to the Developing World: Report and Case Studies', in J. Ives, ed., *The Export of Hazard*. Boston, MA: Routledge and Kegan Paul, 172–92.

Jackson, Marvin R. (1987). 'Economic Development in the Balkans Since 1945 Compared to Southern and East-Central Europe', *Eastern European Politics and Societies*, vol. I, no. 3, Fall, 393–455.

Jacobsen, Jodi (1993). 'Closing the Gender Gap in Development', in *State of the World 1993*. World Watch Institute. New York: Norton, 61–79.

Jameson, Fredric (1972). *The Prison-House of Language: A Critical Account of Structuralism and Russian Formalism*. Princeton, NJ: Princeton University Press.

Jantsch, Erich, ed. (1981). *The Evolutionary Vision: Toward a Unifying Paradigm of Physical, Biological, and Sociocultural Evolution*. Boulder, CO: Westview.

Jencks, Charles (1989). *What is Post-Modernism?*, 3rd rev. edn. New York: St Martin's Press.

Johnson, Stanley P., ed. (1993). *The Earth Summit: The United Nations Conference on Environment and Development (UNCED)*. Boston, MA: Graham & Trotman.

Jones, Gavin W. (1984). 'Economic Growth and Changing Female Employment Structure in the Cities of Southeast and East Asia', in G W. Jones, ed., *Women in the Urban and Industrial Workforce: Southeast and East Asia*. Honolulu: University of Hawaii Press, 17–59.

Julius, DeAnne (1990). *Global Companies and Public Policy: The Growing Challenge of Foreign Direct Investment*. London: Pinter.

Kadane, Kathy (1990a). 'Ex-agents Say CIA Compiled Death Lists for Indonesians', *San Francisco Examiner*, 20 May.

——— (1990b). 'U.S. Officials' Lists Aided Indonesian Bloodbath in '60s', *Washington Post*, 21 May.

Kakabadse, Mario A. (1987). *International Trade in Services: Prospects for Liberalisation in the 1990s*. New York: Croom Helm.

Karns, Margaret P. and Mingst, Karen A. (1994). 'Maintaining International Peace and Security: UN Peacekeeping and Peacemaking', in M.R. Klare and D.C. Thomas, eds, *World Security: Challenges for a New Century*, 2nd edn. New York: St Martin's, 188–215.

——— (1991). 'Multilateral Institutions and International Security', in M.T. Klare and D.C. Thomas, eds, *World Security: Trends and Challenges at Century's End*. New York: St Martin's Press, 216–94.

Katzenstein, Peter (1993). 'Taming of Power: German Unification, 1989–1990', in M. Woo-Cumings and M. Loriaux, eds, *Past as Prelude: History in the Making of a New World Order*. Boulder, CO: Westview.

——— (1987). *Policy and Politics in West Germany: The Growth of a Semisovereign State*. Philadelphia, PA: Temple University Press.

Kaufmann, William W. (1992). *Assessing the Base Force: How Much is Too Much?* Washington, DC: Brookings Institute.

Kay, David (1993). Letter to the Editor, *Foreign Policy*, no. 90, Spring, 169–70.

Keal, Paul (1983). *Unspoken Rules and Superpower Dominance*. London: Macmillan.

Kenwood, A.G. and Lougheed, A.L. (1992). *The Growth of the International Economy 1820–1990: An Introductory Text*, 3rd edn. New York: Routledge.

Keohane, Robert O. (1989). *International Institutions and State Power: Essays in International Relations Theory*. Boulder, CO: Westview.

Kervasdoué, Jean de and Rodwin, Victor G. (1984). 'Health Policy and the Expanding Role of the State', in J. Kervasdoué, J. Kimberly and V. Rodwin, eds, *The End of an Illusion: The Future of Health Policy in Western Industrialized Nations*. Berkeley: University of California Press, 3–34.

Keyder, Caglar (1985). 'The American Recovery of Southern Europe: Aid and Hegemony', in G. Arrighi, ed., *Semiperipheral Development: The Politics of Southern Europe in the Twentieth Century*. Beverly Hills: Sage, 135–48.

Kimberly, John R. and Rodwin, Victor G. (1984). 'The Future of Health Polich: Constraints, Controls and Choices', in J. de Kervasdoué; J. Kimberley and V. Rodwin, ed., *The End of an Illusion: The Future of Health Policy in Western Industrialized Nations*. Berkeley: University of California Press, 257–86.

King, Anthony (1983). 'The Political Consequences of the Welfare State', in S. Spiro and E. Yuchtman-Yaar, eds, *Evaluating the Welfare State*. New York: Academic Press, 7–25.

King, Edmund (1969). *Education and Development in Western Europe*. Reading, MA: Addison-Wesley.

Kitcher, Philip (1982). *Abusing Science: The Case Against Creationism*. Cambridge, MA: MIT Press.

Klare, Michael T. (1994). 'Adding Fuel to the Fires: The Conventional Arms Trade in the 1990s', in M.T. Klare and D.C. Thomas, eds, *World Security: Challenges for a New Century*, 2nd edn. New York: St Martin's Press, 134–54.

——— (1991). 'Deadly Convergence: The Arms Trade, Nuclear/Chemical/Missile Proliferation, and Regional Conflict in the 1990s', in M.T. Klare and D.C. Thomas, eds, *World Security: Trends and Challenges at Century's End*. New York: St Martin's Press, 170– 96.

——— (1989). 'Subterranean Alliances: America's Global Proxy Network', *Journal of International Affairs*, (US Alliance Management Toward the Year 2000), vol. XLIII, no. 1, Summer/Fall, 97–118.

——— (1984). *The American Arms Supermarket*. Austin: University of Texas Press.

——— (1972). *War Without End: American Planning for the Next Vietnam*. New York: Knopf.

Klare, Michael T. and Daniel C. Thomas (1994). *World Security: Challenges for a New Century*, 2nd edn. New York: St Martin's Press.

——— (1991). *World Security: Trends and Challenges at Century's End*. New York: St Martin's Press.

Kogut, Bruce; Shan, Weijian and Walker, Gordon (1993). 'Knowledge in the Network and the Network as Knowledge', in G. Grabher, ed., *The Embedded Firm: On the Socioeconomics of Industrial Networks*. New York: Routledge, 67–94.

Kojima, Kiyoshi (1978). *Direct Foreign Investment: A Model of Multinational Business Operations*. New York: Praeger.

Korner, Peter; Maas, Gero; Siebold, Thomas and Tetzlaff, Rainer (1986). *The IMF and the Debt Crisis: A Guide to the Third World's Dilemma*. London: Zed.

Krauss, Rosalind (1981). 'The Originality of the Avant-Garde: A Postmodernist Repetition', *October*, no. 18, Fall, 47–66.

Kutzner, Patricia L. (1991). *World Hunger: A Reference Handbook*. Santa Barbara, CA: ABC–Clio.

Kwast, Barbara E. (1989). 'Maternal Mortality Levels, Causes and Promising Interventions', *Journal of Biosocial Sciences, Supplement*, no. 10, 51–67.

Landow, George P. (1992). *Hypertext: The Convergence of Contemporary Critical Theory and Technology*. Baltimore: Johns Hopkins University Press.

Lanvin, Bruno, ed. (1993). *Trading in a New World Order: The Impact of Telecommunications and Data Services on International Trade in Services*. Boulder, CO: Westview.

Lappé, Frances Moore and Collins, Joseph (1986). *World Hunger: Twelve Myths*. New York: Grove Press.

——— (1977). *Food First: Beyond the Myth of Scarcity*. Boston, MA: Houghton-Mifflin.

Laszlo, Ervin (1987). *Evolution: The Grand Synthesis*. Boston, MA: New Science Library.

Lebow, Richard Ned (1987). *Nuclear Crisis Management: A Dangerous Illusion*. Ithaca, NY: Cornell University Press.

Lee, Richard (1992). 'Readings in the "New Science": A Selective Annotated Bibliography', *Review*, vol. XV, no. 1, Winter, 113–71.

Leffler, Melvyn P. (1993). 'Negotiating from Strength: Acheson, the Russians and American Power', in D. Brinkley, ed., *Dean Acheson and the Making of U.S. Foreign Policy*. New York: St Martin's Press, 176–210.

——— (1992). *A Preponderance of Power: National Security, the Truman Administration, and the Cold War*. Stanford: Stanford University Press.

——— (1983). 'From the Truman Doctrine to the Carter Doctrine: Lessons and Dilemmas of the Cold War', *Diplomatic History*, vol. VII, no. 4, Fall, 245–66.

Lenin, Vladimir I. (1975). 'Left-Wing Communism: An Infantile Disorder', in V.I. Lenin, *Selected Works*, rev. edn, Moscow: Progress, Vol. III, 291–370.

Lentricchia, Frank (1980). *After the New Criticism*. Chicago: University of Chicago Press.

Lepenies, Wolf (1988). *Between Literature and Science: The Rise of Sociology*, trans. R.J. Hollingdale. New York: Cambridge University Press.

Lévi-Strauss, Claude (1966). *The Savage Mind*. Chicago: University of Chicago Press.

——— (1964). *Totemism*. London: Merlin.

——— (1963). *Structural Anthropology*, trans. C. Jacobson and B.G. Schoepf. New York: Basic Books.

Leys, Colin (1982). 'Samuel Huntington and the End of Classical Modernization Theory', in H. Alavi and T. Shanin, eds, *Introduction to the Sociology of 'Developing Societies'*. London: Macmillan, 332–49.

Lichtenstein, Nelson (1982). *Labor's War at Home: The CIO in World War II*. Cambridge: Cambridge University Press.

Lipietz, Alain (1987). *Mirages and Miracles: The Crises of Global Fordism*. London: Verso.

Lipset, Seymour Martin (1960). *Political Man*. London: Heinemann.

Lipton, Michael (1989). *New Seeds and Poor People*. Baltimore: Johns Hopkins University Press.

Litwak, Robert S. (1984). *Détente and the Nixon Doctrine: American Foreign Policy and the Pursuit of Stability, 1969–1976*. Cambridge: Cambridge University Press.

Lorenz, Edward N. (1964). 'The Problem of Deducing the Climate from the Governing Equations', *Tellus*, vol. XVI, no. 1, February, 1–11.

———— (1963a). 'Deterministic Nonperiodic Flow', *Journal of the Atmospheric Sciences*, vol. XX, 2, March, 130–41.

———— (1963b). 'The Mechanics of Vacillation', *Journal of the Atmospheric Sciences*, vol. XX, no. 5, September, 448–64.

Loriaux, Michael (1993). 'The Riddle of the Rhine: France, Germany, and the Geopolitics of European Integration, 1919–1992', in M. Woo-Cumings and M. Loriaux, eds, *Past as Prelude: History in the Making of a New World Order*. Boulder, CO: Westview, 83–110.

Luard, Evan, ed. (1967). *The International Protection of Human Rights*. New York: Praeger.

Lundestad, Geir (1986). *East, West, North, South: Major Developments in International Politics, 1945–1986*. Oslo: Norwegian University Press.

Lutz, Wolfgang (1994). 'The Future of World Population', *Population Bulletin*, vol. XLIX, no. 1, June, Washington, DC: Population Reference Bureau.

Lyotard, Jean-François (1984). *The Postmodern Condition: A Report on Knowledge*, trans. G. Bennington and B. Massumi. Minneapolis: University of Minnesota Press.

MacGaffey, Janet (1991). *The Real Economy of Zaire: The Contribution of Smuggling and Other Unofficial Activities to National Wealth*. Philadelphia: University of Pennsylvania Press.

Macquarrie, John (1972). *Existentialism*. Philadelphia: Westminster.

Maddison, Angus (1989). *The World Economy in the 20th Century*. Paris: Development Centre of the Organization for Economic Co-operation and Development.

Mak, Grace (1991). 'Continuity and Change in Women's Access to Higher Education in the People's Republic of China', in G. Kelly and S. Slaughter, eds, *Women's Higher Education in Comparative Perspective*. Boston, MA: Kluwer Academic, 31–46.

Mandelbrot, Benoit B. (1982). *The Fractal Geometry of Nature*. San Francisco: Freeman.

Market Share Reporter (1992). Detroit: Gale Research.

Markus, Mario; Müller, Stefan C. and Nicolis, G., eds (1988). *From Chemical to Biological Organization*. New York: Springer-Verlag.

Markusen, Ann and Yudken, Joel (1992). *Dismantling the Cold War Economy*. New York: Basic Books.

May, Lary (1990). 'The Politics of Consumption: The Screen Actor's Guild, Ronald Reagan, and the Hollywood Red Scare', in S. Guilbaut, ed., *Reconstructing Modernism: Art in New York, Paris, and Montreal, 1945–1964*. Cambridge, MA: MIT Press, 332–68.

Mazrui, Ali (1973). 'The Lumpenproletariat and the Lumpenmilitariat: African Soldiers are a New Political Class', *Political Studies*, vol. XXI, no. 1, February, 1–12.

McClintock, Michael (1992). *Instruments of Statecraft: U.S. Guerilla Warfare, Counter-insurgency, and Counterterrorism, 1940–1990*. New York: Pantheon.

———— (1985). *The American Connection: State Terror and Popular Resistance in El Salvador*, Vol I. London: Zed.

McCormick, Thomas (1989). *America's Half Century: United States Foreign Policy in the Cold War*. Baltimore: Johns Hopkins University Press.

McGlothlen, Ronald L. (1993). *Controlling the Waves: Dean Acheson and U.S. Foreign Policy in Asia*. New York: Norton.

McLellan, David (1986). *Ideology*. Milton Keynes: Open University Press.

McNeill, William H. (1982). *The Pursuit of Power: Technology, Armed Force, and Society Since AD 1000*. Chicago: University of Chicago Press.

Meadows, Donella H.; Meadows, Dennis and Randers, Jørgen (1992). *Beyond the Limits: Confronting Global Collapse or Envisioning a Sustainable Future*. London: Earthscan.

Meadows, Donella H. et al. (1974). *The Limits to Growth: A Report for the Club of Rome's Project on the Predicament of Mankind*, 2nd edn. New York: Universe.

Meehan, Eugene J. (1971). *The Foundations of Political Analysis: Empirical and Normative*. Homewood, IL: Dorsey.

Meillassoux, Claude (1994). 'Kapitalistische Produktion von "Überbevölkerung" in Africa', *Das Argument*, vol. XXXVI, no. 2, 219–32.

Meillassoux, Claude (1975). *Femmes, greniers et capitaux*. Paris: Maspéro.

Merritt, Richard L.; Flerlage, Ellen P. and Merrit, Anna J. (1971). 'Political Man in Postwar West German Education', *Comparative Education Review*, vol. XV, no. 3, October, 346–61.

Meulemann, Heiner (1982). 'Bildungsexpansion und Wandel der Bildungs-vorstellungen zwischen 1958 und 1979: Eine Kohortenanalyse', *Zeitschrift für Soziologie*, vol. XI, no 3, July, 227–53.

Michalski, Wolfgang (1991). 'Trends and Developments in the Globalisation of Production, Investment and Trade', in *Trade, Investment and Technology in the 1990s*. Paris: OECD, 7–12.

Milbrath, Lester W. (1984). *Environmentalists: Vanguard for a New Society*. Albany, NY: SUNY Press.

Miller, E. (1991). *Future Vision: The 189 Most Important Trends of the 1990s*. New York: Research Alert.

Mishra, Ramesh (1990). *The Welfare State in Capitalist Society: Policies of Retrenchment and Maintenance in Europe, North America, and Australia*. Toronto: University of Toronto Press.

Mitchell, John G. (with C.L. Stallings) (1970). *Ecotactics: The Sierra Club Handbook for Environment Activists*. New York: Trident.

Miyazaki, Giichi (1992). *Fukugo Fukyo: Posuto Baburu no Shohosen o Motomete* [Complex Recession: In Search of Policy Prescription in the Post Bubble Era]. Tokyo: Chuo Koronsha.

Monahan, Laurie J. (1990). 'Cultural Cartography: American Designs at the 1964 Venice Biennale', in S. Guilbaut, ed., *Reconstructing Modernism: Art in New York, Paris, and Montreal, 1945–1964*. Cambridge, MA: MIT Press.

Moore, Joe (1983). *Japanese Workers and the Struggle for Power, 1945–1947*. Madison: University of Wisconsin Press.

Morrison, Philip; Tsipis, Kosta and Wiesner, Jerome (1994). 'The Future of American Defense', *Scientific American*, vol. CCLXX, no. 2, February, 38–45.

Morgan, Dan (1979). *Merchants of Grain*. New York: Viking.

Müller, Ronald (1979). 'The Multinational Corporation and the Underdevelopment of the "Third World"', in C.K. Wilber, ed., *The Political Economy of Development and Underdevelopment*, 2nd edn. New York: Random House, 151–78.

Nasbaumer, Jacques (1987). *Services in the Global Market.* Boston, MA: Kluwer Academic.

National Center for Educational Statistics (1989). *Digest of Education Statistics 1989.* Washington, DC: GPO.

National Research Council (1975). *World Food and Nutrition Study.* Washington, DC: National Academy of Sciences.

NEA (Nuclear Energy Agency) (1989). *Nuclear Energy in Perspective: Organization for Economic Co-operation and Development.*

Nelli, H. (1987). 'A Brief History of American Syndicate Crime', in T. Bynum, ed., *Organized Crime in America: Concepts and Controversies.* Monsey, NY: Criminal Justice, 15–30.

Neurath, Otto (1959 [1931/32]). 'Sociology and Physicalism', in A.J. Ayer, ed., *Logical Positivism.* Glencoe, IL: Free Press, 199–208.

Nicolaides, Phedon (1991). 'Service in Growing Economies and Global Markets', in *Trade, Investment and Technology in the 1990s.* Paris: OECD, 33–55.

Nicolis, Grégoire and Prigogine, Ilya (1989). *Exploring Complexity: An Introduction.* New York: W.H. Freeman.

Nightingale, Elena O.; Hamburg, David A. and Mortimer, Allyn M. (1990). 'International Scientific Co-operation for Maternal and Child Health', in T. Lambo and S. Day, eds, *Issues in Contemporary International Health.* New York: Plenum Medical, 113–34.

Nisbet, Robert (1986). *Conservatism: Dream and Reality.* Milton Keynes: Open University Press.

Nishimura, Takaaki (1988). 'Ginko Kashitsuke Toshi to Kokusai Kin'yu Shijo (Bank Lending Investment and International Financial Market)', in S. Okumura, ed., *Gendai Sekai Keizai to Shihon Yushutsu* [Contemporary World-Economy and Capital Export]. Kyoto: Minerva Shobo, 135–69.

Noer, Thomas J. (1989). 'New Frontiers and Old Priorities in Africa', in T.G. Paterson, ed., *Kennedy's Quest for Victory: American Foreign Policy, 1961–1963.* New York: Oxford University Press, 253–83.

Noyelle, Thierry J. and Dutka, Anna B. (1988). *International Trade in Business Services: Accounting, Advertising, Law, and Management Consulting.* Cambridge, MA: Ballinger.

Nusbaumer, Jacques (1987). *Services in the Global Market.* Boston, MA: Kluwer Academic.

Nwoke, Chibuzo (1987). *Third World Minerals and Global Pricing: A New Theory.* London: Zed.

OECD (Organization for Economic Cooperation and Development) (1993a). *Economic Integration: OECD Economies, Dynamic Asian Economies and Central and Eastern European Countries.* Paris: OECD.

——— (1993b). *Foreign Direct Investment Relations Between the OECD and the Dynamic Asian Economies.* Paris: OECD.

——— (1991). *The State of the Environment.* Paris: OECD.

——— (1987). *International Investment and Multinational Enterprises: Recent Trends in International Direct Investment.* Paris: OECD.

——— (1981). *Long-Term Trends in Tax Revenues of OECD Countries, 1955–1980.* Paris: OECD.

Ogawa, Naohiro; Jones, Gavin W. and Williamson, Jeffrey G. eds (1993). *Human*

Resources in Development Along the Asia-Pacific Rim. New York: Oxford University Press.

Ohmae, Kenichi (1985). *Triad Power: The Coming Shape of Global Competition*. New York: Free Press.

Okumura, Shigetsugu, ed. (1988a). *Gendai Sekai Keizai to Shihon Yushutsu* [Contemporary World-Economy and Capital Export]. Kyoto: Minerva Shobo.

—— (1988b). 'Sengo Sekaikeizai ni okeru Shihon Yushutsu', in S. Okumura, *Gendai Sekai Keizai to Shihon Yushutsu* [Contemporary World-Economy and Capital Export]. Kyoto: Minerva Shobo, 1–40.

Oman, Charles (1989). *New Forms of Investment in Developing Country Industries: Mining, Petrochemicals, Automobiles, Textiles, Food*. Paris: OECD.

Oppl, Hubert and von Kardoff, Ernst (1990). 'The National Health Care System in the Welfare State', *Social Science and Medicine*, vol. XXXI, no. 1, 43–50.

Osterman, Paul and Kochan, Thomas A. (1990). 'Employment Security and Employment Policy', in K. G. Abraham and R. B. McKersie, eds, *New Developments in the Labor Market: Toward a New Institutional Paradigm*. Cambridge, MA: MIT Press, 155–84.

Ozawa, Terutomo (1993). 'Foreign Direct Investment and Structural Transformation: Japan as a Recycler of Market and Industry', *Business and the Contemporary World*, vol. V, no. 2, Spring, Special Issue: The Asia-Pacific Region: The Impact of Globalization and Regionalization, 129–50.

—— (1979). *Multinationalism, Japanese Style: The Political Economy of Outward Dependency*. Princeton, NJ: Princeton University Press.

Pagels, Heinz R. (1988). *The Dreams of Reason: The Computer and the Rise of the Sciences of Complexity*. New York: Simon & Schuster.

Palma, Gabriel (1978). 'Dependency: A Formal Theory of Underdevelopment or a Methodology for the Analysis of Concrete Situations of Underdevelopment', *World Development*, vol. VI, no. 7/8, July/August, 881–924.

Paterson, Thomas G. (1989). 'John F. Kennedy's Quest for Victory and Global Crisis', in T. Paterson, ed., *Kennedy's Quest for Victory: American Foreign Policy, 1961–1963*. New York: Oxford University Press, 3–23.

Payer, Cheryl (1974). *The Debt Trap: The International Monetary Fund and the Third World*. New York: Monthly Review Press.

Pearce, Fred (1992). 'Third World Fights to Retain its Natural Rights', *New Scientist*, vol. CXXXIV, no. 1822, 23 May, 4.

Peliti, Luca and Vulpiani, A., eds (1988). *Measures of Complexity: Proceedings of the Conference, Held in Rome, Sept. 30–Oct. 2, 1987*. New York: Springer-Verlag.

Pentagon Papers: The Defense Department History of United States Decisionmaking on Vietnam: The Senator Gravel Edition, Vol. I. (1971). Boston, MA: Beacon.

Peters, Guy B. (1991). *The Politics of Taxation: A Comparative Perspective*. Oxford: Blackwell.

Peterson, A.D.C. (1965). 'Secondary Re-organization in England and Wales', *Comparative Education*, vol. I, no. 3, June, 161–9.

Pines, David, ed. (1988). *Emerging Synthesis in Science: Proceedings of the Founding Workshops of the Santa Fe Institute, Santa Fe, NM*. Redwood City, CA: Addison-Wesley.

Piore, Michael J. (1979). *Birds of Passage: Migrant Labor and Industrial Societies*. New York: Cambridge University Press.

Piore, Michael J. and Sabel, Charles F. (1984). *The Second Industrial Divide: Possibilities for Prosperity*. New York: Basic Books.

Piven, Frances F. and Cloward, Richard A. (1977). *Poor People's Movements — Why They Succeed, How They Fail*. New York: Pantheon.

Pomian, Krzysztof (1979). 'The Secular Evolution of the Concept of Cycles', *Review*, vol. II, no. 4, Spring, 563–646.

Portes, Alejandro; Castells, Manuel and Benton, Lauren A., eds (1989). *The Informal Economy: Studies in Advanced and Less Developed Countries*. Baltimore: Johns Hopkins University Press.

Portes, Alejandro and Benton, Lauren A. (1984). 'Industrial Development and Industrial Absorption', *Population and Development Review*, vol. X, no. 4, December, 589–611.

Preston, Samuel H. (1988). 'Urban Growth in Developing Countries: A Demographic Reappraisal', in J. Gugler, ed., *The Urbanization of the Third World*. New York: Oxford University Press, 11–31.

Preston, William Jr.; Herman, Edward S. and Schiller, Herbert (1989). *Hope and Folly: The United States and Unesco, 1945–1985*. Minneapolis: University of Minnesota Press.

Price, Terence (1990). *Political Electricity: What Future for Nuclear Energy?* New York: Oxford University Press.

Prigogine, Ilya (1986). 'Science, Civilization and Democracy: Values, Systems, Structures and Affinities', *Futures*, vol. XVIII, no. 4, August, 493–507.

Prigogine, Ilya and Géhéniau, J. (1986). 'Entropy, Matter, and Cosmology', *Proceedings of the National Academy of Sciences, USA*, vol. LXXXIII, no. 17, 6245–9.

Prigogine, Ilya and Stengers, Isabelle (1984). *Order Out of Chaos: Man's New Dialogue with Nature*. New York: Bantam Books.

Puchala, Donald and Hopkins, Raymond (1982). 'International Regimes: Lessons from Inductive Analysis', *International Organization*, vol. XXXVI, no. 2, Spring, 245–75.

———— (1980). *Global Food Interdependence: Challenge to United States Policy*. New York: Columbia University Press.

Pyle, David (1989). *Tax Evasion and the Black Economy*. London: Macmillan.

Rabe, Stephen G. (1989). 'Controlling Revolutions: Latin America, the Alliance for Progress, and Cold War Anti-Communism', in T.G. Paterson, ed., *Kennedy's Quest for Victory: American Foreign Policy, 1961–1963*. New York: Oxford University Press, 105–22.

Raikes, P. (1986). Flowing with Milk and Money: Food Production in Africa and the Policies of the EEC', in P. Lawrence, ed., *World Recession and the Food Crisis in Africa*. London: James Currey, 160–76.

Ramphal, Shridath S. (1990). 'Third World Grievances', *EPA Journal*, vol. XVI, no. 4, July/August, 39–43.

Rawski, Thomas G. (1979). *Economic Growth and Employment in China*. New York: Oxford University Press.

Reed, Wornie (1993). *Health and Medical Care of Black Americans*. Westport, CT: Auburn House.

Reeves, Edward (1990). *The Hidden Government: Ritual, Clientelism, and Legitimation in Northern Egypt*. Salt Lake City: University of Utah Press.

Rehsche, Guntram (1981). *Brain Drain: Fachleute aus Entwicklungsländern in der*

Schweiz. Adliswil: Institut für Sozialethik.

Reise, Barbara M. (1992). 'Greenberg and the Group: A Retrospective View', in F. Frascina and J. Harris, eds, *Art in Modern Culture: An Anthology of Critical Texts*. New York: Icon Editions, 252–63.

Reuter, Peter (1983). *Disorganized Crime: The Economics of the Visible Hand*. Cambridge, MA: MIT Press.

Reynolds, David; Sullivan, Michael and Murgatroy, Stephen (1987). *The Comprehensive Experiment*. London: The Falmer Press.

Robbe-Grillet, Alain (1972a [1963]). 'Temps et description dans le récit d'aujourd'hui', in *Pour un nouveau roman*. Paris: Gallimard, 155–69.

———— (1972b [1961]). 'Nouveau roman, homme nouveau', in *Pour un nouveau roman*. Paris: Gallimard, 141–53.

———— (1972c [1958]). 'Nature, humanisme, tragédie', in *Pour un nouveau roman*. Paris: Gallimard, 55–84.

———— (1972d [1957]). 'Sur quelques notions périmées', in *Pour un nouveau roman*. Paris: Gallimard, 29–53.

———— (1972e [1956]). 'Une voie pour le roman futur', in *Pour un nouveau roman*. Paris: Gallimard, 17–27.

———— (1972f [1955, 1963]). 'A quoi servent les théories?', in *Pour un nouveau roman*. Paris: Gallimard, 7–15.

———— (1972g [1953]). 'Joë Bousquet le rêveur', in *Pour un nouveau roman*. Paris: Gallimard, 103–19.

Robbins, Thomas (1988). 'The Transformative Impact of the Study of New Religions on the Sociology of Religion', *Journal for the Scientific Study of Religion*, vol. XXVII, March, 12–31.

Roberts, Bryan (1990). 'The Informal Sector in Comparative Perspective', in M.E. Smith, ed., *Perspectives on the Informal Economy*. Lanham, MD: University Press of America, 23–48.

———— (1978). *Cities of Peasants: The Political Economy of Urbanization in the Third World*. London: Edward Arnold.

Rondinelli, Dennis A. (1983). *Secondary Cities in Developing Countries: Policies for Diffusing Urbanization*. Beverly Hills: Sage.

Rosenau, Pauline Marie (1991). *Post-Modernism and the Social Sciences: Insights, Inroads, and Intrusions*. Princeton, NJ: Princeton University Press.

Rostow, W.W. (1960). *The Stages of Economic Growth: A Non-Communist Manifesto*. Cambridge: Cambridge University Press.

Rothman, Barbara Katz (1989). *Recreating Motherhood: Ideology and Technology in a Patriarchal Society*. New York: Norton.

Rouse, Joseph (1990). 'The Narrative Reconstruction of Science', *Inquiry*, vol. XXXIII, June, 179–96.

Ruggie, John G. (1993). 'Territoriality and Beyond: Problematizing Modernity in International Relations', *International Organization*, vol. XLVII, no. 1, Winter, 139–74.

Ryle, Martin (1988). *Ecology and Socialism*. London: Radius.

Sakamoto, M. (1991). 'Public Administration in Japan: Past and Present in the Higher Civil Service', in A. Farazmand, ed., *Handbook of Comparative and Development Public Administration*. New York: Dekker, 101–25.

Salt, John (1981). 'International Labor Migration in Western Europe: A Geographical Review', in M.M. Kritz, C.B. Kelly and S.M. Tomasi, eds, *Global Trends in Migration: Theory and Research on International Population Movements*. New York: Center for Migration Studies, 133–57.

Sanders, Jerry W. (1983). *Peddlers of Crisis: The Committee on the Present Danger and the Politics of Containment*. Boston, MA: South End Press.

Sassen, Saskia (1991). *The Global City: New York, London, Tokyo*. Princeton, NJ: Princeton University Press.

——— (1988). *The Mobility of Labor and Capital: A Study in International Investment and Labor Flow*. New York: Cambridge University Press.

Schaller, Michael (1985). *The American Occupation of Japan: The Origins of the Cold War in Asia*. New York: Oxford University Press.

Schmink, Marianne (1986). 'Women and Urban Industrial Development in Brazil', in J. Nash and H. Safa, eds, *Women and Change in Latin America*. South Hadley, MA: Bergin and Garvey, 136–64.

Schneider, Reinhart (1982). 'Das Bildungswesen in den westeuropäischen Staaten 1870–1975', *Zeitschrift für Soziologie*, vol. XI, no. 3, July, 207–26.

Schultz, T. Paul (1990). 'Women's Changing Participation in the Labor Force: A World Perspective', *Economic Development and Cultural Change*, vol. XXXVIII, April, 457–89.

Schumacher, Ernest F. (1973). *Small is Beautiful: Economics as if People Mattered*. New York: Harper and Row.

Schurmann, Franz (1993). 'After Desert Storm: Interest, Ideology, and History in American Foreign Policy', in M. Woo-Cumings and M. Loriaux, eds, *Past as Prelude: History in the Making of a New World Order*. Boulder, CO: Westview, 179–216.

——— (1987). *The Foreign Politics of Richard Nixon: The Grand Design*. Berkeley: University of California, Berkeley, Institute of International Studies.

——— (1974). *The Logic of World Power: An Inquiry into the Origins, Currents, and Contradictions of World Politics*. New York: Pantheon.

Scott, Peter Dale (1985). 'The United States and the Overthrow of Sukarno, 1965–1967', *Pacific Affairs*, vol. LVIII, no. 2, 239–64.

Selden, Mark (1994). 'The Pacific Rim, The New Co-Prosperity Sphere or Greater China? China and Japan in the Emerging Global Order', unpublished paper delivered at 'Japan in Asia' workshop, Cornell University, 19–20 May.

Selwyn, Enzer and Drobnick, Richard (1978). *Neither Feast nor Famine*. Lexington, MA: Lexington Books.

Sen, Somnath (1990). 'Debt, Financial Flows and International Security', in *SIPRI Yearbook*. Oxford: Oxford University Press, 203–17.

Sharrock, Wes and Anderson, Robert J. (1986). *The Ethnomethodologists*. New York: Tavistock.

Shaw, Robert (1981). 'Strange Attractors, Chaotic Behavior, and Information Flow', *Zeitschrift für Naturforschung*, vol. XXXVI-A, no. 1, 80–112.

Shimura, Yukio (1994). 'Nichibei Handotai Senso: Hachinen burino Koshu Kotai' [Japan–US Semiconductor War: Reversal After Eight Years], *Ekonomisuto*, 15 February, 38–43.

Singelmann, Joachim (1978). 'The Sectoral Transformation of the Labor Force in Seven Industrialized Countries, 1920–1970', *American Journal of Sociology*, vol. LXXXIII, no. 5, March, 1224–34.

Singh, Andrea M. and Kelles-Viitanen, Anita, eds (1987). *Invisible Hands: Women in Home-Based Production.* Newbury Park, CA: Sage.

Singham, A.W. and Hune, Shirley (1986). *Non-Alignment in an Age of Alignments.* Westport, CT: Lawrence Hill.

Sivan, Emmanuel (1992). 'The Islamic Resurgence: Civil Society Strikes Back', in L. Kaplan, ed., *Fundamentalism in Comparative Perspective.* Amherst: University of Massachusetts Press, 96–109.

Sivard, Ruth Leger (1991[1982]). *World Military and Social Expenditures.* Washington, DC: World Priorities.

Skinner, B.F. (1971). *Beyond Freedom and Dignity.* New York: Knopf.

Sleuwaegen, Leo and Yamawaki, Hideki (1991). 'Foreign Direct Investment and Intra-form Trade: Evidence from Japan', in A. Koekkoek and L.B.M. Mennes, eds, *International Trade and Global Development: Essays in Honour of Jagdish Bhagwati.* New York: Routledge, 143–61.

Smith, George D.; Bartley, Mel and Blane, David (1991). 'The Black Report on Socioeconomic Inequalities in Health: 10 Years On', *British Medical Journal,* CCCI, 18–25 August, 373–7.

Smith, Joan and Wallerstein, Immanuel, coordinators (1992). *Creating and Transforming Households: The Constraints of the World-Economy.* New York: Cambridge University Press.

Smitka, Michael J. (1991). *Competitive Ties: Subcontracting in the Japanese Automotive Industry.* New York: Columbia University Press.

Snow, C.P. (1965). *The Two Cultures: And a Second Look.* New York: Cambridge University Press.

Sobchack, Vivian (1990). 'A Theory of Everything: Meditations on Total Chaos', *Artforum,* vol. XXIX, no. 2, October, 148–55.

Soete, Luc (1991) 'National Support Policies for Strategic Industries: The International Implications', in *Strategic Industries in a Global Economy: Policy Issues for the 1990s.* Paris: OECD, 51–80.

Soete, Luc and Verspagen, B. (1991). *Technology and Productivity.* Paris: OECD.

Solomon, Robert (1982). *The International Monetary System, 1945–1981.* New York: Harper & Row.

Soper, Kate (1990). 'Socialist Humanism', in H. Kaye and K. McClelland, eds, *E.P. Thompson: Critical Perspectives.* Philadelphia: Temple University Press, 204–32.

Stahl, Charles W. (1986). *International Labor Migration: A Study of the ASEAN Countries.* New York: Center for Migration Studies.

Stallard, Karen; Ehrenreich, Barbara and Sklar, Holly (1983). *Poverty in the American Dream: Women and Children First.* Boston, MA: South End Press.

Starr, Paul and Immergut, Ellen (1987). 'Health Care and the Boundaries of Politics', in C. Maier, ed., *Changing Boundaries of the Political: Essays on the Evolving Balance Between the State and Society, Public and Private in Europe.* New York: Cambridge University Press, 221–54.

Stein, Daniel, ed. (1989). *Lectures in the Sciences of Complexity: The Proceedings of the 1988 Complex Systems Summer School, Santa Fe, NM, June/July 1988.* Redwood City, CA: Addison-Wesley.

Stein, Herbert (1988). *Tax Policy in the Twenty-First Century.* New York: Wiley.

Stopford, John M. (1982). *The World Directory of Multinational Enterprises 1982–83.* Detroit: Gale Research.

Stopford, John M. and Dunning, John H. (1983). *Multinationals: Company Performance and Global Trends*. London: Macmillan.

Storper, Michael (1991). *Industrialization, Economic Development and the Regional Question in the Third World: From Import Substitution to Flexible Production*. London: Pion.

Sutherland, Margaret (1991). 'Women in Higher Education: Effects of Crisis and Change', in G. Kelley and S. Slaughter, eds, *Women's Higher Education in Comparative Perspective*. Boston, MA: Kluwer Academic Press, 131–44.

Sweet, James A. (1984). 'Components of Change in the Number of Households: 1970–1980', *Demography*, vol. XXI, no. 2, May, 129–41.

Sweezy, Paul (1949). *Socialism*. New York: McGraw Hill.

Tabak, Faruk and Kasaba, Resat (1994). 'Fatal Conjuncture: The Decline and Fall of the Modern Agrarian Order During the Bretton Woods Era', in P. McMichael, ed., *Food and Agrarian Orders in the World Economy*. Westport, CT: Greenwood.

Taylor, Charles L. and Hudson, Michael C. (1972). *World Handbook of Political and Social Indicators*. New Haven, CT: Yale University Press.

Taylor, Michael J. and Thrift, N.J. (1982a). 'Introduction', in M.J. Taylor and N.J. Thrift, eds, *The Geography of Multinationals: Studies in the Spatial Development and Economic Consequences of Multinational Corporations*. London: Croom Helm, 1–13.

——— (1982b). 'Models of Corporate Development and the Multinational Corporation', in M.J. Taylor and N.J. Thrift, eds, *The Geography of Multinationals: Studies in the Spatial Development and Economic Consequences of Multinational Corporations*. London: Croom Helm, 14–32.

Teece, David J. (1991). 'Support Policies for Strategic Industries: Impact on Home Economies', in *Strategic Industries in a Global Economy: Policy Issues for the 1990s*. Paris: OECD, 35–50.

Teichler, Ulrich (1988). *Changing Patterns of the Higher Education System: The Experience of Three Decades*. London: Jessica Kingsley.

Therborn, Göran (1984). 'The Prospects of Labour and the Transformation of Advanced Capitalism', *New Left Review*, no. 145, May–June, 5–38.

Thompson, Edward P. (1978). *The Poverty of Theory and Other Essays*. New York: Monthly Review Press.

——— (1965). 'The Peculiarities of the English', in R. Miliband and J. Saville, eds, *The Socialist Register, 1965*. New York: Monthly Review Press.

——— (1961). 'Review of Raymond Williams, *The Long Revolution*', *New Left Review*, nos 9 and 10, May–June and July–August, 24–33 and 34–9.

Tilly, Charles (1981). *As Sociology Meets History*. New York: Academic Press.

——— (1989). 'Collective Violence in European Perspective', in T.R. Gurr, ed., *Violence in America*, Vol. 2. Newbury Park, CA: Sage, 62–101.

Tournier, Michèle (1973). 'Women and Access to Universities in France and Germany (1861–1967)', *Comparative Education*, vol. IX, no. 3, October, 107–18.

Townroe, Peter M. and Keen, David (1984). 'Polarization Reversal in the State of Sao Paolo', *Regional Studies*, vol. XVIII, no. 1, February, 45–54.

Tyler, Patrick E. (1992a). 'After the Cold War: As Fear of Big War Fades, Military Plans for Little Ones', *New York Times*, 3 February.

——— (1992b). 'U.S. Strategy Plan Calls for Insuring No Rivals Develop: A One-Superpower World. Pentagon's Document Outlines Ways to Thwart

Challenges to Primacy of America', *New York Times*, 8 March.
———— (1987). *Environmental Data Report.* Oxford: Blackwell.
UN (United Nations) (1993). *Report on the World Social Situation.* Geneva: UN Publications.
———— (1992). *Yearbook of Industrial Statistics 1990*, I. New York: UN Publications.
———— (1991). *Yearbook of Industrial Statistics, 1989*, I, II. New York: UN Publications.
———— (1989). *World Economic Survey 1989.* New York: UN Publications.
———— (1986). *Urban and Rural Population Projections 1950–2025: The 1984 Assessment.* New York: UN Publications.
———— (1985). *Report on the World Social Situation.* New York: UN Publications.
———— (1982a). *Report on the World Social Situation.* New York: UN Publications.
———— (1982b). *Yearbook of Industrial Statistics, 1980*, I. New York: UN Publications.
———— (1981). *Yearbook of Industrial Statistics 1979*, I. New York: UN Publications.
———— (1978). *Report on the World Social Situation.* New York: UN Publications.
———— (1977). *Yearbook of Industrial Statistics 1975*, I. New York: UN Publications.
———— (1976). *Yearbook of Industrial Statistics, 1974*, I, II. New York: UN Publications.
———— (1967). *The Growth of World Industry 1953–65.* New York: UN Publications.
———— (1957). *Report on the World Social Situation.* New York: UN Publications.
———— (1952). *Preliminary Report on the World Social Situation.* New York: UN Dept of Social Affairs.
———— (1952–70). *Report on the World Social Situation.* New York: UN Publications.
UNCTC (United Nations Center on Transnational Corporations) (1991). *World Investment Report 1991: The Triad in Foreign Direct Investment.* New York: UN Publications.
———— (1988). *Transnational Corporation in World Development*, United Nations Publications E.88.II.A.7.
UN Center for Human Settlements (Habitat) (1987). *Global Report on Human Settlements.* New York: Oxford University Press.
UNEP (United Nations Environmental Program) (1991). *Environmental Data Report.* Oxford: Blackwell.
UNICEF (United Nations International Children's Emergency Fund (1989). *Children on the Frontline. The Impact of Apartheid Destabilization and Warfare on Children in Southern and South Africa*, 3rd edn. New York: UNICEF.
United States Congress, Senate, Select Committee to Study Government Operations with Respect to Intelligence Activities (1975). *Alleged Assassination Plots Involving Foreign Leaders*, Rep. No. 94–465 (November). Washington, DC: US GPO.
US Department of Agriculture, Foreign Agricultural Service, (1988) *World Rice Reference Tables*; *World Wheat and Coarse Grains Reference Tables* (unpublished printouts), Washington, D.C.: June.
Uyanga, Joseph (1990). 'Economic Development Strategies: Maternal and Child Health', *Social Science and Medicine*, vol. XXXI, no. 6, 649–59.
Vainio, H.; Parkin, D.M. and Tomatis, L. (1990). 'International Cancer Care', in J. Lambo and S. Day, eds, *Issues in Contemporary International Health*. New York: Plenum Medical Book, 165–201.
van Bruinessen, Martin (1992). *Agha, Shaikh, and State: The Social and Political Struc-*

tures of Kurdistan. London and Atlantic Heights, NJ: Zed.

van der Pijl, Kees (1984). *The Making of the Atlantic Ruling Class*. London: Verso.

van der Wee, Herman (1986). *Prosperity and Upheaval: The World Economy, 1945–1980*. Berkeley: University of California Press.

van Ginneken, Wouter and van der Hoeven, Rolph (1989). 'Industrialization, Employment and Earnings (1950–87): An International Survey', *International Labour Review*, vol. CXXVIII, no. 5, 571–99.

Veeser, H. Aram, ed. (1989). *The New Historicism*. New York: Routledge.

Vergopoulos, Kostas (1979). 'L'hégémonie américaine après la Seconde Guerre Mondiale et la formation de la bourgeoisie périphérique en Grèce', *Les temps modernes*, no. 392, March, 1474–1503.

Vernon, R. (1979). 'Product Cycle Hypothesis in a New International Environment', *Oxford Bulletin of Economics and Statistics*, vol. XLI, 255–68.

Volkart, Edmund H. (1981). 'Seventy-five years of It', *The American Sociologist*, vol. XVI, no. 1, February, 64–7.

Wagner, Helmut (1983). *Alfred Schültz, An Intellectual Biography*. Chicago: University of Chicago Press.

Wainwright, Milton (1990). *Miracle Cure: The Story of Penicillin and the Gold Age of Antiobiotics*. Oxford: Blackwell.

Walker, R.B.J. and Mendlovitz, Saul, eds (1990). *Contending Sovereignties: Redefining Political Community*. Boulder, CO: Lynne Rienner.

Wallerstein, Immanuel (1992a). 'The Collapse of Liberalism', in R. Miliband and L. Panitch, eds, *Socialist Register 1992: New World Order?* London: Merlin, 96–110.

——— (1992b). 'Liberalism and the Legitimation of Nation-States: An Historical Interpretation', *Social Justice*, vol. XIX, no. 1, Spring, 22–33.

——— (1991a). *Geopolitics and Geoculture: Essays on the Changing World-System*. Cambridge: Cambridge University Press.

——— (1991b). *Unthinking Social Science: The Limits of Nineteenth-Century Paradigms*. Cambridge: Polity.

——— (1984). *The Politics of the World-Economy: The States, the Movements, and the Civilizations*. Cambridge: Cam bridge University Press.

——— (1983). *Historical Capitalism*. London: Verso.

——— (1982). 'Dutch Hegemony in the Seventeenth-Century World-Economy', in M. Aymard, ed., *Dutch Capitalism and World Capitalism*. Cambridge: Cambridge University Press, 93–145.

——— (1979). 'Kondratieff Up or Kondratieff Down?', *Review*, vol. II, no. 4, Spring, 663–73.

——— (1978). '*Annales* as Resistance', *Review*, vol. I, no. 3/4, Winter/Spring, 5–7.

——— (1954). 'McCarthyism and the Conservative', unpublished M.A. thesis, Columbia University.

Wallerstein, Immanuel and Martin, William G. (1979). 'Peripheralization of South Africa: Changes in Household Structure and Labor-Force Formation', *Review*, vol. III, no. 2, Fall, 193–207.

Wallerstein, Immanuel; Martin, William G. and Dickinson, Torry (1982). 'Household Structures and Production Processes: Preliminary Thesis and Findings', *Review*, vol. V, no. 3, Winter, 437–58.

Watson, John B. (1925). *Behaviorism*. New York: W.W. Norton.

Weaver, Warren (1948). 'Science and Complexity', *American Scientist*, vol. XXXVI, no. 4, 536–44.

Weitz, Morris, ed. (1966). *20th Century Philosophy: The Analytic Tradition*. New York: Free Press.

Wexler, Mark N. (1990). 'Deep Ecology: An Emerging Critique of Conventional Wisdom', *Quarterly Journal of Ideology*, vol. XIV, no. 1, 15–38.

Whaling, Frank, ed. (1987). *Religion in Today's World: The Religious Situation of the World from 1945 to the Present Day*. Edinburgh: Clark.

Whichard, Obie G. (1981). 'Trends in U.S. Direct Investment Position Abroad, 1950–79', *Survey of Current Business*, vol. LXI, no. 2, February, 39–56.

White, Hayden (1987). *The Content of the Form: Narrative Discourse and Historical Representation*. Baltimore: Johns Hopkins University Press.

—— (1978). *Tropics of Discourse: Essays in Cultural Criticism*. Baltimore: Johns Hopkins University Press.

—— (1973). *Metahistory: The Historical Imagination in Nineteenth-Century Europe*. Baltimore: Johns Hopkins University Press.

WHO (World Health Organization) (1988a). *Four Decades of Achievement 1948–1988*. Geneva: WHO.

—— (1988b). *From Alma-Ata to the Year 2000: Reflections at the Midpoint*. Geneva: WHO.

—— (1980; 1992). *World Health Statistics Annual*. Geneva: WHO.

Widgery, David (1976). *The Left in Britain: 1956–68*. Baltimore: Penguin.

Williams, Karel, et al. (1987). 'The End of Mass Production?', *Economy and Society*, vol. XVI, no. 3, 404–38.

Williams, Raymond (1983). *Keywords: A Vocabulary of Culture and Society*, rev. edn. New York: Oxford University Press.

Wilson, Maggie (1991). 'Europe: An Overview', in M. Wilson, ed., *Girls and Young Women in Education*. New York: Pergamon, 203–13.

Wnuk-Lipinski, Edmund (1990). 'The Polish Country Profile: Economic Crisis and Inequalities in Health', *Social Science and Medicine*, vol. XXXI, no. 8, 859–66.

Wolf, Edward (1986). *Beyond the Green Revolution*. Washington, DC: Worldwatch Institute.

Wolfe, Tom (1973). *The New Journalism*. New York: Harper & Row.

Woo, Jung-en (1991). *Race to the Swift: State and Finance in Korean Industrialization*. New York: Columbia University Press.

Woo-Cumings, Meredith and Loriaux, Michael (1993). *Past as Prelude: History in the Making of a New World Order*. Boulder, CO: Westview.

Wood, Robert (1986). *From Marshall Plan to Debt Crisis: Foreign Aid and Development Choices in the World-Economy*. Berkeley: University of California Press.

Wriston, Walter B. (1992). 'The Twilight of Sovereignty', speech given at the Commonwealth Club of California, 10 November.

Yachir, Faysal (1988). *The World Steel Industry Today*. Tokyo: UN University.

Yoshihara, Kunio (1976). *Japanese Investment in Southeast Asia*. Honolulu: University Press of Hawaii.

Yoshitomi, Masaru (1991). 'New Trends in Oligopolistic Competition in the Globalisation of High-Tech Industries: Interactions Among Trade, Investment and Government', in *Strategic Industries in a Global Economy: Policy Issues for the 1990s*. Paris: OECD, 15–34.

Zysman, John (1991). 'U.S. Power, Trade and Technology', *International Affairs*, vol. LXVII, no. 1, January, 81–106.

Index

CPSIA information can be obtained
at www.ICGtesting.com
Printed in the USA
LVHW111430301118
598793LV00002B/378/P